The Football Battalions

The elite footballers who fought in the Great War

Christopher Evans

BLOOMSBURY SPORT
LONDON · OXFORD · NEW YORK · NEW DELHI · SYDNEY

For Julia

BLOOMSBURY SPORT
Bloomsbury Publishing Plc
50 Bedford Square, London, WC1B 3DP, UK
Bloomsbury Publishing Ireland Limited,
29 Earlsfort Terrace, Dublin 2, D02 AY28, Ireland

BLOOMSBURY, BLOOMSBURY SPORT and the Diana logo are trademarks of Bloomsbury Publishing Plc

First published in Great Britain 2025

Copyright © Christopher Evans, 2025

Christopher Evans has asserted his right under the Copyright, Designs and Patents Act, 1988, to be identified as Author of this work

For legal purposes the Acknowledgements on page 234 constitute an extension of this copyright page

All rights reserved. No part of this publication may be: i) reproduced or transmitted in any form, electronic or mechanical, including photocopying, recording or by means of any information storage or retrieval system without prior permission in writing from the publishers; or ii) used or reproduced in any way for the training, development or operation of artificial intelligence (AI) technologies, including generative AI technologies. The rights holders expressly reserve this publication from the text and data mining exception as per Article 4(3) of the Digital Single Market Directive (EU) 2019/790

Bloomsbury Publishing Plc does not have any control over, or responsibility for, any third-party websites referred to or in this book. All internet addresses given in this book were correct at the time of going to press. The author and publisher regret any inconvenience caused if addresses have changed or sites have ceased to exist, but can accept no responsibility for any such changes

A catalogue record for this book is available from the British Library

Library of Congress Cataloguing-in-Publication data has been applied for

ISBN: HB: 978-1-3994-1351-0; ePDF: 978-1-3994-1349-7; eBook: 978-1-3994-1350-3

2 4 6 8 10 9 7 5 3 1

Typeset in Adobe Garamond Pro by D.R. INK
Printed and bound in Great Britain by Clays Ltd, Elcograf S.p.A.

Bloomsbury Publishing Plc makes every effort to ensure that the papers used in the manufacture of our books are natural, recyclable products made from wood grown in well-managed forests. Our manufacturing processes conform to the environmental regulations of the country of origin.

To find out more about our authors and books visit www.bloomsbury.com and sign up for our newsletters
For product safety related questions contact productsafety@bloomsbury.com

Contents

Dramatis personae   4
Prologue Tim Coleman: The man who lived twice   10
Introduction   18
1   Pressure! The world tries to shame football   23
2   Formation: Football does its bit   38
3   Hearts: Scottish football responds to the war   52
4   Vivian Woodward: The journey of a polymath   66
5   Steve Bloomer: A superstar goes to Germany   78
6   Cup Final! A subdued event   87
7   Fix! A Lancashire betting scandal   98
8   Orders: The Battalion makes its way to France   109
9   Winners: Morale-boosting games   120
10   Walter Tull: Leaving the field   132
11   Evelyn Lintott: A teacher on the Somme   142
12   Brothers: Jonas and McFadden   151
13   Frank Buckley: The Major   160
14   Munitionettes: The war on the home front   170
15   John McCartney: Forever Hearts   181
16   Joe Mercer: The hard man who did not break   191
17   Allastair McReady-Diarmid: Conspicuous bravery   200
18   Bookends: The different worlds of Haig-Brown and Tull   209
19   Reunion: All that is left behind   217
Afterword Why we remember   228
Acknowledgements   234
Bibliography   238

Dramatis personae

Steve Bloomer
Steve Bloomer was one of football's first superstars and England's record international goal scorer until 1911. He endorsed football boots and other products, and, when the Queen Mary set out on her maiden voyage in 1936, his image was part of a giant mural in one of the public rooms portraying famous Britons.

Most of his career was with Derby County – there was a controversial transfer to Middlesbrough – but he eventually returned to a hero's welcome, brass band and all, at the Baseball Ground. Just before the war Bloomer had retired and taken up a coaching post in Germany.

Frank Buckley
An England international who made a name for himself at Derby County and Bradford City, Buckley was the third man to sign up for the 1st Football Battalion at its launch at Fulham Town Hall in December 1914.

Tim Coleman
Born in Kettering in 1881, to a father who could never remember the names of his children, John G. Coleman was called 'Tim' like his brothers – and the name stuck. Starting out at Kettering Town, Coleman moved to Woolwich Arsenal in 1902, becoming their top scorer in his first full season.

In 1908, Woolwich Arsenal's difficult financial situation meant that it was happy to accept a bid from Everton. It was here that Coleman became an active trade unionist, maintaining his membership even when this was against Football Association rules.

He subsequently joined Sunderland, then Fulham and was playing for Nottingham Forest when war broke out.

Allen Foster

Foster played for Rotherham Town and Bristol City before transferring to Reading FC in August 1911 for a fee of £75, which was paid in two instalments. The centre-forward was a hero at Elm Park: he scored the only goal as Reading knocked mighty Aston Villa out of the FA Cup in 1912 and his hat-trick made for an improbable 5-0 victory against AC Milan on an Italian tour.

Alan Haig-Brown

Educated in the English public school system, where he excelled in both cricket and football, Haig-Brown graduated from Cambridge before taking up the post of assistant master at Lancing College. In October 1901 he signed League forms to play as an amateur for Tottenham Hotspur Football Club and in February 1906 he joined Clapton Orient.

From 1906 to 1915, Haig-Brown was the commanding officer of the Lancing College contingent of the Officer Training Corps.

Ted Hanney

The son of a soldier, Hanney spent his early years at Reading's Brock Barracks, enlisting in his father's regiment as a boy soldier. He would go on to serve eight years before leaving the army in 1911.

Hanney then played more than 150 games for Reading, Manchester City and Coventry City, and he was part of the gold medal-winning Great Britain team for the 1912 Olympic football competition in Stockholm, which was captained by Vivian Woodward.

William Jonas

Jonas joined the 17th Battalion Middlesex Regiment, along with nine of his Clapton Orient teammates, at the specially convened recruitment meeting at Fulham Town Hall on 15 December 1914. Something of a heart-throb, he was very popular with the women at Millfields Road, so much so that at one stage he was receiving over 50 letters a week from female admirers.

Fred Keenor

Having starred in his school team, and for local side Roath Wednesday, the tough-tackling Keenor agreed to sign for another local side, Cardiff City. Like most footballers of the time, Keenor picked up additional work as a labourer to guarantee a steady income.

When Keenor enlisted, Cardiff City organised regular collections for him and his fellow teammate Jack Stephenson, which contained small keepsakes and encouraging letters from City supporters.

Evelyn Lintott

A teacher, trade unionist who chaired the Players' Union, and an England international, Lintott was born in Godalming, Surrey, on 2 November 1883. He began playing for his local side, Woking, before moving on to Plymouth Argyle, a club close to where he undertook teacher training in Exeter.

Upon qualifying and securing a position in West London, Lintott joined Queens Park Rangers. In 1908 he would become the first QPR player to win a full England international cap. At the same time, Lintott served as chairman of the Association Football Players' Union (AFPU), campaigning for an end to the £4 maximum wage.

Eventually, Lintott moved to Bradford City before joining Leeds City. It was from here that he joined the 15th (Service) Battalion of the West Yorkshire Regiment, better known at the 1st Leeds Pals, on 14 September 1914.

Joe Mercer Senior
Joe Mercer Senior was a tough, no-nonsense centre-half who started out with Ellesmere Port Town before joining Nottingham Forest in 1910. Four months after the start of the First World War, and a day after the 17th Middlesex was formed, Mercer travelled down to London with teammates Tom Gibson and Harold Iremonger to enlist.

John McCartney
In 1914, McCartney was the manager of title-chasing Heart of Midlothian F.C.

Born in Glasgow in 1866, he plied his trade as a footballer with Glasgow Rangers, Newton Heath and Luton. Seeing out his playing days with Barnsley, he was appointed the secretary-manager of the club in 1901, before leaving for St Mirren, taking them to a Scottish Cup Final in 1908.

After being appointed manager of Hearts in 1910, he had steadily built a side which was a real threat to the dominance of Celtic and Rangers in the Scottish First Division. The season 1914/15 looked like the season they would finally make the breakthrough.

Richard McFadden
Born in 1889 in Lanarkshire, Scotland, Richard McFadden played for Blyth Spartans and Wallsend Park Villa, before his eventual move to Clapton Orient in 1911. McFadden once dragged a man from a burning building, saving his life; at Orient he rescued two young children who were struggling in the River Lea; and two weeks later, he pulled a little girl out of a burning building.

His reputation was further enhanced when he signed up to join the 17th Middlesex Regiment and headed off to war.

Allastair McReady-Diarmid

Born in Southgate 1888 as Arthur Malcolm Drew, he changed his name by deed poll in 1915. Privately educated, he was disowned by his parents for a marriage deemed beneath him. Although not a footballer, McReady-Diarmid was to become one of the most significant members of the 17th Middlesex Regiment.

Jackie Sheldon

Sheldon was born in Clay Cross, Derbyshire, in January 1887. He played for Nuneaton and Manchester United before moving to Liverpool, lifting the FA Cup in 1914.

Walter Tull

Born in 1888, the son of a Barbadian father and an English mother, Tull lost both parents before the age of nine. An orphanage boy, he became one of the first Black professional footballers in the UK, playing for Clapton, Tottenham and Northampton Town during his career.

Before the outbreak of the war in 1914, Tull made 111 appearances for Northampton Town, earning the maximum allowable wage for a footballer of £4 per week. He then joined the Football Battalion.

Vivian Woodward

Vivian John Woodward was born in Kennington, London, on 3 June 1879. An architect by trade, Woodward was a prolific centre-forward who starred for Tottenham Hotspur and Chelsea before the First World War and retained amateur status throughout his career. After he netted twice on his international debut in 1903, one journalist lauded him as 'the human chain of lightning, the footballer with magic in his boots'.

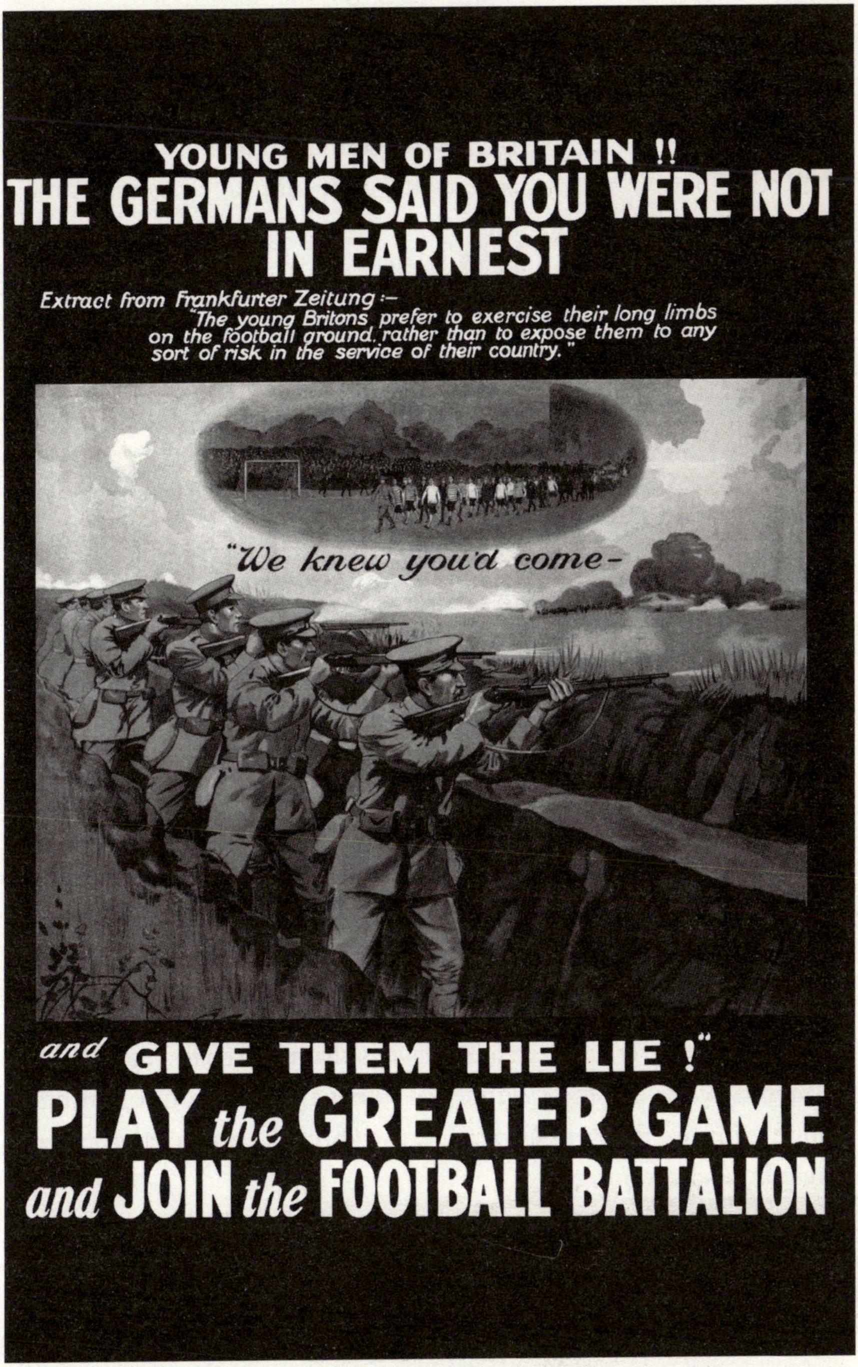

Buyenlarge via Getty Images

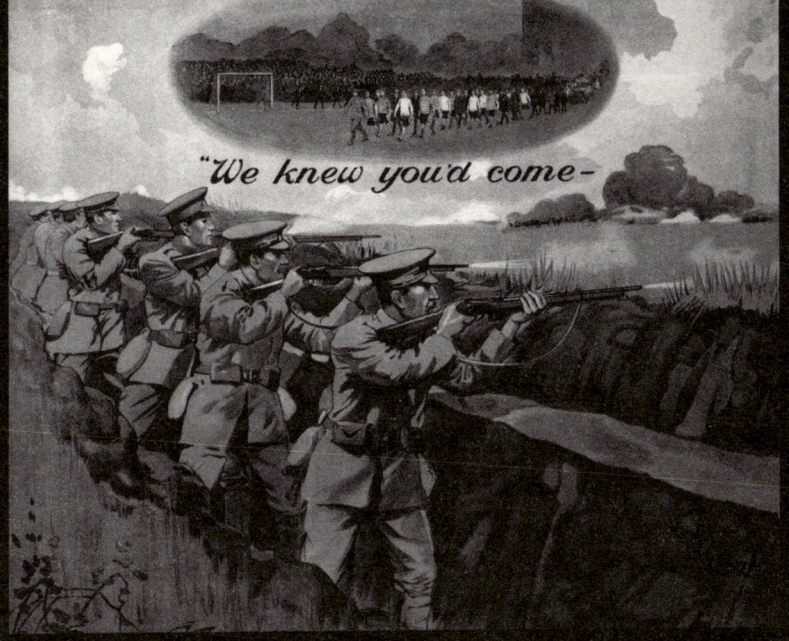

A recruitment poster. After its formation, fans were encouraged to join the 17th Middlesex to serve in the army alongside their heroes.

Prologue
Tim Coleman
The man who lived twice

30 December 1915
The training, the marching and the sheer boredom of waiting around for orders has finally come to an end. The 17th Middlesex Regiment, commonly known as the Football Battalion, will finally see action. Formed in a blaze of publicity just over year ago, they now find themselves in Loos, Northern France, where they will experience the trenches and hear German gunfire for the first time.

Given that there are so many famous names among their ranks, any snippet of news from France is pounced upon by football fans. So reports that one of the more celebrated players of their number, John 'Tim' Coleman, is dead plunge the football world into shock and grief.

The diminutive figure, known as a tricky and clever inside-forward, had made a name for himself at Woolwich Arsenal, Everton and Fulham. To the working man he was something of a hero – a militant who maintained his membership of the Players' Union in defiance of Football Association rules.

However, there can be little doubt: Coleman has been lost. Underneath an article detailing the latest victory of the East End boxer Ted 'Kid' Lewis, the *Daily Mirror* reports that three famous footballers have been killed.

The well-known England international lost his life in the first action encountered by the Football Battalion and fell alongside two comrades: Sergeant Bob Dalrymple of Clapton Orient and Private Bob MacDonald from Norwich City.

It went on to say of both, 'J. G. "Tim" Coleman and R. Dalrymple have laid down their lives for their country. Both were well known to London crowds, and, at different times, both figured in the Fulham side.

'Coleman for England against Ireland in 1907 was a born humourist, and was always the most popular of any party he happened to be travelling with.'

Coleman had recently played for Forest and local newspapers were quick to report the news, confirmed by various sources, that he had been hit and killed on the front. The *Nottingham Journal* and *Nottingham Evening Telegraph* both played tribute, describing Coleman as a 'brainy type' and a 'humourist' who could more than hold his own with comedians of the day.

The *Liverpool Echo* was to say of Coleman, 'These three men were members of the Footballers' Battalion, and the best known of them was undoubtedly Coleman. He was the comedian of the football field and was known the world over for his witty sallies. When his regiment was resting, the captain always made point of fixing his feet wherever Coleman was, so that he might enjoy the little fellow's humour.'

While there was some doubt among the Fulham community as to whether Dalrymple was dead, to the *West London Observer*, Coleman was definitely lost, his wife having been informed by telegram that she was now a widow.

Nottingham Forest were also quick to react to the news, telling reporters they would be arranging a collection at their next fixture against Bradford City in aid of his widow and two children. In the next two days the tributes came thick and fast.

On 29 December, the *Sporting Chronicle* wrote, 'Perhaps the best known of these footballers was Tim Coleman, a wonderfully clever and versatile footballer who represented England against Ireland in 1907.

'Although of roving disposition, he was wonderfully popular wherever he went, for he was a born humourist and was the life and soul of every club he was travelling with. He was an inside-forward and could play right or left but his favourite position was inside-right.

'He was tricky with his feet but did not overdo it and was a good rattling shot. His first important club was Kettering but from there he joined Northampton Town in his first season and then went south to Woolwich Arsenal. Everton next attracted him to the north, later he did excellent work at Roker Park before the more genial climate of the south once more appealed to him and he joined Fulham. From there he went to Nottingham Forest, where he was playing until he heard his country's call.

'Poor Tim, many will miss his cheery face with an ever ready joke.'

On New Year's Eve, the *Liverpool Echo* carried a letter from Jackie Sheldon, formerly of Liverpool and fellow recruit to the Football Battalion, describing the last goal scored by Tim Coleman:

'Just a few lines to let you know that I am still living, and in the best of health. I have done several turns in the trenches, which are thigh-deep in mud.

'On Sunday afternoon we played a team of city lads, who belong to Liverpool. The match caused considerable excitement, the city boys turning up in large numbers to give their old favourites warm welcome. We turned out a pretty strong side as follows: J. Webster (West Ham); A. Foster (Reading), J. Doran (Coventry); J. Limb (Sheffield Wednesday), F. Keener (Cardiff City), Scott (Clapton Orient); J. Sheldon, Tim Coleman (Nottingham Forest); J. Conk (Huddersfield), T. Barber (Aston Villa), and Hunter (Gainsborough).

'The match turned out very one-sided. As could be expected, our side ran out easy winners (7-1). Coleman several times greatly amused the crowd with his clever play and brought the house down when he scored our first goal. The game was played under peculiar conditions, shells from our artillery constantly whizzing over our head, while higher still the Germans were amusing themselves by shelling our airmen.

'Fortunately, the Germans were unsuccessful. After the match myself and "Tim" were entertained to tea, and had a right good time.'

In an appreciation, the column 'Robin Hood' of the *Nottingham*

Journal wrote, 'Never again will Coleman entertain the crowd who gather at the playing fields of Old England. He has died a death of a gallant Britisher and passed on into the Great Silence leaving still eleven Foresters to fight on.'

For those who mourned Tim Coleman, those words would have served as a fitting epitaph.

By Saturday, however, the *Nottingham Journal* informed their readers that the news of Tim Coleman's death on active service with the Footballers' Battalion was, in fact, untrue. 'The famous Nottingham Forest footballer's mother, who resides at Northgate Street, Kettering, received a telegram from Tim's wife which read "John alive and well – Nell."'

The writers of the *Journal* were left to scratch their heads. The first report of Coleman's death had reached Nottingham from three sources, and, moreover, it was afterwards stated that his wife had received the report of his death.

Private John Nuttall, also of the Football Battalion, wrote to Bert Lipsham, the Millwall manager: 'I expect you have read that Dalrymple, Coleman and MacDonald have been killed but the statements are false, as they are all in the pink and MacDonald has been sent back to England.

'Things are very quiet here just now. I trust it will not be long before I will be able to look you up again and in the meantime I wish you a prosperous New Year and ask you to remember me to all players and others connected to the club, and tell Elijah (the dressing room attendant) I could do with one of his Sunday morning baths just now.'

For his part, Coleman was handed a telegram by Tommy Gibson, his captain at Nottingham Forest and now the company sergeant major, telling him of the fuss back home. Ever the joker, Coleman replied, 'I am pleased to say, gentlemen, there is absolutely no truth in the report at all!'

22 August 1916

For a man who had been declared dead some eight months ago, Private Tim Coleman was in remarkably good form when he wrote to the *Liverpool Echo*, 'We are having a little rest, and we need it.'

Those words were nothing short of an understatement. Coleman finally had his letter published seven weeks after British, Canadian and Bermudian troops went 'over the top' on the first day of the Battle of the Somme, in Northern France.

The day of 1 July 1916 became the bloodiest in the history of the British Army. One of the most infamous of the First World War, it began at four in the morning, and by dusk, the British forces had suffered 57,470 casualties, including 19,240 fatalities, many of them succumbing to German machine guns.

The Football Battalion was stationed in a small town, Bryas, and did not see action that day, but one of the casualties would have a profound impact on Coleman and his comrades.

At 3 p.m., Lieutenant Evelyn Lintott was struck in the chest. A report in the *Yorkshire Evening Post* described his demise: 'Lt. Lintott's end was particularly gallant. Tragically, he was killed leading his platoon of the 15th West Yorkshire Regiment, "The Leeds Pals", over the top.

'He led his men with great dash and when hit the first time declined to take the count. Instead, he drew his revolver and called for further effort. Again, he was hit but struggled on but a third shot finally bowled him over.'

Lintott had been a star for the teams of Queens Park Rangers and England before moving north. Furthermore, he had been elected the chairman of the Players' Union in 1910, an organisation in which Coleman played an active role.

Even as the sporting world was just coming to terms with the death of Lintott, Major Hartley, the Commanding Officer of the Leeds Pals, was writing to a Mr J.C. Booth, 'I am deeply sorry to inform you of the death of your brother, while gallantly assisting a Battalion attack. He was killed instantaneously. The Battalion had a real stiff task but acquitted itself more gallantly. Your brother was loved by officers and men and earned his commission through real merit. His place will indeed be hard to fill.'

The subject of the letter was Lieutenant Major William Booth, a cricketer who had played for Yorkshire, and who became the first cricketer to lose his life in the Great War. He had also once played football for Leeds City.

The *Sporting Chronicle* paid tribute to the fallen men in an article of 12 July entitled 'The inevitable toll of war – Reflections on the deaths of two well-known athletes'.

'In a weekly causerie of this kind the passing of two sportsmen as Major William Booth and Evelyn Lintott cannot be passed over in silence, even though the news does not possess the swing quality of freshness.

'Many a year hence, lovers of cricket and football will tell how these brave young men responded to the call, how they attracted attention of their commanding officer, how they received commissions, went to Egypt, were brought back to the Western Front, and laid down their lives when the English lads in the New Army assumed the offensive against the disturbers of peace in Europe.

'Those who live to be old men will recount the story of Booth and Lintott, who had both worn the jersey of Leeds City, and in the imperishable words of Ian Hay in "The First Hundred Thousand" joined the "great company of happy warriors to walk Elysian Fields."'

Just over a week after the obituary had been published, Private Tim Coleman found himself on a train headed to Longueau. For over a week under the leadership of former Bradford City defender Major Frank Buckley, they waited there in the trenches for orders.

Then on 27 July, alongside the South Staffs Regiment and a brigade from South Africa, they battled the Germans for 48 hours at Delville Wood.

By the morning of 29 July, the Battalion had suffered 35 deaths and 192 wounded, among them Major Frank Buckley, who had been hit in the chest by shrapnel from a German grenade. Those who saw Buckley in the field thought their commanding officer had died. He survived, but such was the devastation that only 13 men who died were buried in known graves.

The *Illustrated Sporting and Dramatic News*, a weekly magazine, was a few weeks out of date when Coleman got to read it. On 15 July an article appeared, entitled 'The Sportsman's Roll of Honour', and the former Nottingham Forest forward read, 'Regret will be very general in cricket circles at news of the death in action of Second Lieutenant MW Booth of the West Yorkshire Regiment, who played twice for England in Test matches in South Africa and is the first cricket international to lose his life in this war.'

Then came the words which angered the easy-going Coleman. Indeed, after everything he had endured in the last few weeks, they cut like a knife. Commenting on Booth voluntarily joining the war effort, the article referred to him 'joining the Leeds "Pals" Battalion of the regiment early in the war, thereby setting a fine example to those football professionals who held aloof until compelled to serve.'

So strongly did Coleman feel about the slaughter he had witnessed that he was compelled to write to the *Liverpool Echo*. On Merseyside he was still idolised as a former Evertonian, and was by now familiar with death: of those who travelled to France with him the previous December, William Jonas of Clapton Orient, Norman Wood of Chelsea and Allen Foster from Reading, all famous names, had given their lives for king and country.

Sacrifices like these needed to be known about back home. And Coleman did not hold back: 'I came across a paragraph in a sporting paper which I thought was a little bit off. It said, after paying tribute to Lieutenant Booth, whose death was regretted by everyone of our battalion, where he had set a fine example – not like the footballers who had waited until they were nearly forced to join.

'The man who wrote that must be "up the pole" as we have been on active service for nearly ten months and have been in some very hot places and have also taken our part in the big push. We all joined up to do our bit, and it is rather a big jump from £4 per week to 5 francs. I think we all agree.

'The professional footballers have done their bit. The rest of the players who are left are trying to arrange a match for the benefit for those depending on them, also those who are permanently disabled.

PROLOGUE

We shall have to gain the consent of the authorities of course, but I think they shall see to that, as they always encourage charitable actions. I was hoping this little "tiff" would have been over for next season, but it still wags on.'

By the time his letter was published in the *Liverpool Echo*, Tim Coleman and the 17th Middlesex had arrived at the frontline, east of La Signy Farm. The irony may have been lost on Coleman and his comrades, but the Football Battalion were now standing on almost the very spot where both Major William Booth and Evelyn Lintott had fallen on 1 July.

The popular John 'Tim' Coleman. Widespread press reports of his death on the Western Front in December 1915 were proven to be untrue.

Introduction

To mark the hundredth anniversary of the Armistice which ended the First World War, England's most recognisable footballer sat down with *The Times* to discuss his thoughts on the footballers who fought in the Great War and never came back.

'It's hard to imagine really in the football world we are living in now to be playing football one day then suddenly you are making the ultimate sacrifice.' So said the man who was then England's captain and leading goalscorer.

His comments were especially poignant, because the younger Harry Kane had spent a season on loan from Tottenham Hotspur to Leyton Orient. Every day as he made his way to the Brisbane Road Ground, he passed the memorial in the park opposite.

On top of the memorial, a black marble plaque is flanked by two mythical wyverns (two-legged dragons with wings), which today are found on the official badge of the club. The inscription on the plaque reads: 'Remembering the forty-one players and staff of Clapton Orient Football Club who served with the 17th Middlesex Regiment (The Footballers' Battalion) during the Great War.'

Inside the ground, fans gather on match day in the Supporters' Club, where a glass case hangs on the wall, holding a wooden plaque that lists the names of all the players who gave their lives or were wounded in the war. Above the plaque are three names etched in gold: George Scott, William Jonas and Richard McFadden.

In the stadium itself, where Kane ran out at 3 p.m. on any given Saturday afternoon when Leyton Orient were playing at home, is a permanent banner above the red seats in one corner. White writing on a green background reads: 'CLAPTON ORIENT, THE FOOTBALLERS

INTRODUCTION

Battalion, The Somme 1916'. Next to it is the logo of the O's Somme Memorial Fund, with a red 'V' shape in the middle and the names of McFadden, Jonas and Scott on the outer rim.

With this history around him, is it any wonder that Kane became an ambassador for the Royal British Legion?

While he was sitting down to give his interview to *The Times*, over 200 supporters and friends of Leyton Orient made the trek to Northern France as part of a pilgrimage in honour of the men who had made up the 17th Middlesex Regiment, better known as the Football Battalion. It would be the sixth time that the supporters of the O's had made the trip, to ensure the former players are not forgotten.

Even when Kane broke the record for highest number of goals scored for England, there were reminders of players whose stories became entwined with the Great War.

In the list of England's leading goalscorers sit names such as Rooney, Charlton, Lineker and Greaves, but among their number are two players less familiar today: Vivian Woodward and Steve Bloomer, on 29 and 28 goals respectively. If the highest goalscorer were based on average goals per game, Woodward and Bloomer would easily stand at first and second.

• • • •

For a country which subscribes to the view that modern football began the day Bobby Moore lifted the 1966 Jules Rimet trophy, the exploits of Woodward and Bloomer barely register a mention.

There is no video tape or cinefilm of them in action. Like many footballers of that generation, all that is left behind are sepia-tinged monochrome photographs of ramrod-straight men with handlebar moustaches, greased and severely parted hair, and heavy cotton three-buttoned, long-sleeved shirts, with shorts finishing just below their knees and hobnail boots that would look more at home these days on a building site rather than the football field.

It is fair to say they have nothing in common with the millionaires who grace the game today and yet Woodward and Bloomer could claim to be football's first real superstars, enjoying endorsement and fame. For both men, the First World War would change all of that.

On 1 September 1914, just under a month after Great Britain had entered the First World War, the new football season kicked off. Woodward, though, would be one of the first to abandon his multi-faceted career as cricketer, footballer and architect to join the colours.

At the same time, Steve Bloomer, his former strike partner and the man he bested to become England's all-time highest goalscorer, was in Germany, coaching a local side in Berlin.

Many of us understand the First World War via the reflections of writers and poets. The likes of Rupert Brooke, Siegfried Sassoon and Robert Graves, of J.R.R. Tolkien, C.S. Lewis and Ernest Hemingway. They are only a small number of the millions who served in Northern France in those bloody four years of war.

The Football Battalions is a history of footballers in war. The aim is to describe the First World War experiences of the leading footballers of the day. In doing so it is hoped that these players can jump out of the crumbling photographs and tell their story. Take Joe Mercer, whose son would go on to win the League Championship as player and manager, and who played for Nottingham Forest, a no-nonsense, tough-tackling and brave central defender before war interrupted a promising career.

It is impossible to tell the story of the footballers without touching on the wider society. For example, Woodward, an amateur throughout his career, was born into an upper middle-class family while Bloomer was the son of a blacksmith.

Perhaps the most well remembered of the Football Battalion players is Walter Tull, the second person of Afro-Caribbean mixed heritage to play in the top division of the Football League.

Today, Tull is commemorated and celebrated: a cardboard cutout of his image greets visitors to the archives of the Commonwealth War Graves Commission Headquarters in Maidenhead, school children are taught about his story, and a 50 pence coin is still in circulation which bears his image.

INTRODUCTION

In his lifetime, Tull faced tragedy, poverty and racism. Brought in by Spurs to replace Woodward, he met with abuse from the crowds at away games. Tull rose above all of that and won a commission as an officer in the army, the first Afro-Caribbean person to do so.

By 1914, football was popular across the country, having usurped cricket as the country's national sport. Since the turn of the century, attendances had increased year on year and gates now averaged 23,000 a week.

When George V attended the 1914 FA Cup, football's place in society was assured. In the succeeding months, there followed a public outcry about the sport continuing during wartime. The issue was raised several times in the House of Commons and there were even calls for George V to step down as patron of the Football Association.

By November, public opinion had turned against football and many newspapers were hugely critical of the game. A letter to *The Times* insisted, 'Every club who employs a professional footballer is bribing a much-needed recruit to refrain from enlistment, and every spectator who pays his gate money is contributing to a German victory.'

Jingoistic recruitment posters could be found around football grounds across the country. At The Den, home of Millwall, the slogan was 'Let the enemy hear the lion's roar!' Stamford Bridge asked, 'Do you want to be a Chelsea Die-Hard?' And Tottenham Hotspur fans were told to, 'Sharpen up Spurs, shoot! shoot! shoot!! and stop this foul play.'

The reason this book is called *The Football Battalions* is simple. It was never the intention to cover only the exploits of the original Football Battalion known more formally as the 17th Middlesex. This book also explores the second 23rd Middlesex regiment in which Tull served.

There are also footballers like Leeds City's Evelyn Lintott, a commissioned officer with the West Yorkshire Regiment 15th Battalion, known as the Leeds Pals.

The book goes to Scotland, too, where Heart of Midlothian looked as though they were finally going to break Glasgow Celtic's stranglehold on the Scottish title, sweeping all before them before the breakout of war.

THE FOOTBALL BATTALIONS

With the winds of war blowing once again across the continent of Europe and beyond, it is the right time to look back on all those footballers who served king and country. They are not simply characters in a story, many of them fated to die on the battlefields of Northern France. They were ordinary men who left football to do extraordinary things.

We should not forget them.

British Army soldiers watching a game. Matches like these, as well as tournaments like the Divisional Cup, were won easily by the 17th Middlesex and proved a morale booster for troops on the Western Front.

Chapter 1

Pressure!
The world tries to shame football

The fair weather which Great Britain woke up to on 21 November 1914 was a welcome break from the torrential rain and gale force winds that had hit the country in the past week. Apart from some fog in the North and the low temperatures, which were only to be expected at this time of year, it was shaping up to be a good day for the start of an action-packed weekend of sport.

Across the Channel, the British Expeditionary Forces were fighting to stalemate in the First Battle of Ypres. November had been particularly harsh for the soldiers: a sudden cold snap had brought sleet, biting cold and snow. In Northern France, the first cases of frostbite in soldiers were being recorded.

The fighting, together with the weather, had led many men to collapse with exhaustion or fall asleep while standing up, making them an easy target for a German sniper or grenade from the enemy trenches.

Back home, if King George V was of a mind to follow his favourite pastime, horse racing, Hurst Park in Surrey offered a full programme beginning at 2p.m. In the West Midlands, at the Victoria Grounds in Wolverhampton, there was dog racing; in the East Midlands, Staton in Leicestershire hosted rabbit coursing; and in the north-east, St James' Hall in Newcastle had a packed boxing card.

Boxing was certainly in the news, with Freddie Welsh, the lightweight champion of the world, fighting to a draw against Jimmy Duffy in the Broadway Auditorium, Buffalo, New York. *The Herald* called his compatriot Jimmy Wilde, the flyweight known as Tylorstown Terror, 'the greatest fighting machine in the world' and tipped him to beat Scotsman Tancy Lee after the Welshman dominated Plymouth's Young Symonds in an eliminator for the vacant British, European and World titles.

If anyone in central London was looking for something a bit more sedate and cerebral, billiards offered up two matches: one at Soho Square, with sessions at 2.30 p.m. and 5 p.m., and another game at the Grand Hall, Leicester Square, with their sessions beginning at 3 p.m. and 8 p.m.

Then there was football, which offered a full programme of fixtures. League leaders Oldham Athletic were due to travel to the north-east to take on Newcastle United, and champions Blackburn Rovers were making a trip to Yorkshire to face Bradford City.

There was some excitement in the capital as the two bottom clubs, Notts County and Manchester United, were in town to face Chelsea and Tottenham Hotspur. *Sporting Life* predicted wins for both London clubs, but even at this stage of the season it was close at the foot of the table, with Chelsea on 9 points, Spurs on 8 and both Notts County and United on 7 points each. A win or loss for any of the four clubs could change fortunes overnight.

For the football fans and players, it was not, however, the tussle for the championship at the top or the relegation dogfight at the bottom of the table which occupied minds this November day. It was the constant barrage of abuse the game had faced since war had been declared on 4 August 1914.

An article entitled 'Dark Days' by D.D., published in the *Daily News and Leader* on 20 November, suggested that even the inclement weather which had hit the country in the past week had joined the so-called crusade against football.

'Should yesterday's weather be repeated tomorrow, the workers will have little inducement to attend football matches, and it will therefore be the most depressing Saturday of the season up to date.'

Every week since August and the outbreak of war there had seemed to be another dissenting voice added to the chorus of disapproval at the continuance of the football season, whether it was Arthur Conan Doyle, the creator of Sherlock Holmes, or the Bishop of London.

In late September there had been a court case involving two Fulham officials, who stood accused of manhandling temperance campaigner Frederick Charrington out of Craven Cottage. At half-time in the game between Fulham and Clapton Orient he had tried to speak out against football being played during wartime.

The subsequent civil court case was viewed as spurious and thrown out by the judge, but the campaign against football continued unabated.

For D.D. these attacks on the game were born out of ignorance: 'For those who attack football do so in ignorance of the damage they might cause, not only to wives and families of thousands of who are dependent upon the game as a profession but to the war department.

'Why are not racing (which the King has countenanced), golf and such other professions at this stage attacked? Football from its ranks has contributed 20 recruits to everyone from other sports professions. Then as to contributions to war funds, the clubs have done handsomely.'

Certainly, according to the pages of *Sporting Life*, horse racing had largely escaped the ire of those who wanted football shut down, with the advertised racing fixtures, at Warwick on the 23rd, 24th and 25th of the month, followed by race meetings at Lingfield on the 26th, 27th and 28th, and the racecourse at Manchester holding a meeting on the same days.

Slightly galling for those who had to listen to politicians calling for trains to football games to be stopped, or the fares hiked up for carriages carrying away football fans to matches, was an article which stated, 'In connection with the Warwick meeting on Monday, Tuesday and Wednesday next week, the Great Western Railway Company are running a special carrier excursion which leaves Paddington at 10.23am and is due at Warwick at 12.08pm.'

Then, as the article happily informed readers, there were the convenient ordinary trains which charged a daily fare of 8s 2d or a three-day fare of 11s 6d. On the same page, bookmakers Douglas

Stuart, Alfred Heaton and Alfred Carrington invited readers to write to them applying for a credit account, as their advertisements confidently said it would be business as usual during the winter season.

There was no criticism in *The Citizen* of the large crowd who had gathered under heavy clouds at the last day of the race meeting at Derby on 20 November to witness William's Pride holding off the challenge of White Lie to win the Derby Cup by a head. In fact, horse racing would not be suspended until June 1918 (less than six months before the war's end) and the King continued to attend meetings without a word of complaint from the press.

This attitude to 'the sport of kings' did not pass without comment. The *Daily News and Leader* reported that even though the income of Chelsea had been reduced by 50 per cent owing to the war, the club had sent £1258 to various funds from their gross receipts in the past three months. By contrast, no racecourse company had done anything.

Furthermore, the paper reported, Chelsea had established a special recruiting scheme and 'tomorrow half a dozen speakers will address the crowd at Stamford Bridge. A fortnight later the occasion of the next home game, a special collection for the provision of footballs for soldiers.

'Up to date, the club had received over 500 letters from soldiers from all parts of the country and from Belgium and France asking for footballs, and as many as possible have been sent in advance.'

In addition, according to the same newspaper, on 16 November, 'Chelsea Football Club is endeavouring to raise a company of the South Down Battalion of the Royal Sussex Regiment. Mr Claude Kirby, the chairman of the club, is giving every facility for recruiting at the football matches at Stamford Bridge.

'At the close of a reserve match on Saturday addresses on the duty of young men to the country were delivered outside the club offices with the result that several have now enlisted. The Chelsea players are also performing military drill and a rifle range has been set up.'

It had been an indifferent season for Chelsea. After an encouraging 1-1 draw on the opening Saturday against Tottenham Hotspur,

Chelsea had to wait until 10 October to record their first win, against Liverpool. They would then have to wait another month before easing past Bolton Wanderers on 7 November.

Despite what the soothsayers were writing in their newspapers about football fans, there did not seem to be many shirkers in the crowd of 15,000 that day: a photograph shows men intermingled with lads who look too young to enlist, either dressed as sailors or soldiers. With so many men in uniform, any recruitment campaign would probably have proved futile anyway.

On 16 November anyone watching Chelsea for the first time that season would have been hard-pressed to believe this was the same club that had made such a spluttering start.

Chelsea started in fine style by attacking the Notts County defence. A penalty after 15 minutes gave the blues the lead and concerted pressure from Notts County came to nothing as Chelsea doubled their lead before half-time. After the players had left the pitch for the break, a white-haired man rose to speak to the assembled crowd.

Across the country, politicians and soldiers had made a concerted effort to recruit football crowds to the war effort. At Stamford Bridge that afternoon, Colonel Charles Burn, MP for Torquay and aide-de-camp to the King for the past four years, was tasked with convincing those present to join the army. He now gave a speech amid his deepest grief.

Just three weeks earlier, on 30 October, he had received the news that every parent of a child fighting on a foreign battlefield dreads. His son, Arthur Herbert Rosdew Burn, Second Lieutenant, Royal Dragoons, had fallen at Ypres. He was just 22 years old and his body was now, like hundreds of others, buried in the mud of Flanders.

Clearing his throat and with something of a tremble in his voice, Burn began his address: 'I am a sportsman as well as a soldier. I believe in football, I believe in games being carried on as usual.'

He told the assembled crowd of the story of the Great Retreat from Mons, followed by the First Battle of the Marne and the smashing of the Prussian Guard.

Then he explained his reasons for talking to them that day. 'I have come to ask if there is any young man who has encumbrances to join the forces. I don't say come. I say, "Come for God's sake, you are wanted!"'

Referring to his own tragedy and how recruitment had become a personal crusade, he struggled to maintain his composure. 'I have given my own son. He enlisted at the start of the war. He is now dead. I have given up my own house as a shelter for the care of wounded officers.'

Then finishing with an emotional and patriotic plea, the MP had this message for all the crowd: 'I say to you young men that if I had 12 sons, I would give them all as my own life, for my country and my king.' There was a great round of applause which rang out from all four corners of Stamford Bridge.

Soon the players were back on the pitch. Chelsea picked up where they left off. The continuing pressure on the Notts County goalmouth reaped rewards when Chelsea went three up with a goal after 66 minutes.

Even though Chelsea was largely the dominant side, they were caught cold when, straight from the restart, Notts County hit back and got a goal, leaving the score at 3-1. The goal was the only highlight of a miserable afternoon for the Nottingham side as Chelsea hit home from a corner a few minutes before the final whistle.

In North London, the *Daily News and Leader* claimed 'the light and the war and prejudice played havoc with attendances at White Hart Lane, where Tottenham Hotspur deservedly defeated Manchester United by two goals to nil.' It was also noted that one-third of the 11,000 spectators were in khaki.

Both Chelsea and Tottenham fans could be happy with the performances of their sides: as they walked out into the cold, early evening air, the talk was of the improved prospects of both sides. It is difficult to know if anyone was talking about the speech that Colonel Burn had made at Stamford Bridge at half-time.

• • • •

After a weekend which had yielded only one recruit at football grounds throughout the country, there was only one item the newspapers wanted to write about: the speech by Colonel Burn.

In an article entitled 'One London Football Spectator Out of Thousands Became a Recruit', the *Daily Mirror* was scathing about what it perceived as the indifference of football spectators to the attempts to recruit them to the army.

On its front page it carried a picture of Colonel Burn, dressed in top hat and frock coat, addressing the Chelsea crowd.

Others were even more critical, with the *Pall Mall Gazette* writing, 'The simple and quiet talk of a fine soldier from the fighting line, whose boy had made the great sacrifice for his country, would not (says our contemporary) move this crowd of around 30,000 or more.

'Rome might burn for all they cared so long as they had their football. That was the attitude. And we wonder what the men present in khaki thought of the indifference. Where is the usefulness of the Football Association issuing a poster of appeal with one hand and with the other providing the cause for "the deadening spirit of indifference?"

'The Football Association was forgetful of its duty at the outset of the war. It was a plain and obvious duty. The fanaticism of the game was bound to hinder enlistment.'

The *Pall Mall Gazette* claimed the crowd was 'dumb' even as Colonel Burn was speaking of the fight in the trenches in the defence of Liège. The newspaper even quoted Robert Bridges, the Poet Laureate, who claimed the lack of volunteers for the army was an 'intolerable humiliation'.

The article went on to claim that thousands present at the game were eligible for service and that the Football Association 'can scarcely repair the injury that it had done by making possible the indulgence of the habit of watching football that has become second nature among the masses of the industrial centres.

'But at this late hour it might strive to repair the harm, while there is a spectacle then the habit will not be broken.' The *Pall Mall Gazette* ended with a simple solution. The Football Association should cancel all matches, for as Sir Robert Baden-Powell had said at White Hart Lane: 'We can do our football when we have done the war!'

If the football authorities thought criticism would be confined to London, then they would be sadly mistaken. News of Colonel Burn's speech had reached the Midlands, where the *Stratford-upon-Avon*

Herald claimed there was something wrong with football fans which made attempts to recruit them fail.

Repeating the claim by the *Pall Mall Gazette* that recruiting sergeants were present, it said, 'not a man was induced to join.' Furthermore, it claimed appeals were made at other grounds and also met with failure.

This attitude contrasted heavily with other sports, according to the *Gazette*, which noted 'the wholesale volunteering which has distinguished the performers and devotees of sports. Rugby Union clubs, cricket elevens and rowing clubs throughout the kingdom have placed men into the ranks.'

By Wednesday, the events at Stamford Bridge had reached the ear of the Prime Minister, Herbert Asquith, when Sir John Lonsdale rose in the House of Commons to ask whether it was a fact that last Saturday an appeal to many thousands of people at several football matches produced only one recruit and whether an end could not at once be put to this scandal by the government commandeering football grounds?

The Prime Minister replied that negotiations were ongoing with the football authorities and he did not think the case called for legislation at present.

However, there were some doubts about the accuracy of the reporting of the match. A letter in the *Liverpool Daily Post and Mercury*, from a Mr C.L. Legge, disputed the newspaper's view of events. 'As one of the spectators in the crowd at the Chelsea football ground, which was addressed by Colonel Burn MP on Saturday last, I take exception to the remarks of your London correspondent in today's *Daily Post* as they convey an entirely wrong impression. He says, "Colonel Burn's fine and manly address at Stamford Bridge last Saturday was cut short by a round of applause as the players came on the field."'

According to Mr Legge, this was wrong: 'No one near me either cheered or applauded as Colonel Burn was speaking, looking round, everyone in the vicinity of myself shouted "go on" and did not want him to stop his speech.'

Signing off, Mr Legge said that nearly every individual present was either a soldier or sailor.

PRESSURE!

The question in the Commons led to Chelsea issuing an official statement through the pages of *Sporting Life*: 'The underlying current of indiscriminate abuse of the professional seems to be the crowds of onlookers at his matches.

'These crowds have shrunk this season by some 40–50% and what is the reason? It is that scores of thousands of the younger onlookers have flocked to the colours and thousands more will do so if approached in the right way – not by abusing them, as so many do for "unpatriotic loafers".

'Professional football matches are the finest recruiting grounds imaginable if the authorities only knew it and set about work in an intelligent manner.'

Any calls to end the abuse were to fall on deaf ears, however. The Newspaper Proprietors Association held a meeting in central London on Thursday and agreed that newspapers would publish nothing about football, whether professional or amateur, except the bare results.

According to the letters pages of the *Pall Mall Gazette*, that ban was met with fulsome support from the public. Correspondent S.H. Vaughan of Earl's Court congratulated the *Pall Mall Gazette* before referring to the game at Stamford Bridge, where he claimed that 'Spectators have not the energy or the pluck to enlist and the country wants men and not worms.'

Lying in the Royal Infirmary, Newcastle upon Tyne, with several wounds, Private Morgan wrote a letter to the *Daily News*, in the hope it would 'meet the eyes of those unsportsmanlike people who are criticising our most favourite game, soccer'.

'I certainly think these people who are doing a lot of shouting about stopping football should be made soldiers. I also think people nowadays only want you to go to work, come home and sit looking at the fire. Perhaps those who are so unsportsmanlike will enlist and try and protect their king and country instead of staying at home and criticising the old game of soccer.'

The response from the Football Association to the Newspaper Proprietors Association was particularly robust, openly questioning the various newspaper articles and their reaction to Colonel Burn's speech at Stamford Bridge. In some quarters it had been reported there were 30,000 spectators present and not one had responded.

Not so, said the Football Association: the attendance was 14,852 and of that number 6,702 were soldiers and sailors in uniform and 783 were boys under the age of 14. There were also many ladies present. Crucially, there was not a single recruiting officer at the ground.

Further to this, the FA claimed there were grounds to believe that approximately 500,000 players and spectators had joined the forces since the start of the war – and no other section of the community had produced better results. Furthermore, attendances had dropped by half and the only people watching the games were not of an age or physical condition to join the forces even if they were willing.

This argument was backed up in the pages of the *Chelsea Chronicle*, the match day programme, published ahead of their home game against Sheffield Wednesday on 5 December.

On the front page was a cartoon entitled 'mud slingers' with the caption '*The Times* declare that professional footballers are shirking their national duties, are scared and are preventing recruiting.'

Confirming the view of the Football Association that there were no recruiting sergeants at the game, the editorial said two had been expected but never arrived, delayed by other duties. It added that there had been several enquiries for recruiting sergeants after the match, without result. Therefore, the *Chronicle* now made an appeal to men to enlist through the usual channels – recruiting offices.

Turning to the attitude of the press, it said, 'to say not a single man stepped forward is somewhat akin to lamenting that after a parliamentary candidate had made an impassioned appeal for support at a poll, not a single man stepped forward and voted for him on the spot!'.

The *Chronicle* then focused its attack on pastimes other than football: 'It has been asked what proof is there that the reported shrinking of football crowds by 50% or more is attributable to half the number of those formally attending those matches have enlisted?

'What proof? What the proof afforded to by attending (probably for the first time in the doubter's life) a professional match and noting the number of men in khaki representing the comparatively small proportion of them who have been able to get leave for a few hours on a Saturday afternoon and have seized the opportunity to rush to their "former vice" – the football ground.

'By noting also, the small proportion of those of enlistable age – smaller than that to be found any day at the picture palaces and music halls to say nothing of the racecourses.'

To present further evidence of what they described as bias in the press, the *Chronicle* carried a copy of a letter, written by an old supporter, Dr W. Monro Anderson, and addressed to the editor of the *Pall Mall Gazette*, which they claimed was suppressed.

In the letter, Dr Anderson challenged the editor to enlist if he could persuade any footballer to enlist in Kitchener's Army, even offering to join himself. Then he said if the editor would give a shilling to some fund for every day of Dr Anderson's service, then he himself would give two shillings for every day of the editor's service. The letter was never printed nor answered.

Calling on fans to 'boycott the boycotters', the *Chronicle* published a list of newspapers still giving football reports or favourable to the continuation of football: *Sporting Life*, *Sporting Chronicle*, *Sportsman*, *Daily Citizen* and *Daily Sketch*.

On the same day, the editorial in the *Tottenham Hotspur Football and Athletic* carried criticism of the newspaper boycott of the game. 'The sincerity of the boycott is somewhat open to question when we find that in one instance at least, football news is excluded from a London daily newspaper issuing from the same office as a Sunday newspaper which continues to report and criticise football.

'A more glaring example perhaps is that of a London daily also published in Manchester. The Manchester edition contains the usual reports and criticisms which are rigidly barred from the London edition.'

For Spurs the reason that football was being attacked was simple – class. 'It would certainly appear that the attack is made on football because it is the working man's game, otherwise the same campaign would be employed in respect to horse racing, hunting, golf, theatres, and music halls.'

The editorial went on to cite the example of Europe, where football was still being played in Austria, France and Germany. It was even said the Berlin *Lokal-Anzeiger* newspaper was still publishing comments on several teams, some of which had to be filled by new men who replaced favourites drafted into the army.

Based on these facts it was difficult, Spurs argued, to understand why footballers and those who watch matches were singled out and sneered at as being shirkers.

Certainly, other sports were avoiding censure for reasons that seem convenient. Cricket is traditionally a summer game, which ends in September. The Rugby Football Union announced that there would be no season in 1914/15 – but this was an amateur sport, so there were no financial implications for players who all had alternative careers.

Football was different, and though there were a few exceptions it was played mainly by the working classes. Most players had a contract and were paid a wage. A loss or drop in wages could impact wives, children and elderly parents.

No wonder the FA was grateful for the government's initial announcement that contracts should be honoured. Then there had been the feeling that football could be good for morale. Besides, when the season kicked off on 1 September, there had not been much of an argument to cancel: the war would be 'over by Christmas'.

The theme of an attack on football as being an attack on the working class was taken up by Councillor J.C. Tilloston, president of the Birmingham Football Combination. The *Birmingham Gazette* of 27 November reported his comments at a recent meeting: 'There was no organised sport in the country which has contributed more men to the army than football and personally he was proud that 11 of his own kinsmen, who had been stigmatised by a certain local MP as football loafers, were fighting for their country today.

'The members of the working class were the principal supporters of football, and it was from the ranks of this section of the community that the largest number of recruits had been drawn. The aristocracy and working class were doing their duty, it was the middle-class people who had not made the same sacrifices.'

Even though there was a concerted effort to recruit working class men to fight in the name of democracy when only 60 per cent of men were allowed to vote in the last General Election before the war in December 1910. Only two out of five men, mainly working class, did have the vote when they signed. So, footballers and fans were being asked to defend a system in which they had no stake.

....

On the same day that Chelsea's season finally came to life against Notts County, Heart of Midlothian were continuing their early season dominance of the Scottish League.

Apart from a 2-2 draw with Queens Park at their Tynecastle home on 24 October, they had won every single game of the season, beginning with a 2-0 win over Celtic on the opening day of the season.

The day after, it was reported that on the morning of the match, Tom Gracie, the Hearts centre-forward, opened an envelope in which was enclosed a copy of a *Punch* cartoon berating footballers for not joining the army. The sender was anonymous.

A subsequent match against Partick Thistle was another powerful display by the Edinburgh club. Their opponents were dispatched 2-0, and Hearts fans started to believe the Scottish championship would be resting in the Scottish capital by the end of the season.

Like their Southern counterparts, however, the Scottish Football Association were under pressure to suspend the season.

Since August the entire Hearts playing staff had taken part in weekly drill sessions to prepare them for the possibility of military service. These were conducted by the club's reserve half-back, Annan Ness, who was a former soldier. The Hearts manager, John McCartney, extended an invitation to the players of local rivals Hibernian to join in.

Three weeks later, on Saturday, 14 November, Hearts met Falkirk, hoping to extend their lead at the top of the League. At half-time the Queen's Own Cameron Highlanders made an urgent appeal for volunteers. The initial response was disappointing, but at full time several men stepped forward. Among them was Hearts winger and Scottish international James Speedie.

These actions did nothing to satisfy the anti-football brigade, however. On the night of the victory over Partick Thistle, the *Edinburgh Evening News* carried a letter, signed 'a soldier's daughter'.

The letter was scathing: 'while Hearts continue to play football, enabled thus to pursue their peaceful play by the sacrifice of the lives of thousands of their countrymen, they might accept, temporarily, a nom de plume, say "The White Feathers of Midlothian".' Several letters of this nature had already appeared in the press since the declaration of war but by and large were shrugged off. This one seemed to hit a raw nerve, though, and spurred one man into action.

In Edinburgh, George McCrae was nothing short of a legend. Born in the slums of Edinburgh, he left school at the age of nine to work as a messenger for a bootmaker. There followed a meteoric rise in local politics, and by 1899 he was the Liberal MP for Edinburgh East.

A reservist, he joined as a private but was to become the colonel of his own teetotal battalion, the 16th Royal Scots, known as 'McCrae's Water Rats'. In 1909 he found himself back in his home city, having left Parliament at the request of the Prime Minister to become secretary of the Local Government Board in Scotland, tasked with implementing the government's programme of social reform.

He had resigned in 1913, to look after his wife who had been diagnosed with terminal cancer. Then war broke out, and on 19 November 1914, the *Evening Dispatch* announced that McCrae had volunteered for active service at the age of 54.

The following morning, the *Scotsman* reported that the War Office had accepted his offer to raise and command a battalion in the field. McCrae quickly announced that recruiting would commence on 27 November at a grand public meeting in the Usher Hall. The campaign, he insisted, would last only seven days, because he was confident that the Battalion would be full in that time.

Letters written to the Hearts chairman were read out at the meeting. Mr McDowell of the Scottish Association wrote: 'Bravo! I am proud of the old club', while W.M. Ward, former president of the Scottish League, felt that the formation of the Battalion was the perfect antidote to the anti-football campaign: 'You have indeed given a splendid lead to other clubs, and I hope your example will immediately be followed by all of us. It will be no fault of mine if we in the west do not out patriot you.

'Your action is a splendid answer to "stop the game" croakers and will enlist for the game and those who take part in the goodwill of all right-thinking people "hats off to the patriotic Hearts."'

As part of his recruitment strategy, McCrae and his colleague Sir James Leishman made an appointment to meet with the directors and manager of Hearts at their home ground, Tynecastle Park, with a view to recruiting the playing staff. The *Bradford Telegraph* would later report that McCrae was met with what they termed 'happy results'.

The previous afternoon on 26 November at a press conference at Tynecastle, 11 Hearts players had publicly enlisted in the new battalion: the 16th (Service) Battalion of the Royal Scots, which quickly gained the nickname, 'McCrae's Battalion'.

The *Dundee Courier* called the footballers 'an example to all sportsmen. Their self-sacrifice and patriotism are an example to professional sportsman of all kinds.'

The news quickly reached the English newspapers, the *Northern Daily Telegraph* gleefully reporting McCrae's activities: 'One of his recruiting exploits was the enlistment of no fewer than 11 members of the staff of the Heart of Midlothian at Tynecastle, of the 11 players recruited, six have been associated with the first team and five with the reserves.'

Other newspapers labelled McCrae's efforts 'something of a sensation', the *Bradford Daily Telegraph* claiming, 'Others are now considering the matter. This indeed will give a splendid lead to players in other parts of the country and may have a positive effect on recruiting.'

The pressure was now on the English football authorities. Sir George McCrae had become a hero overnight and his example would be noted by other ambitious men.

Chapter 2

Formation
Football does its bit

To onlookers, the match was a typical cup tie, held in the second week of January, when the ground was unforgiving, the tackles hard and the pitch a veritable mudbath. In a howling wind, Millwall faced Clapton Orient in the first round of the FA Cup at their New Cross home.

Both sides arrived at the match, depleted by injuries. Orient expected to badly miss their star striker, Richard McFadden, who was on the injured list and unable to play. Leading the line in his absence was his strike partner and childhood friend, William Jonas, who would move to the unfamiliar inside left position to compensate.

Millwall scored after half an hour, then made the game safe when they doubled their lead in the second half. According to *Sporting Life*, 'The Orient men were never a beaten side till the end. They were always fighting grimly and with potentialities of success.'

Their pressure finally paid off when a handball gave Orient a penalty. William Jonas converted, and the game was on. In the closing stages, Jonas saw an opportunity for an equaliser to force a replay. With the ball in mid-air, he charged at Joe Orme, the Millwall goalkeeper who was waiting to catch it.

Instead of connecting with the ball, Jonas clattered violently into Orme and both men ended up in a heap on the ground. No one quite heard the angry words that were exchanged, but tempers, which had been threatening to boil over all afternoon, finally exploded into punches being thrown by both men, in the front of the Millwall goal.

After the pair had been separated, the referee, J.F. Pearson, who had travelled to London from Dudley, ordered both players off the pitch.

By the end of the week both the goalkeeper and the striker had made their peace, with *Sporting Life* reporting on 15 January 1915, 'We understand that Orme (Millwall) and Jonas (Clapton Orient) who had a pronounced difference of opinion at New Cross last Saturday towards the close of the cup tie, and were sent off the field, have tendered an unreserved apology to each other, for their momentary loss of temper … the players have furnished to the Football Association their accounts of what happened.'

Punishment was swift, the minutes of the proceedings of the Football Association emergency committee recording, 'Millwall v Clapton Orient – JH Orme of Millwall and W Jonas of Clapton Orient suspended for 14 days from 20th January 1915 for misconduct in this match.'

It was the second suspension that Jonas would serve. Nearly a year to the day of the Millwall match, in another FA Cup first round, Jonas had been given his marching orders at the County Ground, for lashing out in retaliation at Nottingham Forest defender Joe Mercer Sr – who had, he claimed, kicked him first. For that offence the Clapton Orient striker had been suspended for seven days.

There was no doubt these events were embarrassing for both the player and his club. And matters were further complicated by the fact that Jonas, Orme and Mercer were all members of the 17th (Service) Battalion (Football) of the Duke of Cambridge's Own (Middlesex Regiment), more commonly known as the Football Battalion.

Jonas' club had won plaudits just a month earlier when the Battalion was founded at Fulham Town Hall on a cold December afternoon, 10 days before Christmas.

Around 3.30 p.m. on 15 December 1914, as darkness began to descend on the London streets, Jonas and McFadden had gathered with an estimated 400 professional football players, directors and officials of London clubs, at the council chambers of Fulham Town Hall.

They were there at the invitation of the Football Association to meet with Lord Kinnaird, president of the Football Association, Mr W. Hayes Fisher MP, president of Fulham FC, and Mr Joynson-Hicks MP with a view to forming a battalion made up of footballers.

Casting his eye over the packed meeting, the beleaguered FA secretary, Frederick Wall, could feel a sense of satisfaction: professionals who had been demonised in the press had now gathered to do their bit for the war effort.

Just as well. North of the border, George McCrae reported that the Heart of Midlothian players who had volunteered for 'McRae's Battalion' had now been joined by players from Dunfermline, Falkirk, Raith Rovers and Mossend Burnside, as well as many supporters.

...

Just two weeks earlier, England had been hit by heavy rain, resulting in *The Times* reporting on 30 November that attendances at Saturday's matches in the three principal football leagues totalled 173,000 against 234,000 on the previous Saturday.

The weather, which had been mainly wet and windy throughout November, was to have an adverse effect on recruitment efforts that weekend. The report continued: 'No attempts were made to obtain recruits at the matches at Fulham, Bradford, Sheffield, Manchester, Birmingham and Sunderland.

'At league champions Blackburn Rovers, boy scouts distributed leaflets imploring men to "fall in" but there was no recruiting officers at the ground should anyone want to join up.'

Down in West London, where Fulham took on Barnsley at Craven Cottage, it was said that there had been no attempts to obtain recruits. The Football Association added that no communication of any kind had been received from the War Office regarding recruitment. Further, as *The Times* noted, any attempt to recruit would have been futile because rain fell heavily during the match and attendances were in their hundreds.

Even as the adverse publicity continued, it was reported that all 11 London clubs said they were prepared to discontinue the game by closing their grounds. However, there were conditions attached: this would happen only if racecourses, golf links, theatres, music halls and cinemas all closed their doors at the same time.

But things were changing daily. The news of McRae's Battalion was simply adding to the pressure. And the success and fame that George McCrae had suddenly found in forming the 16th Scots made those who sought the limelight sit up and take notice.

One of those men was the Clapton Orient chairman, Captain Henry Wells-Holland, who had hit on the idea of starting his own platoon consisting entirely of his own players and staff. He may not have been the only man to consider such plans, either: there had been calls for a football battalion right at the start of the season, but plans had failed to get off the ground.

Now, though, there was a renewed call for a football battalion – and it came from an unlikely source.

William Joynson-Hicks had come to prominence by defeating Winston Churchill in a by-election for his seat in Manchester North-West, after Churchill was appointed President of the Board of Trade and joined the Cabinet. At that time, anyone appointed to the Cabinet was required to resign his seat and fight a by-election. He would normally expect to be returned unopposed, but Churchill had crossed the floor several years earlier and the Conservative Party was determined to put up a candidate against their turncoat

During the hard fought by-election, Joynson-Hicks was described by Labour leader Keir Hardie as 'a leprous traitor' while the distinguished science fiction writer H.G. Wells said of him that he 'represents absolutely the worst element in British political life … an entirely undistinguished man … and an obscure and ineffectual nobody.' Perhaps, but he won by a few hundred votes.

Known widely as 'Jix', he tended to focus on transport-related matters. When war broke out, he became the head of a movement to supply the British Red Cross with ambulances. He also headed up committees to drum up recruitment.

He earned plaudits in some quarters for this work, but he wanted more. The flamboyant Jix now secured an appointment with the Under-Secretary of State for War, Harold Tennant.

The official reason may have been to see what more he could do to help with the war effort, but this did not mean he would be averse to replicating the role of George McCrae, south of the border. A successful campaign to form such a battalion could ensure future promotion to the Cabinet.

By the time Jix met with Tennant, *The Times* was reporting that 20 players from Hull City had enlisted, along with one director, and £75 been given to relief funds. From Everton, the title challengers and League leaders, came eight players, one director and several sons of other directors. The club had also contributed £500 to the Prince of Wales Fund, £10 10s to the Princess Mary Fund and £75 to other war-related charities.

Other clubs like Burnley and Plymouth Argyle had erected rifle ranges or given over their grounds and other apparatus to the disposal of local troops.

After the conclusion of the meeting with Tennant, Jix wasted no time. At Russell Square, headquarters of the Football Association, he met with the president, Lord Kinnard, and secretary, Frederick Wall.

The two men were keen to do anything to address the adverse publicity that football had been receiving. Considering the positive reaction to McCrae's initiative in Scotland, a pals' battalion which allowed players and supporters to serve together seemed like the best way forward. It was the same idea that both Kinnard and Wall had dismissed when put to them by Frederick Charrington in September.

A letter of 5 December invited the chairmen of the 11 London clubs to Russell Square for a meeting, where the formation of a 'Footballer's Battalion of Kitchener's Army' would be discussed officially for the first time.

The letter arrived just two days after the four National Football Associations had voted during a conference convened by the Scottish FA, to suspend international matches for the duration of the war. The conference had also agreed that both the FA and Scottish Cups could continue as normal without any disruption.

The meeting on 8 December was attended by every single club in the capital. There had been months of hard pressure from the press, clergy and now the government – and to make matters worse, the Scottish FA now decided not to proceed with the Scottish Cup, claiming it was honour-bound to suspend matches despite its earlier agreement.

At the meeting in London, there would no arguments about pay or contracts; Jix had decreed there was to be a football battalion and any dissension would not be tolerated. If an indication was needed that he meant business, this came from the presence of Captain Thomas Whiffen, who had been appointed by the War Office as the chief recruiting officer for London.

At the end of the meeting a motion was voted upon: 'That this meeting with the directors of London professional clubs heartily favours the project of the formation of a Footballer's Battalion.' There were no dissenting voices.

The second resolution was the formation of an executive committee to oversee accommodation, clothing and equipment for the proposed battalion alongside recruitment. And, just to ensure that Jix would be mentioned in the same breath as George McCrae, he was appointed the chairman.

The new battalion was officially named the 17th (Service) Battalion (Football), Middlesex Regiment as part of the Duke of Cambridge's Own (Middlesex Regiment) – which just so happened to be local to Jix's constituency of Brentford.

One of the first acts of the new executive committee was to ensure that the usual height requirements for the army would be foregone; that players who joined up would be given leave to play for their clubs in League and Cup matches for the rest of the season; and that the headquarters of the new battalion would be located at Richmond Athletic Ground.

Other officers of the executive committee were Frederick Wall, the FA secretary, who agreed to act as honorary secretary, and Sir Henry Egger, a former solicitor to the Indian government, who agreed to be treasurer. Also on the committee were W.C. Kirby of Chelsea, J.B. Skeggs of Millwall and Captain H. Wells-Holland of Clapton Orient, the one person to rival Jix with a nose for publicity.

Now only one point remained: to invite the players to form a battalion. The meeting was arranged – to take place where?

The Mayor of Fulham, Henry Norris, offered up the use of Fulham Town Hall. Norris was a controversial figure in footballing circles. A multimillionaire property developer, he had first drawn attention as the chairman of Fulham FC in the early 1900s, before joining the board of Woolwich Arsenal in 1910 while remaining in position at Fulham.

He then suggested merging the two clubs, a proposal so unpopular that he had to resign as chairman of Fulham. His ability to upset people continued when he moved Arsenal from Woolwich to Highbury in 1913, this time falling out with the other London clubs who opposed such a move.

Looking for a way to gain some much-needed positive publicity, Norris offered up the use of the town hall, where all professional players would be invited to join the new football battalion. The date was set for 15 December.

Over the next few days, adverts were to appear in the press: 'The Football Battalion wants players, officials, and club enthusiasts. Are YOU fit and free?'

• • •

According to a report in *The Times* on 16 December, Joynson-Hicks launched into an opening speech, where he said 'Nobody who took an interest in football could be ignorant of the great deal of correspondence and numerous articles in newspapers which contained attacks on football, football clubs, upon anyone who looked on while a match was being played.'

Getting into his stride, Joynson-Hicks was reported as saying, 'This meeting was not to answer those attacks. After the war was over there would be plenty of opportunities for recrimination.'

Then directly quoting him, *The Times* reported the politician as saying, 'I am certain that those who played and those who managed the game could endure any attacks and if they felt inclined, answer them later. The very best answer that could be given would be the success of the Football Battalion and I say the success of the Football Brigade.'

According to *The Times* report, the gathered crowd applauded and cheered as Jix warmed to his theme, 'I am not going to ask you to join in any picnic. I tell you that this war is one of bitterness and danger. We are fighting not merely for Belgium, not merely a scrap of paper, not merely for the honour of Great Britain but also our own homes, our wives, and our children.

'Remember, that even as Germany has treated Belgium so she would treat England, aye, tenfold more so if she were allowed to gain a footing in the country.

'Men, I solemnly assure you the best way to fight for England is to fight in Flanders. Let each one ask himself the question whether as an Englishman he ought not to take some part in the infliction of revenge upon the barbarians for the manner they have treated Belgium.'

Finishing with a flourish, Jix implored those gathered to do their bit. 'Yes, we must do our part and I shall not be satisfied until we have two or three Footballers Battalions fighting in Flanders.' As the chairman sat down, he could be satisfied with the several minutes of applause.

Sporting Life reported that Jix 'appealed to them, for what they were, he appealed to them on behalf of their children, the children that were to be, to give themselves to their country and in doing so they would be doing something that would rebound on the honour of footballers and its fame would resound not merely from one end of England to the other, but from the confines of Flanders to the centre of Berlin.'

Next to speak was William Hayes-Fisher, who told the audience that he spoke not as the local MP but as the president of Fulham FC. According to *Sporting Life*, he said, 'Footballers and spectators had had a lot to put up with of late and he had read in the campaign against footballers and spectators some of the worst nonsense he had ever read in his life.'

After Hayes-Fisher sat down, the floor was open for questions, there were a few queries on pay. It would be 7s for a single man, 12s 6d for a married man and 3s 6d extra for men who lived in London, with extra allowances for children and travel.

According to *The Times*, 'After dwelling on the risk of injury, which might ruin the earning capacity of a footballer, but would not impair the efficiency of the clerk, Fisher said the committee were considering the possibility of setting up some system of insurance, and concluded by stating the House of Commons was engaged in considering the question of pensions given in case of disablement or death and remarked, "I am perfectly certain they are going to be raised to a far better standard than ever before."'

The chairman of Crystal Palace, Sydney Bourne, enquired whether it might be possible to secure the transfer to the Footballers Battalion of some of those who had recently joined but would prefer to be with their old football friends? Jix as chairman replied that it would be a matter for the War Office, but the committee would certainly make representations.

The FA president, Lord Kinnaird, told the meeting he had sent three sons and four nephews to the front and there was not a single person he had spoken to, who had been there, had regretted it. He then asked those present to set an example and join up.

Colonel Grantham, Chief Recruiting Officer for London, and the secretary, Frederick Wall, appealed to the gatherings for recruits. They could apply either at the Football Association Headquarters, 42 Russell Square, or here today at the meeting.

There was a minute or two of silence, then one man stood up and proceeded towards the stage.

With his receding dark hair, swept back by hair cream from his lined forehead, he could have been taken for being a decade or two older than his 28 years. Frederick Parker was the captain of Clapton Orient, known since his days growing up in Weymouth as 'Spider' for his spindly frame. He weighed only a little over 70 kg (11 stone) despite standing at 1.8 m (5' 11").

Years before joining Clapton Orient in 1907, Parker had attempted to join the army, as described by *Reynolds's Newspaper*, 'As soon as he reached the minimum age for recruiting, Parker, then a tall, lath-like looking lad "took the shilling". He was passed by the doctor and appeared before the colonel.

'That officer, evidently not impressed with Parker's physique, told him to return to the doctor, with his compliments for a second examination. The medical officer promptly took the hint and would not pass him. This ended, for the time being, Parker's vision of wearing His Majesty's uniform, on account of "Spider's" slender build.'

For years, Parker would often joke that he had considered himself a soldier for the space of about an hour! There were no such fears today. When Parker volunteered, he was promptly signed up, officially becoming the very first recruit of the 17th (Service) Battalion (Football) of the Duke of Cambridge's Own (Middlesex Regiment).

The second man to volunteer was a done deal. Just the previous week, on Thursday, 10 December 1914, the *Birmingham Mail* reported that, 'Frank Buckley, the Bradford City half-back, and former member of the Aston Villa and Birmingham Football Club, has offered his services to the Association for the Footballers' Battalion now in the process of formation.

'Buckley was a sergeant instructor in the 2nd Battalion King's Liverpool Regiment for three and a half years before joining the Aston Villa club as a footballer in April 1903.

'He comes of a military family, for his father was a sergeant-major in the regiment for over thirty years. Buckley played for Villa for two seasons and was then transferred to Manchester City.

'He subsequently joined Birmingham, for whom he played for several seasons, and then threw in his lot with Derby County, left that club to join Bradford City. He was for several years a farmer at Redditch, and at present resides at the Bury Mound Farm, Warstock, near King's Heath.'

Like Parker, Buckley was a leader and someone who would take no nonsense. According to the *Derbyshire Advertiser and Journal*, 'when up before a Football Association Disciplinary Committee for punching an opponent he told the disciplinary committee he would do it again if necessary.

'A committee member recalled: "The other man he said used filthy language every time he came near an opponent and as he persisted after being warned 'he let him have it'."'

Other players stepped forward. Teddy Foord, Chelsea star winger, stood up alongside Brighton & Hove Albion half-back, Archie Needham. *The Times* was to write, 'In singles and couples others left their seats, until 35 players had offered themselves.' Among those to step forward were William Jonas and Richard McFadden.

By the end of the meeting the following players had also volunteered for the Football Battalion: Thomas Ratcliff (Arsenal assistant trainer), Ralph Routledge, Frank Spencer, John Woodhouse (Brighton & Hove Albion); William Krug, David Girdwood, (Chelsea); Jimmy Hugall, Nolan Evans, Harold Gibson, Bob Dalrymple, Edward King, Arthur Tilley, Thomas Pearson (Clapham Orient); Ernie Williamson, Thomas Newton, Dick Upex, Cyril Smith, Albert Tomkins, Percy Barnfather (Croydon Common); James Bowler, William Middleton (Crystal Palace); Hugh Roberts, Frank Lindley (Luton Town); Frederick Robson (Southend United); George Bowler, William Oliver (Tottenham Hotspur); Reginald Williams, Alexander Stewart and Joe McLaughlan (Watford).

When it came time to move the vote of thanks, William Hayes-Fisher was enthusiastic in his praise of the chairman, William Joynson-Hicks, and the oratorical skills of all the speakers, thanking them for attending.

Seconding the vote of thanks, Captain Wells-Holland was at pains to make it clear that none of the players were forced or coerced into joining the colours, although, he did express the hope that Clapton Orient would form a platoon of its own. *The Sportsman* reported him as saying, 'The battalion would be a splendid answer to the unjust strictures in the press.'

Unsurprisingly, the vote of thanks was carried with great cheers and enthusiasm. Standing at the front of the meeting, with all the footballers who had enrolled behind him, Jix knew he had scored a huge political victory and would have felt extremely pleased with his day's work.

There was no need to thank him, he insisted; today was not about him. Turning to the group of players and addressing them directly, he told them that they themselves should be thanked for the expression of loyalty that they as footballers had given to king and country.

The meeting ended with the singing of 'God Save The King'. With that the players filed out into the pitch-blackness of the cold December night.

• • •

News of the Football Battalion was quick to break. Nestled next to an advertisement which spoke of the delight of the French Rivera in the winter, where you could travel by train to Cannes, Monte Carlo or Nice and enjoy golf, lawn tennis and motor excursions, the *Sporting Life* columnist G. Wagstaffe Simmons wrote of its formation providing 'ample refutation of the frequent statements by anti-footballers that those who control and play the association game are so absorbed in the pastime that they pay no attention to the urgent demands for men for the New Army.'

Wagstaffe Simmons then went on to launch an attack on the press and their reporting of football: 'When the campaign against association football was begun, after the outbreak of war, wide and sweeping denunciations were made by detractors.

'For several weeks, I made an assiduous collection of letters and articles which appeared in the press and a careful analysis of their writers revealed the fact that those who led the campaign and a great majority of those who supported it were men who never identified with the game. One of the most virulent of the critics thanked heaven that he had not seen a professional match in a decade.

'The savage attacks made on the association footballers have largely petered. They were so grotesquely untrue that the publication of the facts overwhelmed most critics with ridicule.'

An editorial in the *Kensington News and West London Times* said, 'Every man, woman and child of British blood will wish the Football Battalion God speed. It is indeed a feather in the footballers' cap and best of all, not a white feather, but a glorious plume. The whole incident serves to exemplify, if example were needed, how cheerfully Britons may be led, and how difficult it is to drive them over in the right direction.'

At the weekend's football matches, the clubs would also have their say. In the Millwall official programme, J.B. Skeggs, the club chairman, wrote, 'What was considered impossible in August is now an accomplished fact and we have in existence a Football Battalion of the 17th Middlesex Regiment (the Die-hards).

'A meeting was held at the Fulham Town Hall, on the invitation of the Mayor of Fulham, my good friend, Mr HG Norris JP, who is in social and municipal work, is a gentleman and a patriot, but who, because of his love of football, is likewise a coward, a shirker and a traitor if one is to accept the opinion of Lord Northcliffe's hired writers.'

In conclusion Mr Skeggs ended by saying, 'And to those time and great facilities for good have prostituted by a vicious abuse of a good body of sportsmen, may I express a hope that the coming year may find them more honest, more charitable and less ready to sit at home in comfortable armchairs concocting lies about a body of men their superiors as Englishmen.'

In the days that followed the meeting, recruitment continued at a pace. On 17 December the *Globe* noted, 'The following professional players had joined the football battalion yesterday – Millwall; Orme, Williams, Kirkwood, Nuttal and Borthwick.

Luton – Dunn, Frith, Wileman, Rowe, Simms and Wilson.

'The only London professional clubs not represented in the Battalion were West Ham and Fulham.

'Joseph Mercer, the Nottingham Forest centre-half, had joined the colours yesterday. Notts Forest were now only fourteen players.'

On 22 December, the *Daily News* reported Arsenal players G. Ford, Spittle, Butles and Houston had signed up, as had the assistant trainer, Tom Ratcliffe. They joined Northampton's Walter Tull, who had taken the oath the day before.

FORMATION

On 11 January 1915, just two days after Clapton Orient's William Jonas and Millwall's Joe Orme had slugged out in the goal mouth at New Cross, they joined their new comrades to march side by side, without pomp or ceremony, through the London streets towards their eventual destination, White City, where they would go through special training before being drafted into service.

The march started from West Africa House, Kingsway, where the men received their pay and conditions, though not their uniforms. Nor was the Battalion yet at full strength, though the previous week it had been estimated that 600 people had joined: 200 from London and 400 from further afield.

In the parade was Colonel Grantham, the senior officer, Captain A. Elphinstone, an old Cambridge athlete, Captain Wells-Holland, the chairman of Clapton Orient, and Lieutenant W.W. Scotland, a director of Crystal Palace.

Also marching that day were the first commissioned officers of the Battalion, Vivian Woodward of Chelsea, Evelyn Lintott of Leeds City and Frank Buckley of Bradford City, all-star players but now all soldiers about to begin their training in preparation for the frontline.

It had been an incredible effort by the football community. It had taken hard work and patience, but finally there was a Football Battalion. And as hard as the last few months had been, the soldiers who marched knew that things were going to be much tougher.

Chapter 3

Hearts
Scottish football responds to the war

It is a clear beautiful morning in June; the atmosphere has a celebratory air. Many of the men who march are used to crowds, but none as big as this. Usually, the city is split between the maroon of Hearts and the green of Hibernian – but not today. Today, Edinburgh stands together as one.

The windows of the shops and houses are bedecked with banners, girls wave and blow kisses, and parents point and ask children to wave small flags. Everyone has come out to greet the lads, many of them already heroes to the vast crowds.

As they march, they sing patriotic songs and the crowd joins in. For anyone who does not know the country is at war, the scenes could easily be mistaken for a summer parade. The crowds are happy, for they have taken to the streets to bid farewell to McCrae's Battalion.

Some of the more eagle-eyed soldiers have seen the few older women dotted around, dressed in black and not joining the festivities. Some with tears in their eyes stand silent, grieving and perhaps remembering the scene as their husband, son or brother marched to war, never to come back.

On through the main street the soldiers march, boots striking the ground in time to the band leading them, arms swinging just as they have been taught since joining up six months previously in November. Finally, they arrive at their destination, Waverley train station, where the crowd has only become heavier and more intense with their singing.

Eventually, the men are told to halt. Each of them knows why they are here, to board a train and travel 188 miles to Ripon, Yorkshire, for more training, then on to Salisbury Plain and finally, the Western Front, Northern France.

Many men are looking forward to the change of scenery. The initial training in drill and musketry, together with demanding route marches around the Lothians and Lanarkshire countryside, have taken their toll.

The large crowds are held back to allow the soldiers a route through. They look out to the gathered throng for one last glimpse of a loved one. The crowd gazes back, mothers and wives holding their emotions in check while the men, some fathers and brothers, proudly call and cheer. Some of those watching to support the soldiers are so overcome by fear they faint and have to be helped.

In single file, slowly, they board the train. Among their number are Sergeant-Major Annan Ness, Sergeant Duncan Currie, Corporal James Low, Corporal Thomas Gracie, Corporal Norman Findlay, Corporal Alfred Briggs, Private James Boyd, Private Ernest Ellis, Private Henry Wattie and Private Patrick Crossan.

They should have been joined that day by Bob Preston and Willie Wilson, but Preston is in hospital with influenza and Wilson is having problems with a shoulder injury. For now, they remain in Heriot Watt School, where they have been billeted since joining up in November 1914.

Of all the men of the 16th Royal Scots Battalion 'C' Company who march that day, their faces will have been some of the most recognisable. For the past few months, they have thrilled and entertained the people of Edinburgh dressed in another uniform. Not khaki and polished army regulation boots, but the maroon shirt of Heart of Midlothian Football Club.

••••

Just four months earlier, the soldiers now boarding the train had looked as though they were about to claim the Scottish League Championship pendant as their own. Then, on 20 February, everything caught up with them.

The howling February wind sweeping across Tynecastle Park suddenly felt more bitter as John McCartney, the Heart of Midlothian manager, pulled out his fob watch from his waistcoat pocket to check the time.

The 17,000-strong crowd, many in uniform, had been stunned into silence watching their team, the current League leaders and unbeaten at home, fall four goals behind to Glasgow Rangers.

The trusty gold watch provided no comfort, either. Time was running out; there were just eight minutes left. For months the team in maroon had been dominating nearly every team they faced, but now they were being humbled by Glasgow Rangers. Running against the breeze, the men from Ibrox had scored twice in the first half with goals from their strikers, Willie Reid and Tommy Cairns.

In the second half, Reid of Rangers completed his hat-trick. Hearts' enviable home record was coming to an end. Inadvertently, Rangers had done their Old Firm rivals, Celtic, a favour.

Back in Glasgow, Celtic had taken an early first-half lead and were bombarding the Dumbarton goal. It was only a strong defensive display from the visitors which kept the deficit to one goal.

This had been a day for shocks. South of the border in the third round of the FA Cup, holders Burnley had been dumped out of the competition, Bolton Wanderers coming out on top, 2-1.

League leaders Oldham Athletic made it through to the next round with a 3-2 win away at Birmingham, as did fellow title chasers Everton, who got past Queens Park Rangers. Both Sheffield United and Chelsea also recorded wins, securing their places in the draw for the next round.

English football teams were still playing for a cup – in contrast to Scotland. At a meeting of the Scottish Football Association on

22 December 1914, a motion had been passed by one vote: 'The delegates, feeling strongly the honour Scottish football is at stake commend that this Association respects the requirements of the War Office, and to withdraw international matches and ties from this year's programme.' Crucially, they also asked footballers to take a pay cut.

The decision was devastating for Hearts. In any other season, they would have had every right to feel confident that this was going to be their year – for the first time since 1897. In the intervening years, either Celtic or Rangers had taken home the title – with only two exceptions, Hibernian in 1903 and Third Lanark of Glasgow in 1904.

Manager John McCartney had been a man with vision ever since his appointment. He arrived at the club after a career as a player and with previous experience as a manager, as outlined by the *Portsmouth Evening News*. 'He first came to real prominence as a footballer with Glasgow Rangers and was one of the best-known full-backs in the game. His clubs in England were Newton Heath (now Manchester United) which club he captained, Luton then Barnsley.

'He was successful with all the clubs he was associated with, not only welding together at a small cost a successful team but stabilising the finances and in assisting the clubs to raise money for the erection of new stands. He directed the operations of Barnsley for four seasons, placing that club on a sound financial basis, and for the next six years he was with Paisley St Mirren.'

In his first full season for the club (1910/11), he struggled to make progress. Regular changes to the club before his arrival meant that Hearts never had a settled side. When first appointed, McCartney was shocked by the fitness levels of the players. Some 18 League defeats, and an equal 14th place in the championship, reflected the size of the rebuilding job on his hands.

The following season the team was strengthened with several additions. Performances significantly improved and Hearts finished equal fourth in the League. Progress was being made.

The 1912/13 season saw Hearts finish equal third in the League, their best performance in seven years. The team made a promising start with some notable results, including a 10-3 victory over Queens Park in the league at Tynecastle. They also beat the eventual champions, Rangers, at Ibrox, before hitting a poor spell at the end of the year and dropping out of the title race.

By the 1913/14 season, many supporters felt John McCartney had built the nucleus of a strong side, the Tynecastle club again finishing equal third in the League with a new club record of 54 points.

Hearts were unbeaten in the first 12 League fixtures; in September they beat Rangers and Celtic in the space of three days. They fell to their first defeat against St Mirren and although they bounced back, they stumbled again in the early weeks of 1914 and lost ground.

Still there was no doubt that these results represented progress, so Hearts chairman Elias Furst handed the manager a new five-year contract.

By the beginning of the 1914/15 season, McCartney's influence could be felt throughout the club. Hearts now boasted a strong side built around midfielder Bob Mercer and when they faced Celtic on the opening day of the season, it was in front of a state-of-the-art, 4,000 all-seater main stand. Coming at a cost of £12,780, it would be completed in October that year.

The construction of the stand had come at some cost. Percy Dawson, who had become something of a star at Hearts after scoring 63 goals in 80 League and Scottish Cup games, and was sold to English League champions Blackburn Rovers for a massive of fee of £2500. Much of the profits of this transfer were directed towards the new stand.

After looking long and hard for Dawson's replacement, McCartney thought he had found his answer on Merseyside, where he heard that Scottish centre-forward Tom Gracie was unsettled. In May 1914, he made his move. The *Scottish Referee* wrote of the £400 transfer, 'Manager McCartney, of the Hearts, has made a notable capture in Tom Gracie, of Liverpool, who has not quite "filled the bill" at Merseyside.

'When Gracie was with Morton he was selected as reserve centre to W. Reid (Rangers) in 1911, when the international was played at Goodison Park, and at the same time he signed for Everton. Gracie now returns to fill the place of a potential English Internationalist, Percy Dawson, of Blackburn Rovers. The Anglo-Scot is a capital shot, a strong dribbler, and powerful enough to beat the most robust defence … Gracie naturally wanted to come home. In new colours he is expected to reproduce his best form.'

For McCartney, Gracie was the final piece in the jigsaw, citing the former Liverpool man's deft touch and footballing brain as a better fit for the Hearts side he was building than the prolific Dawson.

After beating reigning champions Celtic 2-0 on the opening day of the season, Hearts prepared to take on Rangers on 19 September. The *Scottish Referee* wrote, 'The Tynecastle club travels to Glasgow tomorrow with all the glory of an unbeaten record to maintain.

'They have already beaten Celtic, Raith Rovers, Third Lanark, and St Mirren, and only lost one goal in the process, while they have notched 14, which spells superb attack and resolute defence.

'Unfortunately, Mercer is an enforced absentee owing to the knee injury he sustained against Celtic, in his place Scott, of the reserves, has done splendidly.

'Then Boyd, once of Bo'ness, is a rare goalkeeper, Crossan is voted the best right back in Scotland, and of course, everyone knows Peter Nellies. Briggs, too, is a fine half. However, it is the Hearts' forwards that deserve most of the credit for the succession of victories.'

Then referring to the big summer signing, Tom Gracie, the *Scottish Referee,* said, 'Gracie, late of Liverpool, has proved a distinct capture, and flanked by artists like Graham and Wattie he can hardly fail to do well. Low and Wilson are admirable foragers.

'The Hearts are, indeed, a happy company. On the other hand, the "Light Blues" have not proved a convincing side this season, though the draw at Dundee last week was capital business.

'No club in Scotland, bar Celtic, rises to the occasion against the "Light Blues" better than the "Maroons", and on this season's form a rare football treat is in store for the spectators at Ibrox Park.'

On the same day, McCartney placed an advertisement in the *Edinburgh Evening News* informing fans that 'a special train to Ibrox leaves Princes Street station on Saturday 19th September at 13.50 and Mercherson at 13.54.' There would be a return train from Glasgow Central in the evening.

In front of 41,000 spectators, Rangers raced into an early lead after only 90 seconds, when a mishit from Rangers' Bowie hit striker Reid on the chest and ricocheted past a stricken Boyd in the Hearts goal. Despite claims of a handball from Hearts players, the referee waved them away and the goal stood.

The match was played against a backdrop of both rain and sun, an equaliser came when Gracie charged at Rangers keeper Lock, bowling him over and putting his head and shoulders over the line with the ball in his hands. The goalkeeper, backed up by his Rangers teammates, claimed the ball never crossed the line, but the referee dismissed any claims of a foul and granted the goal.

After only 14 minutes, Wattie wrapped it up for Hearts, shooting through a crowd of players. He fell as he hit the winner, sustaining a head injury which he soon shook off. Hearts had now made it six League wins in a row.

Writing in the *Dundee Courier* on Monday, 21 September, 'Lynx' wrote of the match, 'The Rangers' halves were the best in the division but the fact the Tynecastle forwards availed themselves of a few chances offered entitled them to the points.

'Hearts are yet unbeaten. In fact, they have the most possible points. Twice only this season has their defence been pierced and 16 goals on their credit record. This indicates championship form.'

The only real cloud on the horizon for Hearts in those early days of the new season was the loss of George Sinclair and Neil Moreland, who were Army Reservists. Soon, Sinclair would be engaged in heavy fighting at the Battle of Mons.

Their amazing run continued and a thumping 4-0 win over Raith Rovers on Boxing Day meant they could go into the New Year full of belief.

When Hearts lined up to face Falkirk on 2 January 1915, their confidence seemed justified: a win would mean the opening of a comfortable gap over Celtic, who had lost to Rangers on New Year's Day. The disappointing 1-1 draw, and another 2-2 scoreline with Third Lanark three weeks later, meant the trip to face Celtic on 30 January took on extra significance.

The performance of the team saw the *Evening Telegraph and Post* asking whether Celtic could overtake Hearts in the race for the League Championship. 'The race for the league flag between the two clubs named is going to be a protracted one. Only four points separate Hearts and Celtic; a slip by the leaders, and the aspect of affairs might assume a totally different appearance.'

The newspaper then went on to highlight that Hearts had yet to visit Airdrie, Aberdeen and Greenock, with Partick Thistle and Rangers scheduled to arrive at Tynecastle Park.

Hearts were in a good position, but the *Evening News Edinburgh* was increasingly concerned about the effect of military training on the large group of players who were preparing for 'a much bigger cause'.

When Rangers came to Tynecastle Park on 20 February, the gap between Hearts and the champions Celtic stood at only four points. With nine games left, a slip-up could be fatal to Hearts' championship hopes.

As Hearts' goalkeeper Boyd picked the ball out of the net for a fourth time, McCartney took a deep breath. He had feared this would happen, the team having looked lethargic the previous week.

There were explanations, of course. The *Daily Record* reported that, in addition to inoculations, those players in McCrae's Battalion had been undertaking manoeuvres amid snow and rain on the Pentland Hills, training through the night – vital experience, it was felt, for when the men finally made it to the trenches but not so for footballers with a heavy schedule.

As vital as the match was to Hearts, there was only one thing on the minds of the players in the lead-up. The *Daily Record* noted, 'There is sadness in the Heart of Midlothian camp this week over the death of Alexander Lyon, assistant trainer to the club. He died suddenly in the Edinburgh Royal Infirmary on Sunday.'

The Hearts match day programme carried a tribute. 'Without doubt, he was an unsung hero behind the scenes, helping the head trainer, Jimmy Duckworth, with players' fitness, coaching, discipline, and performance assessment. Alex also looked after the kit and assisted with work around the ground. In addition, he was always available to help the soldier-players who were suffering from military related injury or illness.'

With the players grieving, McCartney tried to use letters from the front to motivate the players. One such letter appeared in the *Edinburgh Evening News*: 'George Sinclair, the Heart of Midlothian footballer, who has been at the front since August, writing to Mr McCartney, the Hearts manager, says the weather is "a shade rough," but is well seasoned now and is living off the fat of the land.

'Referring to the financial troubles which are besetting the football club at home, he says he thought that the Edinburgh club was Scotland's best and would have been better patronised … Sinclair expresses his satisfaction with the news that his old club are continuing to sweep in the points and keep their place at the top of the League table.'

With Hearts four down against Rangers, the spectators began to file out of Tynecastle Park. The old fob watch which McCartney held in his hand told him 83 minutes had passed; just seven minutes left. He closed the lid on the watch and put it back in his waistcoat pocket.

Then he looked back at the game, the referee pointing to the penalty spot. Gracie took the kick, hit the back of the net and scored. For McCartney, a 4-1 scoreline looked more respectable. Hearts pushed on and McCartney took out his watch again, and with just three minutes left, a Hearts corner was met by Low, who scored to make it 4-2.

Rangers, a team who looked like they were cruising to victory 10 minutes earlier, were suddenly panicked. Almost from the restart, Wilson scored again and the Tynecastle crowd roared back to life. McCartney, along with everyone else, was on his feet. It was now 4-3.

The hands on his fob watch ticked by faster than they had ever done and, with seconds left, Hearts were awarded a corner. Surely this would be the last kick of the match. The crowd fell silent in anticipation, only for the ball to float harmlessly over the heads of the players. Heart of Midlothian had lost at home for the first time that season.

This first home defeat of the season was undoubtedly a damaging result, because Celtic, as expected, beat Dumbarton by 1-0 and the Parkhead side were now only two points behind Hearts.

The *Daily Record* was quick to explain Hearts' current form: 'That their defeat by Rangers is to be laid at the door of the effects of the Army training need not be doubted.'

Crucially, as the *Edinburgh Evening News* noted, 'Between them the two leading Glasgow clubs, Celtic and Rangers, have not sent a single prominent player to the Army. There is only one football champion in Scotland, and its colours are maroon and khaki.'

The Edinburgh derby could not have come at a worse time for the team. McCartney and his trainer Jimmy Duckworth wereable to spend less and less time with their players as army training took precedence.

In any other time, a 2-2 draw in a local derby would have been a respectable result, but Hearts needed points and these were suddenly becoming hard to find, with the *Daily Record* reporting, 'Hearts appeared to have lost much of its attacking sparkle and a tired-looking group was punished for two defensive lapses.'

For McCartney, it was only a matter of time before he would lose all his players to the front, where heavy fighting and associated casualties around Ypres were being reported every day. A charity football match was being planned for Tynecastle in support of the Belgian Relief Fund.

The following day, the *Sunday Post* greeted Hibs' draw and Celtic's win over Partick Thistle with the news, 'Celtic going straight for the flag, Hearts lagging when pace is the hottest.' The gap at the top was now one point.

On the playing field, Hearts could afford no more slip-ups and the team's next opponents were Dumbarton, at home, on 6 March 1915. A crowd of 12,000 saw a much-needed return to form, with a resounding 4-1 win over the hapless Dumbarton.

However, the 5-1 victory recorded by Celtic over Hibernian showed a side that was coming into form at the right time of the season. With only six games left, Hearts had 55 points and Celtic had 54.

There was some good news for the Tynecastle outfit when the *Daily Record* told its readers that the military authorities had just allowed the soldier-players to report to Tynecastle for practice two nights a week: 'It is wonderful how much tuning-up can be done in an hour or two by a master hand like Trainer Duckworth.'

There was an unexpected opportunity to increase the lead to three points when Celtic opted to rearrange their scheduled League match and play a friendly match against Glentoran. Meanwhile, Hearts travelled to North Lanarkshire to face Airdrieonians.

Then disaster struck. After the death of Alex Lyon, Jimmy Duckworth had been working himself into the ground. At almost 65, he was no longer a young man and despite warnings, he now fell seriously ill, and was admitted to the Royal Infirmary.

After visiting him in hospital, John McCartney told him to rest, but Duckworth did not listen. Discharging himself from hospital against doctors' orders, he immediately returned to work – only to suffer a complete nervous breakdown.

In Duckworth, Hearts had the closest thing to an assistant manager, involving himself in the treatment of injuries, fitness and preparation, as well as coaching, discipline and player assessment. His loss was a real blow.

At their next match, their opponents were an improving Airdrieonians, who did everything in their power to frustrate Hearts, the game ending in a disappointing 2-2 draw.

With only five games left to play, Hearts remained on top of the Scottish League, two points ahead of Celtic. However, the Glasgow side had a game in hand and this became two when Celtic did not play on Saturday, 20 March 1915.

At Tynecastle, Hearts returned to winning ways with a 3-1 victory over Partick Thistle. This won them an important two points and allowed them to maintain their impressive record of having scored in every League game that season. They were now four points ahead of Celtic, although the Glasgow side did have those two games in hand.

In blue shirts, Hearts faced Clyde at home on 27 March. The *Daily Record* reported that for a second week, the supporters were treated to splendid football, in which Hearts dominated the game but showed a distinct lack of scoring ability.

However, the *Record* went on to explain why the Hearts' attack looked ineffective. Those military men – Gracie, Currie, Briggs and Low – had been given vaccinations earlier in the week. Nevertheless, a 2-0 victory was welcome.

That afternoon, Celtic beat Raith Rovers by 3-1. At the top of the League stood Hearts on 60 points from 35 games and Celtic on 56 from 33 games. There were now only three games to play and there could be no mistakes. If they won every game, Hearts would either be champions or force a play-off against Celtic.

A trip to Aberdeen on 3 April 1915 would be first up, but they would have to do it without top scorer Tom Gracie, who was sick, and Willie Wilson, who had a serious shoulder injury. There would be very few away fans because there was a reduced train service.

Therefore, a small crowd of only 6000 saw a dour 0-0 draw. That afternoon, Celtic beat Airdrieonians by 3-0 and at the top of the League it was Hearts with 61 points from 36 games and Celtic with 58 from 34 games. The *Daily Record* noted that, 'For the first time this season, Heart of Midlothian now sees the winning of the Championship taken out of their hands. They now need Celtic to fail.' On Monday, 5 April, Celtic played one of its games in hand and defeated Queens Park by 3-0 at Hampden Park. They had 60 points from 35 games.

On Saturday, 10 April at Greenock Morton, Hearts lost by 2-0. The headline in the *Sunday Post* summed it up: 'Hearts hopeless fail at two penalties'.

The paper did, however, point out, 'as an example of the handicap the Edinburgh men have had to undergo, it may be said that several of the eleven were out with their battalion on a night march on Friday and did not get back to barracks till the early hours of Saturday morning. That is not good training for hard football, and the contest at Greenock was a particularly trying one.'

That afternoon, Celtic beat Aberdeen by 1-0 and the Glasgow side had 62 points from 36 games. Hearts had 61 points from 37 games.

John McCartney did not need to tell his players that Celtic needed only two points from their final two games to be champions.

It looked as though Hearts had fallen short. The *Sunday Post* reported, 'The destiny of the flag is practically settled for another season. It is hard lines on Hearts. They have made a good fight of it, but their military handicap has been too much for them. But they have all the glory.

'The honour goes to Parkhead, but the glory goes to Tynecastle. Morally, the championship is for Edinburgh. No doubt remains that the enlistment of the bulk of the Hearts players tended to reduce the power of the team's play. But most people will agree that in giving themselves to the Army, they did the proper thing.

'Better by far to lose the race than not to respond to the call of the country when the men are young and for the most part, unfettered. A Hearts win would in the circumstances have been tremendously popular. In their hard luck they have the sympathy of the football public.'

Even though they were reliant on Third Lanark and Motherwell doing them a favour, a tired Hearts lost their final game 1-0 at Love Street at the hands of St Mirren. The Championship was lost after Celtic defeated Third Lanark by 4-0. The Glasgow club had 64 points with a game left, while Hearts had finished with 61 points from 38 games.

The *Scotsman* felt that Celtic were to be congratulated on retaining possession of the flag, but much sympathy had to go out to Hearts, who put up a great fight, and at one time seemed almost certain champions: 'What effect military training may have on the form of footballers is a matter for argument, but the fact remains that it was only after the majority of the Tynecastle players had enlisted that a deterioration of play set in. It was a glorious failure.'

The *Daily Record*'s view was that, 'This season's competition has been remarkable for the long leadership of the Hearts, and their subsequent dethronement. Their success, for reasons known to all, would have been the most popular outcome possible, yet they, along with others, will readily pay tribute to the resolute rally of the Celtic since the New Year time.'

There was some consolation in the fact that Tom Gracie had finished as the top scorer in the Scottish League. The *Daily Record* confirmed the club's and the *Evening News'* opinion that one of the two own goals scored at Dumbarton earlier in the season should be credited to Gracie. As a result, the Hearts marksman finished with 30 League goals, a new club record.

By any stretch of the imagination, it had been a remarkable season. After the final whistle at St Mirren, the players returned to their barracks for more drills and training. John McCartney and his players may have lost a championship, but they had won the admiration of a city and an entire country.

Hearts take on Celtic in 1911. After leading the table throughout 1914/15, it looked as though the Edinburgh side were finally about to break the Old Firm's stranglehold over the Scottish title.

Chapter 4

Vivian Woodward
The journey of a polymath

Even though George Webb had not played football for the past two seasons, and was only 26 when he succumbed to tuberculosis, leaving behind a young widow, Nellie, the huge crowds his funeral procession attracted were testament to the way people felt about 'one of their own'. Webb would hold the distinction of being West Ham United's first international footballer.

The rain which had been drizzling all morning had now turned torrential. To some it felt as though the entire populations of Stratford, Newham, Barking and Ilford had turned out. Soaked to the skin in their overcoats, men both young and old had taken off their hats and held them to their chest as a mark of respect. And children openly wept into the arms of their mother or grandmother.

Streets usually alive with the noise of people selling their wares or children playing had fallen silent. The only sound on 3 April 1915 was the sound of the hooves of the horses clip-clopping along the road to their destination, West Ham cemetery.

As the horses pulled the glass-fronted hearse, a procession walked slowly behind them. At the front marched two young men, one carrying a floral tribute in claret and light blue, the colours of West Ham United, which came from the club directors, and the other carrying white and sky-blue flowers, representing Manchester City. The floral tributes were so large, a special car had to be arranged to transport all the flowers to the graveside.

Once the funeral and interment of Webb was at an end, many of those in the crowd would be heading to the Boleyn Ground, where the flag was fluttering at half-mast. That afternoon, West Ham United of the Southern League would run out to face Watford, both teams wearing bands made of black crepe on their arms as a mark of respect.

A native of Poplar, an amateur centre-forward, Webb played for seven seasons for West Ham United, attracting attention with his goal-scoring exploits. It was not long before the bigger clubs began sniffing around, so there was no surprise when he joined Manchester City in the First Division of the Football League.

However, after playing the first two games of the season for his new club, he resigned when he discovered that a transfer fee had been paid for his services. After that, Webb would never kick a football in a competitive match again.

In 1910 he represented England at amateur level against Switzerland. The following year he played against Wales, Belgium, Germany and Holland. Webb won his first full international cap for England against Wales on 14 March 1911.

According to *The Times* report of that match, 'Webb forced his way through in splendid style to score.' It was the second of three goals scored that day as England recorded a resounding 3-0 win over the Welsh.

....

The man responsible for the other two goals was on the other side of London, pulling on the royal blue shirt of Chelsea as George Webb was being interred.

Like Webb, Vivian Woodward was an amateur, and if his club, Chelsea, had ever needed him, it was now. Coming off back-to-back defeats against Newcastle United and champions Blackburn Rovers, Chelsea had played the role of giant-killer when they dumped League contenders Everton out of the FA Cup to reach the final at Old Trafford.

Since the turn of the year, though, the Stamford Bridge outfit had failed to win a single game, apart from a 3-1 win over Aston Villa on 6 February. By 2 April, when they had recorded a 2-0 win over Bradford City, they found themselves locked in a relegation dog fight with Notts County, Bolton Wanderers, Manchester United and Tottenham Hotspur.

There were high hopes on 8 March, when Vivian Woodward, England captain and leading goalscorer, made his first appearance for the Blues at Bramall Lane. His absence had been explained months earlier in *Sporting Life*, on 19 September 1914: 'The non-appearance of Vivian Woodward in the ranks of Chelsea so far this season has occasioned some surprise in certain quarters.

'His return to the team will be further delayed for he has joined that fine sporting regiment, the London Rifle Brigade, in which many of the best Southern athletes are enlisted.'

Even after Woodward had enlisted in the Rifles, it was hoped he would turn out for Chelsea. *Sporting Life* reported on 16 October, 'It was a great disappointment to many onlookers of the match at Chelsea yesterday that Vivian J Woodward, the famous international did not turn out for the Chelsea team.

'It was his intention to do so, but an injury received last Saturday while playing for the Rifle Brigade team compelled him to cry off.'

Those Chelsea fans who had travelled to Yorkshire, hoping to see a vintage performance from the veteran superstar, were left disappointed. The months of army training had clearly caught up with Woodward, however, and it was Chelsea's one-eyed striker, Thomson, who put the visitors ahead after only 17 minutes.

Reporting on the match, the *Sheffield Daily Telegraph* said of Woodward, 'He played fairly well in his first match of the season. He has played quite a lot of company football since he joined the colours, but probably found the pace of yesterday's game rather different.'

Now a month later and a day after Chelsea had recorded a morale-boosting 2-0 win over Bradford City, it was hoped that Woodward would rediscover his old form against mid-table Sunderland. With Spurs taking on fellow strugglers Notts County in North London, it was vital that the spark of good form continued.

On 20 February 1914, high-flying Everton travelled south, to London and Stamford Bridge, the home of Chelsea, for the third round of the FA Cup. However, it would not be the team nicknamed

'The Pensioners' that the double-chasing 'Toffees' would be facing.

Instead, it was the blue and white hoops of Southern League outfit Queens Park Rangers who would provide the opposition. On the morning of the match, the *Sports Argus* explained: 'Owing to Park Royal being required for military purposes, Queens Park Rangers take their tie with Everton to Stamford Bridge.'

Having dispatched Leeds City and Glossop, all at their home ground of Park Royal, Queens Park Rangers had nothing to lose in facing Everton, who had been the season's pacesetters alongside Oldham Athletic and Manchester City.

Their fellow title contenders, Manchester City, awaited the arrival of Chelsea at Maine Road; no one was expecting great things from the West London side. The Citizens could feel confident, because the *Week and Sports Special Star Green 'Un* was reporting that 'Chelsea would love to choose Vivian Woodward, but military rules forbade it.'

The last time Woodward had played any sort of match for Chelsea was on 8 August 1914. Then he was dressed all in white, waiting for a small red leather ball and carrying a bat as he waited for his first delivery of the day in a cricket match against Tottenham Hotspur.

Even though both sides were better known for their footballing exploits rather than their prowess with willow and leather, the game served as the traditional opener of the football season in London. That game had found Woodward in spectacular form. Describing his performance, the *Biggleswade Chronicle* wrote, 'Tottenham were well beaten, for they were dismissed for 90 after Chelsea had made 172. Vivian Woodward, the famous amateur forward compiling a faultless 110. The latter's leg play and driving were the leading factors of the match.'

It was nothing new for Woodward to see out the cricket season before playing football. The *Scottish Referee* reported on 25 September 1914, 'Vivian J Woodward is one who does not desert cricket until the weather is less summer like and whilst his Chelsea colleagues were engaged in football, he produced 77 (not out) for Spencer CC v IBIS.'

The *Chelsea Chronicle*, the official match day programme, published on the morning of the QPR and Everton match, depicted a cartoon caption, 'Two Minds with a Single Thought'. The Toffee Man remarks, "Scuse me, Sir, I'm trying to find my way to the Fourth Round, can you assist me?' The Ranger replies, 'That's strange, you've taken those very words out of my mouth; I want to get there also.'

For the 33,000 crowd, there was excitement aplenty. Everton, who were clearly more superior in attack, missed a penalty only six minutes after kick-off, but if QPR thought this incident would in some way dent Everton's confidence, they would be sorely mistaken.

Just 10 minutes later, constant pressure from Everton paid off when they won a corner. Floating in above the QPR defence, the ball found the head of Everton's Galt, who promptly nodded it into the back of the Rangers net, giving the team from Merseyside a deserved lead.

The *Football Echo* described what followed: 'When Galt scored the first goal of the match an enthusiastic supporter of Everton, clad in khaki, rushed on to the ground, and following Galt to the centre of the field insisted on shaking hands with him.'

Up in Manchester, at Hyde Road, Chelsea had a plethora of chances, but both sides were still locked in a goalless draw as the teams went in for the half-time break.

In London, as the teams trudged in at half-time, the players of QPR could count themselves lucky to be only a goal behind, while Everton were left scratching their heads wondering why they had failed to convert chance after chance.

· · · ·

At half-time, during the QPR v Everton game, all the crowd could see was the drum major controlling the pace. Next came the pipers, then the crowd finally caught a glimpse of the man they all secretly wished was in Manchester with the rest of the Chelsea team.

Vivian Woodward, now a lieutenant in the 17th Middlesex Regiment of the Footballers' Battalion, having accepted a commission just two weeks earlier, shouted out the marching instructions to the soldiers – 'Left, right, left, right' – as they began to parade around the stadium he had graced so many times as a player.

Even though his wavy hair was now slightly receding from his temples, he still looked very much like the player described by the *Boston Independent and Lincolnshire Advertiser* as 'the most talked about amateur footballer of the day … he is tall, rather sallow and thin though he weighs 11 stone.'

As the band struck up a rendition of 'God Save The King', members of the Football Battalion marched around the perimeter. In the crowd were soldiers dressed in khaki, some on leave, many with young boys on their shoulders, anxious to catch a glimpse of their heroes.

Some called out for Lieutenant Frank Buckley, an England international who had been the subject of a move from Derby County to Bradford City in the summer. Others would have been thrilled to see the Clapton Orient pair, William Jonas, and Richard McFadden, but there was only one man the whole of Stamford Bridge would have paid money to see.

As he walked past, the youngsters, who had idolised him, called out to him: 'Jack, Jack over here, look this way.' Woodward did not react to hearing the familiar name the fans knew him by. His only focus was ensuring his men stayed in formation.

Even if he had not been playing in the royal blue of Chelsea for the past five years, Woodward's very presence would have guaranteed a crowd. He was not only the star of the Stamford Bridge side, but also a double gold medallist, captain of England and his country's leading goalscorer, as well as a handy tennis player.

Simply put, Vivian Woodward was football's first superstar. The seventh of eight children, Woodward was born on 3 June 1879 at the family home of 10 Crown Villa, Kennington, Surrey.

Woodward began playing football while attending Ascham College, a fee-paying private school in Clacton. Then he joined Clacton Town FC, of the North Essex League, followed by Harwich & Parkeston FC and Chelmsford FC.

A move to Tottenham Hotspur in March 1901 was something of a step-up. Already champions of the Southern League, they faced Sheffield United in the FA Cup Final at Crystal Palace a month after Woodward joined.

If it was a shock that Spurs held the Football League's Sheffield United to a 2-2 at Crystal Palace on 20 April 1901, then the replay held a week later at Burden Park, the home of Bolton Wanderers, was earth-shattering as non-League Tottenham dominated the Yorkshire side to win 3-1 and lift the Cup.

By the time Spurs were promoted to the Second Division in 1908, such was Woodward's fame that the *Cricket and Football Field* carried an advertisement which told the world, 'You Can't Play Football in Badly fitting Boots, which soon lose their shape.... You Can't Shoot Straight With ill made Boots.'

Readers were told: 'Look here – we guarantee JJB, football boots (made to measure; with perfect fit) are the best wearing boots in Europe.' Furthermore, they were endorsed and used by none other than 'Vivian J. Woodward and other expert players who know a reliable boot.'

'Football phenomenon' was the only description for Woodward's first performance in the Football League when Spurs faced FA Cup holders Wolverhampton Wanderers in September 1908. The *Morning Leader* asked the question, 'Who was answerable for what must be regarded as a Tottenham triumph?'

The answer? 'Many players may participate in the glory, but the lion's share must go to that phenomenon of the football field, Vivian J. Woodward, no longer the shining light illuminating the darkness of amateur football. Never in his glorious career has Vivian J. Woodward shown better form than he displayed against the Cup-holders.

'It should be sufficient that he scored two goals, against a splendid defence, to mark his work with the 18-carat stamp. Believe me, his goals were mere negligible incidents in his display. He would run an anchorite close for the stakes of unselfishness. Woodward, in the game under consideration, never existed for himself.'

By the time of his exploits against Wolves, Woodward was already a full England international, having made his England debut in February 1903 and getting on the scoresheet twice in a 4-0 win over Ireland at Wolverhampton.

The *Athletic Chat* were fulsome in their praise of Woodward: 'In the front-rank, Vivian Woodward was undoubtedly the man who continually sparkled with grand effect. His goal was a gem—and I can see no other centre for England v. Scotland, for this youngster is to me Tinsley, Lindley, Archie Hunter, and G. O. Smith all rolled into one.'

In October 1905, the *Morning Leader* reported that Woodward was to meet President Theodore Roosevelt. 'The Pilgrim Association Football team are the guests of Mr. Elliot, president of Harvard University, to whom they have explained the Association game in detail.

'Mr. Milnes the captain, and Mr. Vivian Woodward the Spurs' centre-forward, leave for Washington tomorrow to try and interest Mr. Roosevelt in the Association game for American colleges.' By November, it was reported by the *Daily News* that the proposed meeting with Roosevelt had fallen through and with it the opportunity to make the case for football to be organised in the United States.

On 3 February 1908, Woodward was appointed England captain. Lining up with Woodward was schoolmaster and QPR midfielder Evelyn Lintott. On 10 February, England faced Ireland at Wolverhampton, with Woodward scoring the second goal from close range in a dominant 3-1 win. He was to retain the captaincy until 1911, scoring 29 goals in 23 senior appearances.

At the time, England played only three games a season, in the Home International Championship. However, two European tours in 1908 and 1909 presented Woodward with the opportunity to boost his tally and he did so by banging in 15 goals.

He also scored four goals in three unofficial international games with South Africa in 1910 and represented England Amateurs in 44 internationals between 1906 and 1914, with an amazing goalscoring return of 57.

When the Great Britain side won the gold medal at the London Olympics in 1908 and again in the Stockholm Games four years later, it was Woodward who led the side to glory. On the occasion of his first Olympic success, he was described by the *Sporting Chronicle* as having 'a subtle craft tucked away in his toes.' It continued: 'Woodward is a great initiator, the personification of unselfishness, is quick to grasp the ever-changing situation of the game, and, above all, is very cool.'

However, just a year after his greatest sporting success, his first gold medal, it seemed that Woodward's many interests were taking their toll.

Not only was Woodward pursuing a dual cricketing and tennis career in the summer, turning out regularly for the Spencer Cricket and Lawn Tennis Club, but he also had an architectural business that was thriving. He also held a position on the Tottenham board of directors.

The constant calls on Woodward's services in both full and amateur internationals meant that he missed matches at the end of the season. Woodward went on tour with the England team in June 1908. This included a 11-1 victory over Austria, with Woodward scoring four of the goals.

Though his appearances for Spurs were inevitably curtailed to 169 games, scoring 73 goals was not a bad return for a player with so many outside interests. The pressure would soon begin to tell on Woodward, so much so that it seemed almost inevitable that he would announce his retirement from the game sooner or later.

The first time Woodward's potential retirement was mentioned was in *East & South Devon Advertiser* on 26 January 1907: 'Vivian J. Woodward. England's centre-forward has, it is stated, made up his mind to retire from the game, and will not be seen in first-class football after this season.

'The decision has been hastened by the unfortunate accident that occurred to him during the replayed English Cup tie at Hull, when he was so badly kicked in the back that he has since been confined to his bed.

'Regarded as a pure accident.' Woodward, it is alleged, is strongly of the opinion that a prominent amateur playing with a professional club is not given a fair chance but is at once marked out by the opposing defence.'

The final decision came when the *Morning Leader* reported, 'The retirement of Vivian Woodward from the Tottenham Hotspur directorate leaves no room for doubt now that the famous International has decided to give up playing in first-class football.

'The announcement was made in an interview published some weeks back, but his resignation was not considered by his co-directors until this week, when Woodward attended a meeting of the board for the last time.

'Players and spectators alike will regret the decision of the amateur, whose loss will be a severe blow to the Spurs and to the football world generally.'

On 20 November 1909, Woodward returned to football, playing for Chelsea. The *Chelsea Chronicle* wrote, 'The most cheering news we have had during our time of desolation is the intimation that Vivian John Woodward is going to assist Chelsea. Had the great Vivian been a professional player his transfer fee, I fancy, would have been something near a record one.

'Instead, Woodward comes to us for love, and we may take it that he is already the idol of Stamford Bridge. Vivian Woodward has been and ever will be the people's favourite. Small wonder. Great as he is as a player, his first claim to popularity lies in the fact that he has ever been first and foremost a gentleman.

'I question if any footballer has ever been so universally popular, and he carries his honours with the air of a bashful debutant.' He was also appointed a director at the Stamford Bridge club.

The *Dundee Evening Telegraph* speculated on the reason for Woodward's about-turn: 'Two reasons are given for Woodward's actions – one which reflects the Tottenham club, and one which reflects on Woodward. Both are unworthy of credence, and, after all, an amateur player is entitled to choose his club if he is good enough. As Woodward's relations live in the district, that will be found the probable reason for the change.' Over the next six seasons Woodward played 116 times for Chelsea, scoring 34 goals for a side that was often battling relegation.

· · · ·

The rain, which had been torrential during George Webb's funeral, had shown no sign of easing as Woodward ran out with his Chelsea teammates in front of a crowd estimated to be between 18,000 and 33,000, depending on which newspaper you were reading. There was little or no shelter at Stamford Bridge, but the spirits of the crowd were not dampened. After all, Chelsea had overcome Manchester City in the quarter-finals and they had pulled off something of a shock by besting title chasers Everton in the semi-final 2-0 to book their place in the 1915 FA Cup Final.

From the off, it was clear that the Sunderland defence would not offer much resistance to the Chelsea attack. Chelsea striker Thomson was in fine form, running through the Sunderland defence to score with a low drive that gave Chelsea the lead.

As reported by *Sporting Life*, 'Vivian Woodward after a fine start slowed down, but that apart, there was not a weak spot in the side.' Chelsea left the field after the first half, one goal to the good.

The second half continued in much the same way, Chelsea on the attack and Sunderland on the back foot. Then on the 65th minute, Ford's shot from a Chelsea corner was met by the forehead of Vivian Woodward. The Sunderland goalkeeper, Scott, managed to get a closed fist on the ball, only for it to rebound off the upside of the cross bar and over the goal line, doubling the home side's lead.

The *Evening Dispatch* reported, 'When Lieutenant Vivian Woodward scored Chelsea's second goal against Sunderland on Saturday, an excited spectator ran on the ground to give the famous amateur a congratulatory smack on the back which nearly knocked him down.'

A powerful shot from Thomson after a McNeil centre wrapped up the game for the home side. According to the same report in the *Evening Dispatch*, the enthusiast who had handed out a congratulatory slap on the back to Woodward, 'repeated the performance when Thomson scored the third goal. Mr Pellow (the referee) would not proceed with the game until the intruder's buoyant sprit had been curbed.'

Including the FA Cup semi-final win against Everton, this was Chelsea's third win in a row. Beating both Bradford City and then Sunderland a day later certainly eased relegation fears, and there were even some who dared to predict that Chelsea could lift the FA Cup.

According to *Sporting Life*, on Monday, 5 April, 'As Chelsea played against Sunderland on Saturday, they are good enough to win the Cup Final from Sheffield United or any other team for that matter.'

The *Daily Citizen* were similarly fulsome in their praise of Chelsea and of Vivian Woodward in particular: 'No side has improved during the last few weeks as much as Chelsea and the 25,000 spectators who assembled at Stamford Bridge saw their favourites in the happiest vein.

'The famous international forward, Vivian Woodward, relieved for the time being from his military duties, took his place in the forward line. None the worse for his patriotic duties, he exhibited all his cleverness that always seemed to inspire his colleagues.'

According to the *Football Echo* (Sunderland) on 17 April, 'Vivian Woodward seems to be able to secure any amount of weekend leave and is making regular appearances with Chelsea. The Commanding Officer of the Footballers' Battalion has certainly acted up in every way to the promise to provide players to join their teams.'

Even though Woodward was England's leading international goalscorer, holder of two Olympic gold medals and generally seen as one of the greatest players ever to lace up a pair of football boots, he still had no domestic honours to show for his long career.

With only three weeks before the FA Cup Final and with his improved form, it looked as though that was all about to change.

Vivian Woodward sits proudly in the centre as captain of Great Britain's gold medal-winning football team at the 1908 Olympics in London. The team would repeat the feat with Woodward as skipper four years later when the Games were held in Stockholm.

Chapter 5

Steve Bloomer
A superstar goes to Germany

On the day that Great Britain declared war on Germany, Vivian Woodward was looking forward to padding up for Chelsea against Tottenham Hotspur in the annual cricket match, and the one man who rivalled him as a footballing superstar was preparing for a very different experience.

The following day, just after 9 a.m. on an unseasonably chilly summer morning, a gentleman set out to report to the British Consulate in Berlin.

He was carrying a small suitcase and anyone noticing him might have assumed he was a manager on his way to open up his business for the day – rather than an internationally renowned football star.

With his broad round face, framed by dark brown hair swept away from his forehead, Steve Bloomer had graced Ogden's cigarette cards for years. At least, his portrait had – which was just as well for when he smiled, he displayed a set of yellowing, nicotine-stained teeth.

Cigarette cards were not the only product that carried his image: during his playing career he had advertised Lucky Striker boots as well as another brand, Perfergrippe, with their moulded studs that were said to be 'the boot that took the football world by storm'. Another product bearing his name was 'Phosphoric Tonic' marketed as the 'Remedy of Kings'.

Armed with his outstanding salary from his employment in the city, Bloomer had grabbed everything he owned and hoped now to get home to his family in Derby.

••••

Steve Bloomer was born in Bridge Street, Cradley, Worcester, on 20 January 1874, the youngest of six children. However, it was Derby he called home, having moved there when he was five years old after his father, Caleb, secured work as a puddler at Ley's Malleable Castings Foundry.

After leaving St James' School, Bloomer initially joined his father at Ley's, where he worked as a smith's striker at the forge. There he made a name for himself playing football on the plot of land next to the foundry and he was soon playing for Derby Swifts, where he scored 14 goals in one game, and then Derby County, who signed him as a professional at the age of 18 for the sum of 7s 6d.

By the time he accepted a coaching role in Germany in the summer of 1914, Bloomer had turned out 525 times for Derby County, becoming the club's record scorer with 332 goals. His service for his hometown side was broken by a four-year spell at Middlesbrough, between 1906 and 1910, for which he bagged 61 goals in 125 appearances. His 23 goals in 28 games for England meant he was joint highest goalscorer.

However, unlike his strike partner, Bloomer was no amateur and played for money. When he did leave Derby County, Middlesbrough had to pay £750 for his services. And though it was football which brought him fame, he was also a renowned baseball player, with the *Derby Evening Telegraph* claiming, 'He was the best second batsman in England according to BG Knowles, one of the most capable judges of the game.'

On the morning of 5 August, Bloomer was not the only Briton who wanted to escape the city. As tensions had mounted over the previous few days, the mood in Berlin took on a sinister turn. Great Britain was now the enemy; in the city's cafes, Bloomer's broad Derbyshire accent earned sneers; in the beer halls, loud anti-British songs were sung by patrons late into the night; and on the streets, the tension was so heavy it was feared that violence could break out at any moment.

Bloomer never reached the consulate. Accosted on the way, he was instead escorted to the local police station. After waiting and waiting for what seemed like an age, he was finally brought before an officer. The old footballer may have been able to pay his way and then some for safe passage back home, but as he was told through the same translator who had been supplied by his club, there were no trains – for him or any other British national.

How old are you, he was asked. Forty, he replied. *What is your business?* Football, he meekly answered. He had retired from football after Derby County had been relegated the previous season and was now coaching a local side, Berlin Britannia.

When two guards brandishing bayonets entered the room, Bloomer feared the worst. Neither the police officers nor the translator said anything. The guards moved on the seated Bloomer, prodding him in the back, indicating he should stand before pushing him into a crowded room which contained many British nationals, who like him were now stranded in a hostile land.

As the lock turned in the door, leaving the people there in the dim light of the crowded room and the air thin because so many bodies huddled together, Bloomer might have been forgiven for regretting the choice he had made earlier that year.

By January of 1914, it was clear that his illustrious Derby County career was winding down. On the football pitch, the team was sliding towards relegation and already there was speculation that his teammate, the highly regarded centre-half Frank Buckley, was agitating for a move. As for Bloomer, he had scored 332 in 525 games, but at the age of 39, he knew his career was coming to an end.

On 12 May 1914, the *Special Green 'Un* reported that Frank Buckley had left the now-relegated Derby Country to join his fellow England international Evelyn Lintott at Bradford City. And that Steve Bloomer had been released by the Rams. It was time for Derby County to look to the future. For Bloomer, the *Green 'Un* were confident enough to announce that he would be taking up a coaching position with Shirebrook, champions of the Central Alliance.

Just two days later, Bloomer, who had been advertising for a position after being released, was quick to write to the *Derby Evening Telegraph* and explain that reports he was signing for Shirebrook were not true.

On 15 July, the *Uttoexter Advertiser and Ashbourne Times* wrote, 'Steve Bloomer, the famous footballer, has accepted an engagement as a football coach for a Berlin club.

'It will be remembered the ex-international was by no means a regular member of Derby County's team last season and the club have not re-signed him.

'His name has been mentioned in connection with the Shirebrook club, but though the colliery team would have liked him, the announcements were more than premature.'

The minutes of Derby County's Annual General Meeting explain: 'It was noted that Steve Bloomer's name did not appear in the list of players signed on again for next season nor had he been mentioned among those who had been transferred … it was stated he was to take up a coaching position with Britannia Berlin.

'Last season he had only played for the first team five times but had appeared frequently for the reserves, where he had also acted as something of a coach. It was felt he would be a magnificent coach and his friends and fellow players wanted to wish him well in his new position in Germany.'

. . . .

There was a sense of trepidation when the bolts of the locked doors were pulled across and German guards entered the room, some carrying bayonets and others holding pistols.

Aggressively, the British were pushed out of the room and out into the wide open. The welcome comfort of the fresh air gave way to the fear of what was to happen next as the foreigners were lined up side by side and forced to march through the streets of Berlin.

Pushed along with bayonets in their back, there was an air of menace, and the men felt they would pay for a wrong move with their lives. To begin with, only a few people came out of their homes to see the procession.

As the men, who had simply found themselves in the wrong place at the wrong time, marched through the city, the thin crowds got heavier – and the larger the crowd, the angrier it got. The faces of men, women and children were twisted in hate.

Some spat on the men while others threw anything they could get their hands on, rotten vegetables or stones, which occasionally missed their intended target and grazed the guards.

By the time they arrived at their destination, Alexanderplatz, the crowd were close to lynching the men. It was fair to say that everyone, including the guards, was relieved to be inside the courthouse and away from the baying mob, who were by now demanding English blood.

Inside the courthouse, the men were again ushered quite forcibly into an anteroom and there was some trepidation as each man was called one by one and led out. For Bloomer, this was not his first brush with the law.

In the *Liverpool Echo*, of Thursday, 7 April 1898, it was reported, 'At Derby Police Court yesterday, Stephen Bloomer, the well-known footballer, was summoned for having been drunk and disorderly on Sunday last.

'He had only just returned from Glasgow, where the previous day he kicked two of England's goals against Scotland. Defendant did not appear but was represented by a solicitor, whose only statement was an expression of regret. A fine of 10s. and costs were imposed.'

On 3 December 1902, the *Derby Daily Telegraph* had reported, 'The Derby County directors have suspended Stephen Bloomer for "gross insubordination". It is officially announced that he will not play this week, and his selection after Saturday next depends upon whether he offers suitable apology for his alleged breach of discipline.'

Finally, the door was unbolted and the same two heavy-handed guards who had forcibly dragged him from the consulate building hours earlier called out, 'Bloomer, Stephen Bloomer!' The famous old footballer straightened himself and followed the two men.

After being shown into an oak-panelled courtroom, Bloomer was introduced to the chief magistrate. He was asked the same questions he had already answered when he had been arrested.

What was his name? How old was he? And what was his business in Berlin? Bloomer answered truthfully. The magistrate nodded and wrote down his answers. Then, after addressing Bloomer in German, he was handed papers which forbade him from leaving Berlin. He was free to leave and go about his business provided he reported to the police station twice a week so that they had knowledge of his whereabouts.

....

For Bloomer, who knew nothing but football, there was very little to do except busy himself around his club, where he was manager. Britannia Berlin 92 Sports Club was now going under the name of Berliner Sport Veren 1892; such was the anti-British sentiment, the title 'Britannia' had been dropped.

A city which just three weeks earlier had been welcoming and open was now dark and hostile. In a short space of time, Berlin had become volatile and unpredictable to any foreigner, especially if they spoke with an English accent.

While Bloomer worked at the football club by day, by dusk it was no longer safe to be out in the open. It was not uncommon for young men to get drunk and, filled with nationalist fervour, to roam the streets looking for trouble. By and large, Bloomer kept his temper. To do anything else could invite injury or something much worse.

Back home, his wife Sarah had no idea of what was happening to her husband. Bloomer was far away from her and their three daughters, Hetty, Violet and Doris, who would have had no idea what had happened to him in the German capital.

On 5 August 1914, the Aliens Restriction Act passed by Parliament the day after war was declared on Germany required foreign nationals (aliens) to register with the police and, where necessary, they could be interned or deported. This act was chiefly aimed at German nationals and, later, other enemy aliens living in the United Kingdom, but the legislation and subsequent Orders in Council affected all foreign nationals.

The first Aliens Restriction Order was issued on 5 August 1914 and this was quickly followed by two other Orders in Council on 10 and 12 August and a third on 20 August. These were brought together as the Aliens Restriction (Consolidation) Order 1914/1374 on 9 September.

Men of military age who were categorised as enemy aliens were arrested and interned, although for the most part this was done peacefully and they reported to temporary holding camps while more permanent internment camps were set up. It was only a matter of time before the Germans responded in kind.

For Bloomer's family, the last they had heard from him was a letter, a week earlier, telling them of his plans to visit the consulate and to make his way home. They were in the dark about the events that had followed.

As time went on and news began filtering through from the front, it was only natural that worries about the whereabouts of Steve Bloomer would reach the press. The *Birmingham Daily Post* reported on 12 August, 'Anxiety is felt in Middlesbrough by a large number of friends as to the safety of Steve Bloomer, the ex-Middlesbrough and Derby County footballer and well known international player who recently went out to Germany to coach a team.'

Two weeks later, on 25 August 1914, the *Hamilton Daily Times* tried to strike a reassuring note: 'About a month ago, Steve Bloomer, the famous international footballer, left Derby to be a coach in Berlin.

'His relatives received a letter from him to the effect he was contemplating coming home as soon as he could but up to Saturday, he had not turned up in Derby and his friends are naturally anxious about him or rather not having received any news concerning him.

'No doubt Steve is fit and well, but he would rather be home under present circumstances than in Germany.'

However, there was still no word from Bloomer in Germany, which could confirm his whereabouts. For his part, he simply busied himself with menial tasks around the club. Any hope of escape by train had all but disappeared.

The *Special Green 'Un* gave an insight into life in Berlin when Jack Brearley, a former Notts County and England international, managed to get a letter smuggled out of Berlin. Brearley was also engaged as a coach in the German city.

According to the newspaper, Brearley was nominally a prisoner but free to move about the city, only having to report himself every few days. He was quoted as saying, 'Food is quite plentiful and cheap in Berlin and there is no panic or excitement.'

Two weeks later, on 26 September, Brearley managed to get another letter out of Berlin: 'Things are not very pleasant in Berlin. I don't see much of Steve Bloomer, his engagement finished when the war started. He is engaged again but I do not know the terms.'

Further news came on 3 October 1914, when the *Special Green 'Un* carried a story telling readers that James McPherson, the trainer of Newcastle United, had received a letter sent from Berlin stating that 'Steve Bloomer, who is special trainer to one of the leading association clubs in the German capital, was quite safe and meeting with sympathetic treatment from his employers as well as the people generally.'

Another letter arrived on the doormat of 35 Portland Place, Derby, the first piece of good news the Bloomer family had received since Steve had left for Berlin. It reassured his wife that he was quite well and still discharging 'coaching duties to young athletes in Berlin'. It was signed by her husband.

Whatever the press had reported and regardless of what he told his wife, time was running out for Bloomer and his fellow British citizens in Berlin. If Britons were free to go about their business in the German capital, the same could not be said of their German counterparts in Great Britain.

By 5 November 1915, thanks to government legislation, German subjects, like their British counterparts, were required to register their names with the police, obey local curfews and refrain from entering what were termed prohibited areas.

These included the entire east and greater part of the south coast of the country, and further to this, Germans were not allowed to own cars, motorcycles, cameras, military maps or homing pigeons.

These measures were also enforced in all the British Empire's territories and dominions. The Germans issued an ultimatum to the

British, telling their enemy that unless all restrictions were dropped against German nationals then all British subjects living in Germany would be rounded up and interned. Bloomer's fate was sealed.

The following day, as was now his usual routine, Bloomer reported with other British nationals to the police station in Berlin. The appointment usually lasted only five minutes, but on this day, Bloomer was informed he was being arrested as a 'prisoner of war'.

Again, he and anyone else who was able-bodied and deemed to be of fighting age (between 17 and 55) was marched to the Alexanderplatz to board a train. However, their carriage was not about to take anyone back home to Britain.

When asked where they were going, the guards remained silent. After half an hour in cramped conditions, they arrived at their destination: an old racecourse, just west of Berlin, at Ruhleben.

News of Bloomer's predicament finally reached the British press over a week later, when the *Special Green 'Un* reported on Saturday, 14 November 1914, 'Steve Bloomer, the famous international, is a prisoner in Germany. He went to Berlin shortly before the outbreak of the war as coach to a football club.

'His wife who lives in Derby has received a postcard dated November 5th from Steve. On this he says he is one of 2,500 prisoners and that he is well under the circumstances.'

For the next four years, the overcrowded Ruhleben, with its barbed wire and armed guards, and its meagre rations the only source of sustenance, would be the place Bloomer would call home.

Chapter 6
Cup Final!
A subdued event

The grey clouds and swirling mist suggested early morning rather than mid-afternoon as the dignitaries took their seats at Old Trafford for the most anticipated game of the season, the 1915 FA Cup Final. This year it would be contested between Sheffield United and Chelsea.

The return of Vivian Woodward to the Chelsea ranks had failed to stop the inevitable slide towards relegation. So when they travelled to the north-west for the Cup Final, they found themselves placed second to last, above Tottenham Hotspur.

If League form had been disappointing, the FA Cup had proved to be something of a silver lining. After dumping out the title-chasing Manchester City in the third round of the competition, the Pensioners played giant-killer a second time, when they turned their League form on its head, sweeping aside champions elect Everton at Villa Park to reach the final with a fine 2-0 win.

Meanwhile, Sheffield United, who were comfortably nestled in mid-table, earned their place in the final by beating Bolton Wanderers 2-1 at Ewood Park, home of the 1914 League champions, Blackburn Rovers. The game was notable for a wonder goal by their captain, George Utley, who had gone on a 30-yard run before slotting the ball home. In the League, Chelsea and Sheffield United had drawn each other 1-1, home and away. By virtue of their positions, the press felt before the game that the team from Sheffield would just have the edge.

When assessing both sides, the *Hull Daily Mail* wrote, 'Sheffield United must thank their glorious defence for their present proud position, as only one goal has been conceded in the six matches which were necessary to reach the final.

'Chelsea are quite a different type. They play a class of football not supposed to prove successful in cup ties and is often termed the drawing room game. Even with their position in the First Division of the League seriously threatened the Pensioners continue to play the type of football we all admire, but whether it will prove equal to meet the strong, bustling tactics of Sheffield United remains to be seen.'

One thing was certain going into the match, though: this would be the last game of professional football that anyone would witness for the foreseeable future. This had been confirmed at the end of the FA Amateur Cup Final when a journalist approached Charles Crump, FA vice-president, for a comment: 'There will be no more serious football until the war is over.'

Days later, in an interview with the Press Association, Crump's statement was confirmed by FA secretary Frederick Wall, who said the decision had been taken by the FA Council.

As the *Bradford Daily Telegraph* reported, 'It is perfectly definite, and leaves no loophole for misunderstanding, unless over the question of what will constitute the end of the war. It is reasonable to assume that the game will not necessarily be discontinued until the actual signing of peace, but only until virtual peace has been brought about.'

The week before the FA Cup Final, it was clear that the announcement had failed to have the desired effect on the anti-football campaigners. A public announcement printed in the *Manchester Courier* informed citizens of a protest meeting at Albert Hall, Peter Street, which was to be addressed by the prominent anti-football campaigner, Frederick Charrington.

The advertisement went on: 'All sympathisers are cordially invited, come in your thousands and protest against Manchester incurring the disgrace of the Cup Final being played here.'

Over the past few months there had been no let-up in Charrington's campaign to ban football. In a letter to the editor of the *Manchester*

Courier in early April, he explained why the Cup Final had been switched from its traditional home of Crystal Palace to Old Trafford: 'The Football Association, having abandoned the idea of playing the Cup Final in the south, public opinion is too strongly against them, have decided the Cup Final should be played at Manchester.'

According to the *Hull Daily Mail*, the reason for the change was twofold. Crystal Palace was not available because it was the headquarters of the Naval Brigade and the London press had failed to give the FA their support.

On the morning of the Cup Final, the *Sportsman* previewed the game: 'The Londoner in the trenches has rejoiced that for the first time since the days of the Boer War, there is a chance of the Cup finding its home in the metropolis.'

By the time George Utley led out his Sheffield United side, the heavy rain of the morning had turned into a light drizzle. As for the pitch itself, a hard season meant that it was difficult to spot a blade of grass even before a ball had been kicked, the ground resembling a mud bath.

As the team in red and white vertical stripes ran out, the roar from the ground made it sound as though Blades were playing at home, such was the show of support on display that day.

The reception for Chelsea, who were led out by their captain, Fred Taylor, was far more muted, which had more to do with the lack of Chelsea fans. There had been next to no transport from London, as reported by the *Manchester Courier*: 'The English Cup Final at Old Trafford on Saturday will, of course, result in an invasion of the city by thousands of football enthusiasts.

'But unlike previous Cup Finals the crowd, it is expected, will consist mainly of Lancastrians, for railway companies will not this year be offering the customary facilities for enthusiasts outside the immediate district in which the match is being played.

'There will only be one special train to run on account of the match, and that will be from Sheffield. The L and NW railway company have not made any arrangements which will allow admirers of the Chelsea team to travel much cheaper than usual from London, as no specials at all will run.'

One man who had managed to make the trip from London to the north-west was Vivian Woodward. While never having played in a single round of the FA Cup, he was now listed in the official Cup Final programme (alongside advertisements for music hall shows at the Manchester Hippodrome and Ardwick Empire) as a replacement for Bob Thomson.

As the *Yorkshire Evening Post* reported on the morning of the Cup Final, 'Another and in all probability a more important wounded warrior was Thomson, the Croydon man, whom not a few judges regard as the best centre-forward the Chelsea club have ever possessed.

'Last Wednesday week, Thomson had the misfortune to be heavily charged in the first minute of a league match with Bolton Wanderers with the result he fell and dislocated his elbow.'

The *Sheffield Daily Telegraph*, writing at the same time as the *Yorkshire Evening Post*, claimed, 'It is different with Thomson, who sustained a badly fractured arm a week ago and though desperate efforts are being made to patch him up, there is a big doubt whether he will turn out.'

The *Telegraph* went on: 'If he does not play, then we may see Lieutenant Vivian Woodward taking up his old position as pivot.' However, Woodward would watch the game from the Old Trafford stands.

Despite being a lieutenant in the 17th Middlesex, Woodward had been given leave to play, and had made the journey to Manchester for the Cup Final. The day Chelsea were due to face Sheffield United, Woodward had also been named in a Football Battalion 11 to face the Second Sportsman Battalion, a game they would lose 2-1.

As the *Yorkshire Evening Post* reported, for Thomson 'it was a painful injury, but careful treatment had worked wonders.' Dressed in his military uniform, Vivian Woodward would have blended into the crowd – a sea of green and beige, such were the number of men watching the game dressed in uniform. Little wonder that the game was dubbed the 'khaki final' in the press the following day.

Dotted among those who were serving and had taken leave to watch the final were the casualties of war. As the *Sussex Agricultural Express* observed, 'More grim news of the evidence of the dreaded realities of the war was the inclusion among the khaki men of numbers of soldiers who had been under enemy fire. Bandaged heads, strapped limbs, crutches here and there, the support of a crippled hero on the shoulder of his comrades.'

There was no doubt the atmosphere of this year's Cup Final was more subdued than the previous year. In 1914, George V had travelled from Buckingham Palace to Crystal Palace to witness Burnley dispatch Liverpool 1-0 and present the Cup to the winning captain, Tommy Boyle.

Perhaps more remarkable than the result was the very fact that George V was even there. This had been the first time a monarch was present at a football match – and to many, the presence of the King was a firm endorsement of the game which was quickly becoming a national obsession.

The difference in this year's final to the previous year's was noted by the *Hull Daily Mail*: 'What a change has come over sport since the last final for the greatest of all football trophies. Then, the country was at peace and the Crystal Palace was the rendezvous of lovers of the game from all parts of the country.

'To complete the success, His Majesty King George V presented the Cup to the victors. This season football has been carried out under great difficulties, and the final for the first time since 1894 is being decided in the provinces.'

Frederick Charrington, meanwhile, had suggested in his letter to the *Manchester Courier* that the best person to hand over the trophy would have been the Kaiser himself, such was the disgrace the game had brought to society. The person who would hand over the Cup to the winning captain was Lord Derby.

Lord Derby was one of the main advocates for the so-called Pals' Battalions, formed by men who enlisted together, from the same town or workplace. As the *Daily News and Leader* reported on the morning of the Cup Final, 'Today at Old Trafford, Manchester, will be decided the English Cup Final tie between Chelsea and Sheffield United, a classic match which on this occasion will be decided under a cloud.

'Lord Derby will attend the match and at the conclusion of the game will present the Cup to the captain of the winning team and medals to the members of both elevens. Prices of admission have been raised excepting for soldiers, who will be strongly in evidence, including many wounded who will be guests of the English FA.'

Soon the two captains came together to shake hands, their expressions as glum as the weather. The referee, a young-looking man named Mr Taylor, wearing a black blazer with gold buttons teamed with long, white, oversized shorts, reached into the left-hand pocket of his jacket and pulled out a coin. It was the Sheffield United captain George Utley who called correctly and elected to play before the Stretford End.

From the kick-off, it was clear that Sheffield United were the stronger team. With doubts about the fitness of Bob Thomson, it certainly was not helpful to the London side when winger Harry Ford went down injured in the first few minutes, meaning he had to leave the field for treatment before rejoining the game.

By the time Ford returned to the field of play, Sheffield United were firmly in control. As had been true for most of the season, goalkeeper Jim Molyneux was the man who kept Chelsea in the game. After 15 minutes, it seemed as though Sheffield United were sure to score – only for Chelsea defender Jack Harrow to clear off the line.

The *Sunday Pictorial* described the early play: 'Sheffield United played fast, robust football, keeping the ball always on the move and, as a matter of fact, showing considerably more combination than the Londoners' front line.'

The *Special Green 'Un* claimed the match was as good as over after only 10 minutes, claiming, 'I put down my pencil and remarked to a colleague, "There is no need for excitement over this game. The Cup is won."'

The *Sheffield Daily Telegraph* wrote, 'To put it shortly, Chelsea were inferior at all points to their rivals. That is not over-stating the matter. The Chelsea forwards were as clever as one could wish. But they carried that virtue to a point at which it became a weakness.

'In our opinion it was a mistake to play Thomson, who was not fully recovered, and whose fear of further injury, it is natural to assume, would affect his play.'

The *Lancashire Evening Telegraph* agreed about the omission of Woodward: 'Vivian Woodward would have been mishandled, it may be, but at all events he would have been more useful, with the ball so much in the air, than the smaller man, who was simply overwhelmed.

'But the Chelsea forwards as a whole plainly did not relish the character of the opposition they had to overcome, and they were smitten so forcibly and well by the United half-backs that it is safe to say no pair of backs have ever gone through a final tie with such little cause to exert themselves as Cook and English.'

The only surprise about the first goal was how long it took to be scored. A centre from Utley was missed by Molyneux, but efforts by Jack Harrow to head the ball away were in vain as the ball fell to Sheffield United's Jimmy Simmons, who slammed it into the net from close range.

As the Sheffield United man wheeled away in delight, Molyneux and Harrow started to push and shove each other, blaming one another for not clearing the ball before it fell to Simmons to score. The *Manchester Guardian* sided with Harrow, who they believed was at fault for the goal.

However, *The People* wrote of the opener, 'This came after 36 minutes play and they richly deserved the lead. It was in the concluding half that Sheffielders asserted a marked superiority and, at times, the Chelsea goal was all at sea, and it was really a brilliant exhibition of goal keeping on the part of Molyneux that prevented the Pensioners from receiving a more severe drubbing.'

Chelsea had their best chances just before half-time when shots from Harold Halse and Tommy Logan were saved by Harold Gough and Ford struck one wide. So, it was 1-0 at the interval, during which the band marched and played 'It's a Long Way to Tipperary', the song adopted and sung by the British troops as they marched off to war.

There was also a collection on behalf of the East Lancashire branch of the British Red Cross Society, undertaken by soldiers, many of whom were Boer War veterans wearing South African army colours, including one who had lost an arm. They held up khaki-coloured sheets into which spectators threw pennies –

'something after the manner of firemen catching one who leaps from a window,' said *The Times*.

Play was muted at the start of the second half as a thick fog descended over the pitch, preventing spectators from seeing any action on the opposite side of the pitch, though *The Times* commented that they were not missing much.

As the second half began, the fog became thicker, preventing a good view of the pitch from the stands and terraces.

For a spell the play of both sides was poor, Chelsea's especially so. Their forwards' passing was muddled and they were often easily robbed of possession, but Sheffield United failed to capitalise on Chelsea's mistakes. Molyneux made several good saves. Sheffield United's inside-forward, Wally Masterman, did manage to beat the Chelsea goalkeeper, but his effort was ruled offside.

The weather, which had seemed to affect Chelsea more than Sheffield United, now began to clear, but the light began to deteriorate. By the time the match moved into the final minutes, Sheffield United had the game by the scruff of the neck.

It was no surprise to anyone when Sheffield United added a second goal. A shot from the always dangerous Wally Masterman rebounded from the crossbar, to fall on the head of inside-forward Stanley Fazackerley, who directed the ball past the Chelsea keeper.

Four minutes later, Sheffield United centre-forward Joe Kitchen scored what *The People* described as 'the finest goal of the match'. The paper went on to report, 'Kitchen accepted a pass from Utley at the halfway line and brushing aside the opposition gave Molyneux not the slightest chance with his final drive.

'Before this, Chelsea had played very disjointedly and were a thoroughly beaten team when the final whistle sounded. In every department of the game Sheffield were the superior force and Gough had quite a holiday compared with Molyneux.

'He was ably supported by two dashing and fearless backs. The middle line, of whom Utley was the shining light, kept the forwards well together. Kitchen proved a splendid pivot, swinging the ball across to each wing in the most delightful manner.

'On the one side as previously stated the Southerners were very disjointed especially forward and had they taken advantage of the support given by Logan, Sheffield would not have won by a margin of three goals.'

Molyneaux emerged from the Chelsea goal, but Kitchen dodged him and placed the ball in the open net. At this point, before the final whistle, large numbers of the spectators began to leave.

After the third and final goal was scored, some of the crowd ran on to the pitch in the mistaken belief the game was over. 'A number of over-excited youths and men rushed on to the ground, wrung the hands of Kitchen and Utley in fine frenzy, and looked as though they meant to stay there,' reported the *Sheffield Daily Telegraph*.

Apart from some good play in spurts by Chelsea, especially in the first few minutes, it had been a one-sided match. In short, Chelsea had been outplayed, but there were no complaints from the team captain at the end of the game. 'We lost to the better team on the day. They gave us no rest and little chance,' Fred Taylor said of his team's poor performance.

The winning captain, George Utley, said, 'There was only one ball, and we had it most of the time.' Even the referee was moved to say, 'I think the better team won.'

The *Athletic News and Cyclists' Journal* reported that, 'United simply brushed Chelsea aside as if they were novices', and the *Special Green 'Un* wrote, 'If United had won by five goals, they would not have been flattered.' *The Times* agreed with the general sentiment of these reports, stating that United's two late goals gave them a lead 'more commensurate with their merits'.

'If it be a crime for United to squelch the fritter and glitter of the Chelsea men, then United were criminals of the deepest dye, and if the southerners are to be commiserated with upon having their preconceived plans dashed to nothingness, then they have all our sympathy.'

The *Sheffield Independent* wrote: 'United's forwards were generally enterprising and speedy, the best of them being Simmons, whose dazzling runs delighted the crowd, Fazackerley, who passed well and unselfishly, and Kitchen, who swung the ball out to his wings with certainty and accuracy and was always on the spot when a chance presented itself.'

The *Lancashire Evening Post* commented, 'There is no room for two opinions as to the justice of the verdict of the struggle. It was too one-sided to admit of any qualification of the Sheffields' success. It was a triumph of the moral and material power of physical superiority and condition.

'Most of us would have liked to see a little artistry in the game, a few of the moves which prove that football has its brainy as well as its brawny side. In this scientific sense Sheffield United have their distinct limitations.'

After presenting the Cup to George Utley, Lord Derby rose to give a recruitment speech to a crowd who were already serving in uniform.

Even though he did his best, the noise and cheering drowned him out. To those who could hear, he said, 'Everyone should now concentrate their efforts on fighting for the safety and security of Britain and its Empire. The appeal would not be in vain; it was hoped every man must face his duty and do his best.'

After the match Sheffield United directors and players gathered for a subdued celebratory tea. In a short speech, the chairman, Mr Tom Bott, congratulated the team. To him, they were gentlemen, on and off the field.

'They had been told that by taking the Cup to Sheffield they were causing disgrace to the city, but that was not his view at all. He hoped that the writer of "Current Topics in the *Sheffield Telegraph*" would have the good sense to apologise for what he had once written on this matter.'

Mr J.C. Clegg's opinion of the team was reported by the *Sheffield Telegraph* in a short speech: 'They were men with whom it was a pleasure to associate, and he was convinced that even those who had gone to the ground with strong prejudices in favour of the other side must have been convinced that the better team had won, and won in a manner which was a credit to them. He wished every one of them every prosperity during the rather trying times immediately ahead.'

Then quoting Clegg directly, the *Telegraph* went on to write, 'There has been some talk of disgrace being attached to winning the Cup this year, but I do not hold with that opinion. I take the victory to be an honour to Sheffield. So far as I am concerned, I take the responsibility for the statement that the action which the Football Association took at the outset would be repeated were the same crisis to arise again.

'We have suffered more than usual from ill-judged criticism, and people who criticise sometimes get their popularity in proportion to their ignorance, but I think, after all, we acted wisely – having regard to our knowledge of all the circumstances – when we had to come to a decision.

'I am as proud as anyone that we have won the Cup. It is sheer twaddle talking about disgrace. The disgrace lay with those who made such suggestion, and not with the players, or the club. I have had a pretty long experience, and in the past have never hesitated to express my opinion of anything not sport, straightforward, or sportsmanlike, and I shall continue to do so whether I please anyone else.'

There was to be no fanfare for Sheffield United when they returned home by train. Even though some fans appeared at the station to greet the team, George Utley did not show off the Cup and Sheffield did not hold a parade. There was only one preoccupation now – and that was war.

For Chelsea, who quietly returned to London, there was one football matter to consider: whether the Pensioners would still be in the top flight, come the end of the war. Events taking place just a few weeks earlier, close to the same ground where they had played the Cup Final, would put their status in doubt.

Wounded soldiers watch the 1915 FA Cup Final between Sheffield United and Chelsea. The game was known as the 'Khaki Final' for the large number of spectators dressed in military uniform. Within a few months many would be in the trenches of Northern France and Belgium.

Chapter 7

Fix!
A Lancashire betting scandal

Just around the corner from Old Trafford, a backstreet pub, the Dog and Partridge, was a favourite of footballers and fans alike. On a Saturday evening after the game, when Manchester United were playing at home, the players, who were known to regulars by their first names, happily mingled with the railwaymen and factory workers who made up the clientele.

By about 5.30 p.m. after a home fixture it was almost impossible to find a path to the main bar. With no tables or chairs, the men gathered in large groups. Unlike the gentlemen of the day, they were dressed in their patched-up tweed jackets and trousers, topped off with flat caps. It was wartime, so one or two of the patrons could be spotted in army tunics, wounded or on leave from the army.

As the evening turned into night and the beer began to flow, drunken disagreements could become aggressive, punches might be thrown and blood fall on to the floor, which was spread with sawdust to mop up the combination of blood, saliva and beer.

Those who could not find a spot in the main bar would spill into the hall, where they were served from the hatch. Those who simply wanted a quiet drink at home could bring in a jug to be filled up with beer.

It was midweek when three men entered the pub. Even though they were familiar to the thousands who made the pilgrimage to Old Trafford or Anfield, barely anyone raised an eyebrow on this Thursday night as they made their way into the back room.

There, the smell of beer was mixed with the aroma of cigarettes, more than earning its name as the smoke room. On the wall was a stern warning: 'The licenceholder requests the assistance of Women customers in avoiding complaints that there have been recently received of excessive drinking, by not remaining on the premises longer than is necessary for obtaining reasonable refreshment.'

As they settled down with their jugs of ale, the men who gathered in the corner of the smoke room were not there to exchange pleasantries. This was not a social gathering: Tom Miller, Bob Pursell and Thomas Fairfoul had caught a train from Liverpool Lime Street to make the one-hour trip to Manchester.

They had found the pub easily enough, following instructions from Jackie Sheldon. The four men had one thing in common: they had all played in the 1914 FA Cup Final for Liverpool against Burnley. In tandem, and nervously, they supped on their beer, waiting.

If there were any nerves from the men, these quickly subsided when Sheldon walked in. After ordering his drink, he joined his Liverpool teammates at their table. It would not be long before they were joined by three other men: Sandy Turnbull, Arthur Whalley and Enoch West, who wore the red shirts of Manchester United.

Of those three, Sandy Turnbull was the most well-known: not only had he won two League titles and an FA Cup with United, but he could also lay claim to being the first man to score at the newly opened Old Trafford in 1910.

As Sheldon settled down on one of the stools around the bar table, all of the men knew why they had come to this pub. They had first met up weeks ago, when it was clear professional football would soon be at an end.

If any of them had found a copy of the *Lancashire Evening Post* lying around, they might have had a chuckle at a story on the second page, which informed the country that the King was willing to set an example by abstaining from drink for the duration of the war.

In a letter through his personal secretary to the Chancellor of the Exchequer, David Lloyd George, 'The King impressed with the necessity of the most "vigorous measures" in coping with the grave situation in our armaments which had been delayed by the drinking habits of the workers ... The King offered to set an example by abstaining from all alcohol liquor himself and forbidding it from the Royal household.'

If any of the players looked around the smoke room, which had quickly filled up after they had taken their seats, they could be sure that there were very few takers willing to join His Majesty in his campaign of abstinence. As the men moved on to their second and third pints of the evening, the laughing and joking got serious.

All the men agreed they would soon have to join up and take their chances in the trenches of Northern France. No one would be able to escape the war.

There was another option: the players could stay in the country and be conscripted into a munitions factory. With the mood of the country firmly against footballers and other able-bodied men not 'doing their bit', this was something to take seriously.

Whatever the players chose to do, Sheldon pointed out that they would all see a drop in their weekly income. And the way the war was going, they would be too old to come back to play football at any level by the time peace was secured. Sheldon himself had just turned 28 in January – a year or two out and that would be the end of his playing career.

However, the war inadvertently brought an opportunity: one final chance for them all to land some big money before the entire game was stopped. Sheldon told the players he had done some research and discovered that some bookmakers were offering odds of between 7 and 8 to 1 for Manchester United to beat their Lancashire rivals 2-0. This was an opportunity that was simply too good to pass up.

All the players needed to do was work out how they were going to ensure they could deliver that scoreline. The major concern was how to prevent Manchester United's proven matchwinner, Welsh international Billy Meredith, from getting the ball.

At 41, Meredith ranked alongside Vivian Woodward and Steve Bloomer as one of the first football superstars. Though by now he was way past his best, alongside Sheldon he too had won two titles and an FA Cup with Manchester United.

There had been some scandal around Meredith's transfer from Manchester City to United in 1906, when he was accused of offering an opposing player a bribe, but to the players gathered in the Dog and Partridge he was beyond reproach.

And though he had seen better days, the Welshman was still able to summon up the flashes of the brilliant player he had once been. Ironically, Sheldon and Meredith had history: Meredith had once lost his place in the United side to blood the youngster, Sheldon.

It was agreed that the way around the problem of Billy Meredith was simple: however good he was, there would be very little he could do if he did not see the ball. All the United players present agreed they would not pass to the mercurial Welshman.

There was still an elephant in the room. It had been only two years since the Liverpool players had been accused of, at best, not trying or, at worst, throwing a match against Chelsea, on Easter Monday, 1913.

Though ultimately the allegations were not proven, the wounds from the ensuing investigation were still very raw and the Liverpool players wanted reassurances there would be no repeat. As Sheldon explained, there had been an investigation only because Henry Norris, Mayor of Fulham and chairman of Woolwich Arsenal, had by chance decided to holiday on Merseyside.

At a loose end over the Easter weekend, he decided to take in a football match. Not any football match, but one that directly affected him. The result of the Liverpool and Chelsea game would influence the fortunes of his club, Woolwich Arsenal, who had found themselves rooted at the bottom of the First Division.

The man who would later be so important in forming the Football Battalion bought a ticket to go to Anfield and witness mid-table Liverpool lose to strugglers Chelsea 2-1. The shock result meant Woolwich Arsenal would be playing Second Division football. Standing on the terraces, Norris was sure he smelt a rat.

In his weekly column in the *West London and Fulham Times*, Norris did not hold back: 'Would that I had stayed away [from the Liverpool and Chelsea game at Liverpool], for I should then have been spared the infliction of witnessing the worst game of football it has ever been my misfortune to see.

'It was early apparent to me what was happening, and the final result of a win for Chelsea by the odd goal in three occasioned no surprise either to me or the many thousands who left the field in disgust.

'I have no hesitation in saying that many matches played as this one was would effectually kill professional football in this country as surely as professional running and cycling were killed in the olden days.

'I was told by certain of the Chelsea officials that I was talking nonsense and was prejudiced. Was I prejudiced and was I talking nonsense?

'If I am prejudiced, is the same charge to be levelled at the critic of the Lancashire "Sporting Chronicle"? This is what he wrote on Tuesday morning:

"Liverpool terminated their Easter holiday engagements by one of the worst exhibitions of football during their career in the league.

"They allowed Chelsea to defeat them after a display which must assuredly cause their faithful followers much food for genuine complaint. It was not merely the fact that they were beaten that aroused dissatisfaction, but the way their defeat was brought about that led to universal condemnation of their methods.

"Never before have the Liverpool first team been guilty of such palpable inefficiency as was the case in this game, and Chelsea's success was due not to their superiority, but to the pandering of their opponents, who practically added to their own discomfiture by their crude unintelligence and utterly feeble efforts.

"In the early stages, Campbell, Longworth, and Tosswill were sterling strivers, but even during this period there were palpable passengers in the Liverpool ranks, who seemed determined to give the Chelsea men every chance of making headway. Liverpool never appeared desirous of obtaining a goal, whereas they allowed their opponents every opportunity of so doing.

"Never in their career have they given a worse exhibition, and few of the team will emerge from the contest with added reputation. Genuine performers on the Liverpool side could be numbered on the fingers of one hand. Their opponents were feeble in the extreme, yet they won."'

Action from the Football League was swift. On Friday, 4 April, according to the minute book, 'A meeting of the Management Committee of the Football League was held in London last evening, Mr. J. McKenna presiding.

'With regard to the statements made recently concerning the defeat of Liverpool by Chelsea on Easter Monday, the committee decided as follows: The Football Association, having received a request from Notts County to make a full inquiry into the alleged indifferent play of certain members of the Liverpool Football Club in the match with Chelsea on Easter Monday, the Football League report will be withheld until the Football Association inquiry has taken place, so that both reports may be issued simultaneously.'

On Friday, 11 April, the *Derby Evening Telegraph* reported, 'The joint Commission of the Football Association and the Football League, appointed to inquire into allegations by Mr. H.G. Norris as to the conduct of certain Liverpool players in the match between Liverpool and Chelsea, Liverpool, on 24 March, sat at the offices of the Football Association, London, on Friday.

'Messrs. Crump, Pickford, Davis, and Skeggs represented the Football Association; and Messrs. Lewis, Keys, Dickinson, and Hall the Football League. Mr. J. McKenna attended on behalf of the Liverpool Club, and Mr. W.C. Kirby on behalf of Chelsea.'

The deliberations extended over three and a half hours, and at the close the following report was drawn up and issued to the press:

'The Commission is satisfied that no inducement was offered to the Liverpool players to influence the result of the match. Indeed, Mr. Norris assured the Commission that he did not suggest any corrupt or ulterior motive. There is evidence that the form displayed by the Liverpool players was unsatisfactory, but the Commission is satisfied that the allegation that they did not desire to win the match is unfounded.

'Mr. Norris admitted that he was indiscreet in giving publicity to the Football Association and the Football League.'

As a result the Football League seriously warned Norris about making any further allegations of this type and suggested that directors of clubs most certainly did not go around denouncing other clubs. One more outburst and he could be banned from football.

As Sheldon explained, things were different now: Norris was tied up with the Football Battalion and, besides, he would not be interested in their game, thanks to Chelsea's win over the Reds in 1913, Woolwich Arsenal had fallen out of the First Division and were firmly rooted in the second tier. Whatever happened at Old Trafford would have no bearing on what happened to the North London club.

· · · ·

On this Bank Holiday weekend, the weather which had been dire all year showed no signs of letting up. By the time both sides ran out, the 15,000 spectators who had come to Old Trafford on Good Friday, 2 April 1915, were soaked to the skin.

Even before the game kicked off, there had been so much money laid on a result of 2-0 in favour of Manchester United that the market had moved. The best odds to be found as the two captains shook hands in the centre circle were 4-1, down from 8-1 just a couple of days earlier.

On the way to the game, Sheldon almost undermined his plot. Hoping to recruit Fred Pagnam, he offered him £3 to throw the match as they travelled in a taxi to Old Trafford. Outraged, Pagnam lost his temper and threatened to score on purpose. It was only threats of making life difficult for Pagnam and his family which stopped an honest man following through on wrecking the players plot.

From the off, the home side played as though they were competing for honours rather than staring relegation in the face. Their form came as a complete surprise because they had taken to the pitch without Sandy Turnbull.

The only worry United had was their seeming inability to convert the plethora of chances gifted to them by a largely ineffective Liverpool back line.

The breakthrough finally came in the 38th minute, when Manchester United centre-forward George Anderson scored to give the home side a much-deserved lead. To many watching, Liverpool had been so bad that United could have been walking in at half-time four or five up. The overall view of the first half was summed up by the *Liverpool Daily Post*: 'A more one-sided first half would be hard to witness.'

For the conspirators who had carefully laid out the match in the Dog and Partridge a few days earlier, disaster almost struck when Liverpool defender Bob Pursell conceded a penalty by handling the ball in the 48th minute. Patrick O'Connell stepped up to take the kick and blasted it so far wide some spectators claimed he almost hit the corner flag with the ball!

Instead of showing any disappointment, he laughed out loud and took his place for the ensuing goal kick with a big smile on his face. At the time it was thought he was laughing more out of embarrassment than anything else.

A few minutes later, Fred Pagnam nearly followed through on his promise to score when he went close for Liverpool, hitting the United crossbar. A few of the players directed abuse at Pagnam as they ran back to take their places. Apart from those two incidents, there was nothing during the match to arouse suspicions that something was amiss.

For the players who had met at the Dog and Partridge, nerves were spared in the 75th minute when George Anderson pulled off the plan by finding the net for the second time and delivering the intended final score of 2-0 with a goal scored in both halves.

If anything, the reporters who watched the game were less than impressed after watching what they deemed a boring display, especially in the second half.

The *Sporting Chronicle* wrote, 'The Liverpool forwards gave the weakest exhibition in this half [the second] seen on the ground during the season. Despite conceding two goals, Elisha Scott performed excellently in goal.'

The *Manchester Daily Dispatch* said, 'The second half was crammed with lifeless football. United were two up with 22 minutes to play and they seemed so content with their lead that they apparently never tried to increase it. Liverpool scarcely ever gave the impression that they would be likely to score.'

As the referee signalled the end of the match, Sheldon, alongside Sandy Turnbull, could feel quite smug: they had pulled off quite a coup. Apart from a few hairy moments no one would know the game was predetermined.

The result would mean that FA Cup finalists Chelsea would be relegated and that Manchester United, against the odds, would survive. Then there was the bonus that Sheldon and Turnbull had enjoyed a final payday as football was finally ended for the duration of the war, even if that did come at the expense of paying customers, who were unwittingly watching a rigged football match.

If either player had picked up the *Sporting Chronicle*, a cold shiver would have gone down his spine reading about a bookmaker who described himself as the 'Football King'.

In the newspaper he published a notice which charged, 'We have solid grounds for believing that a certain First League match played in Manchester during Easter weekend was "squared", the home club being permitted to win by a certain score.' A reward of £50 was offered to anyone who could come forward with more information.

On Sunday, 25 April, news of the scandal had reached the London newspapers, with *The People* running the headline, 'A squared match'. It went on to report, 'A sensation has been caused in football circles by the following report issued by a commission appointed by the Football League, "We have made very careful enquiries and full investigation into certain rumours that an important league match played recently had been squared but in view of the facts herein after setting forth, we are withholding any report at present.

"'A football coupon issued last week has been brought to our notice … further we have information that several players of both teams were involved."'

Over the rest of the year, each player suspected of being involved in the plot was interviewed individually.

On 27 November 1915 'Wanderer' in the *Manchester Evening Chronicle* claimed, having talked to several players who had just given evidence, 'There is reason to believe the inquiry has taken a very serious turn. It has been stated, I believe, and with some pretence to authority that the whole thing would end in smoke and that no suspensions would follow – that the indictment would be found not proven. That is not my information.'

Whereas the investigation into the allegation of match-fixing into the Liverpool v Chelsea game two years earlier had been over in a matter of months, it would not be until 23 December 1915, some eight months after the final whistle blew on the match at Old Trafford, that the commission would report.

Its findings were damning: 'It is proved that a considerable sum of money changed hands by betting on the match, and that some of the players profited thereby.

'Every opportunity has been given to the players to tell the truth, but although they were warned that we were in possession of the facts some have persistently refused to do so, thus revealing a conspiracy to keep back the truth.

'It is almost incredible that players dependent on the game for their livelihood should have resorted to such base tactics. By their action they have sought to undermine the whole fabric of the game and discredit its honesty and fairness.

'We are bound to view such offences in a serious light. The honesty and uprightness of the game must be preserved at all costs, and although we sympathise greatly with the clubs, who are bound to suffer seriously, we feel that we have no alternative but to impose the punishments which the players have been warned repeatedly would be imposed.

'We are satisfied that the allegations have been proved against the following: J Sheldon, RR Purcell, T Miller and T Fairfoul (Liverpool), A Turnbull, A Whalley and EJ West (Manchester United), L Cook (Chester) and they are therefore permanently suspended from taking part in football or football management and shall not be allowed to enter any football ground in the future.

'There are grave suspicions that others are also involved, but as the penalty is severe, we have restricted our findings to those as to whose offence there is no reasonable doubt.'

The commission had heard that Liverpool's Fred Pagnam and Manchester United's George Anderson refused to take part. At the hearing, Manchester United player Billy Meredith denied any knowledge of the match-fixing but said that he became suspicious when none of his teammates would pass him the ball.

The *Liverpool Echo* reported in December 1915 that 'The excuse, if such it can be called, has been made that the players were tempted into the sordid business through the belief that the war would prevent football in 1915–16, and summer wages would not be the rule. But it is too paltry a claim in connection with a grave charge and can be ignored.'

By the time the FA had reached its verdict Jackie Sheldon was no longer in the country: he had enlisted with the 17th Middlesex Battalion. It was later claimed he joined up to avoid any potential scandal. The same was said of Sandy Turnbull, who had joined the 23rd Middlesex Battalion.

On 10 April 1916, *Athletic News and Cyclists' Journal* published a letter while Sheldon was in Northern France. 'I emphatically state to you, as our best and fairest critic, that I am absolutely blameless in this scandal and am still open, as I have always been, to give any Red Cross Fund or any other charitable institution the sum of £20 if the FA or anyone else can bring forward any bookmaker or any other person with whom I have had a bet. Assuming I return safely from this country, I intend taking action against my suspension.'

However Sheldon got around the ban, he went to Anfield in September 1916 to watch Liverpool play Burnley and got in for free as a wounded soldier. Eventually, he would return to play for Liverpool after the war, even though he admitted his guilt in a court case in 1917.

Chapter 8

Orders
The Battalion makes its way to France

To onlookers, the procession moved more slowly than in previous years. There was less colour and though those who took part were trying to keep up appearances, the grimness of war hung over the proceedings.

Buses and other transport had been converted for war purposes, their usually gaudy colours shrouded in a coating of paint which matched the grey skies above the crowds of Londoners. They were there to greet the new Lord Mayor of their city, who appeared at the Guildhall adorned in a bright red coat and the shining gold chains of office.

The procession trundling along the London streets through a deluge of rain that year included an aeroplane and four guns captured recently at the Battle of Loos. All served as a further reminder of the army on the other side of the channel.

Guns of the Anti-aircraft Corps, designed to protect London and mounted on motorcars, also figured in the procession, and behind them came a searchlight.

Even though the rain did its best to spoil everything, the troops from overseas who figured so prominently in the show would still have preferred to be marching through the streets of London than the alternative of the trenches.

The *Grantham Journal* said of the 1915 Lord Mayor's Show, 'The new Lord Mayor had a very popular reception, and it was gratifying to notice the facilities everywhere afforded to wounded soldiers from the hospitals to get a view of the pageant.

'Even the grandstand outside the Law Courts had been given over to them, the men afterwards being taken inside and entertained with tea by members of the Bench and Bar. Londoners, who were rather inclined to deprecate the holding of the show at all this year, came to criticise, but went away to praise, so essentially patriotic was the whole display.'

The purpose of the 1915 Lord Mayor's Show was to encourage men to join the colours. Recruitment meetings were held at 10 points along the procession's route, addressed by MPs and army men; those who did join up could then participate in the parade. The procession was unambiguously military.

The *City Press* correspondent declared that only the 'veriest slacker' would not be stirred by such a display, but its success as a recruiting exercise remains unclear. Abysmal weather, varying from drizzle to downpour, deterred men from hearing recruiting speeches lasting 'thirty or thirty-five minutes'.

At the Royal Exchange, according to the same *City Press*, there was a warning of 'the march of German soldiery into the city' should the war be lost, which chilled a crowd 'only of moderate dimensions'. At St Paul's Cathedral, listeners 'preferred to remain under the shelter of the railway bridge nearby and were not beguiled therefrom by the eloquence of the recruiting speakers'.

The parade comprised 'soldiers – soldiers all the way', including many 'direct from the trenches'. Among their number was the 23rd Middlesex Regiment, commonly known as the 2nd Football Battalion, whose express purpose was to remind any young men in the crowd that they could serve with their footballing heroes.

After the success of recruiting for the 1st Football Battalion, the 17th Middlesex, its founder William Joynson-Hicks, was soon agitating to form a second battalion. This was announced in a letter to the *Sheffield Daily Telegraph* on Friday, 9 July 1915:

'Sir, May I ask the hospitality of your columns to appeal for recruits for the 2nd Footballers' Battalion? The 1st Battalion has been encamped for upwards of ten weeks in my park at Holmbury and has improved out of all knowledge in appearance and in drill.

'They have now marched away, 1,100 strong, for a few months' brigade training in Nottinghamshire, after which it is hoped they will go to the front, and carry the fame of the Footballers' Battalion into Germany.

'It is, however, felt that there are still a large number, both of football players and football enthusiasts, who would like to join a similar regiment. Men can join any recruiting office, when they will be provided with a railway pass to Cranleigh, or Gomshall, near the camp. I may add that the Football Association is supporting the Battalion in every possible way.'

. . . .

In the Wiltshire town of Pernham Down, after parade and inspection, the first Football Battalion stood to attention.

All had known this day would eventually come: just a fortnight earlier, two teams from the Battalion were sent to The Dell, Southampton, and St Andrew's, Birmingham, to participate in what was billed by the press as the Battalion's 'farewell matches' before they departed for France.

When the two respective battalion teams ran out over 100 miles apart to face Birmingham and Southampton on 31 October 1915, there was an air of excitement and trepidation in the air. This marked the end of their months of training.

On 1 May, the *Dorking and Leatherhead Advertiser* had reported, 'The Footballers' Battalion (17th Middlesex Regiment) has left the White City, which has been its headquarters since the corps was raised, to take up training in camp. Until they receive the call for active service it will remain at Holmbury Park, the country residence of Mr. Joynson-Hicks MP who founded the Battalion.

'It includes in its ranks many prominent professional footballers. The corps, which now numbers 1,400, has recently received War Office sanction to raise its strength to 1,600. The departure of the

Battalion was witnessed by many people, and the fine athletic-looking men as they marched through the streets to Waterloo were loudly cheered.'

Although players were still permitted at this point to turn out for their clubs at weekends, if they so wished, the Battalion had got down to the serious, sometimes tedious, work of preparing for war. There was early morning kit inspection, physical training and route marches as well as trench digging and weapons training.

The *Surrey Advertiser* described the routine: 'For some time now the Footballers' Battalion have been encamped at Holmbury St. Mary, and high old times they have been having.

'Notwithstanding this, they have plenty of work to do, there is no fear of them getting stale, three nights a week there is evening drill, and midnight Thursday week Col. Grantham ordered the sound of the fire alarm to see how quickly they could turn out.

'The football season may have closed under F.A. rules, but two dozen footballs have been presented to the battalion by Col. Fenwick, second in command, and every field in the vicinity of the camp is used nightly, one of the participants being Lieut. Vivian Woodward, the well-known International and Chelsea forward.

'At the formation of the Battalion, Col. Grantham promised the professional players that they would be assisting their clubs at Christmas and Easter, and thus not get the usual military leave.

'The Wednesday night previous an impromptu concert was given by the officers, whilst Saturday night another concert was given in the sergeant's mess, many from the neighbouring village had been invited guests.'

Artist Cosmo Clark of the 17th Middlesex was to offer a slightly different picture, writing of his concerns about the quality of the training. 'My platoon of sixty men are a mixed mob who haven't (through bad teaching) realised what is expected of them as soldiers.

'In fact, the whole battalion are the same – many of the junior officers let unforgivable little crimes slip by without saying anything.

'During a lecture by a sergeant major on musketry I spotted a man who was fitting a live cartridge into the chamber of a rifle! Men were all about him and his rifle was pointing into the midst of them.'

After watching a recruit struggle on the rifle range, Clapton Orient player Richard McFadden, who was now a sergeant in the Battalion, was heard to quip, 'He could not shoot as a soldier, just as he could not shoot as a footballer.'

With recruitment for the first battalion having gone so well, there would soon be talk of another battalion being raised. On 10 July, the *Dorking and Leatherhead Advertiser* wrote of a new football battalion, 'As the Footballers' Battalion the 17th Middlesex Diehards, which has been training for the past ten weeks near Dorking, has now gone for brigade training. 'A second battalion has been authorised and will be known as the 23rd Middlesex (Football Battalion). The Football Association president (Lord Kinnaird), the chairman (Mr J. C. Clegg), together with representatives of the clubs, are members of the battalion committee.'

Recruitment for the original battalion was still ongoing, with the *Mansfield Reporter* writing, 'Captain Frank C. Buckley, of the 1st Football Battalion of the Middlesex Regiment, needs twenty football players to complete his company.

'In the course of his career at Manchester City, Brighton, Birmingham, Derby County, and Bradford City, Captain Buckley must have been in close touch with many players, and through the "Athletic News" columns he desires to appeal to twenty of them to join him.

'There are only these twenty vacancies to complete the strength, and Colonel Grantham has undertaken to post a party of professionals to Capt. Buckley's company so that they will all be football comrades in arms.

'The Football Battalion now brigaded at Clipstone Camp is a fine body of men, and rapidly getting ready for bolder operations on foreign soil. Men who join at once will get a week's leave after they have been up a month.

'We would impress upon football players the manifest advantages of being among "Pals" instead of joining so many scattered units, and we advise our friends to do honour to the game and themselves by writing at once to Capt. Buckley.'

When the players ran out at The Dell, for a game billed as a 'farewell match' for the Battalion, the *Hampshire Advertiser* noted that no major stars were present, 'Southampton entertained the Footballers' Battalion (17th Middlesex) at the Dell on Saturday, and though Vivian Woodward and other stars were absentees, the visitors brought a strong side even though there were several last-minute alterations.'

Among the Battalion team that day was Clapton Orient's centre-half, George Scott, and William Jonas, the strike partner and lifelong friend of Sergeant McFadden. Both had joined up with the rest of their teammates at Fulham Town Hall.

Running out that day was Fred Keenor of Cardiff City, whose recruitment had been announced by the *Lancashire Evening Post* on 10 February, on the same day that Vivian Woodward accepted a commission. 'Vivian J. Woodward, who has been serving in the ranks with the Rifle Brigade in Surrey, reported himself yesterday at the White City, London, for the first time to take up his position as lieutenant with the Footballers' Battalion.

'Recruiting was brisk yesterday, and among those attested at Kingsway were the following professionals: Bullock (Huddersfield Town); Slindoe and Keenor (Cardiff City)'. It was further reported by the *Western Mail* that Keenor had become the ninth player to sign up to the Battalion.

. . . .

Joining Keenor, Scott and Jonas was Tim Coleman, who had made a name for himself as a striker at Woolwich Arsenal and Everton, and was plying his trade at Nottingham Forest when he joined the Football Battalion. He was well known to fellow players, for what was described as his 'cheery good humour in all circumstances', 'great natural wit' and 'buoyant optimism'; he was also an 'inveterate joker' and a 'comedian-footballer'.

A committed trade unionist, Coleman was also a founding member of the Players' Union. Once threatened with suspension by the football authorities if he went on strike in 1910, he stood in solidarity with his fellow trade union members.

On 4 September the battalion played Reading and won 1-0. The *Berkshire Chronicle* claimed there was an attendance of 3000, including 944 soldiers who had paid the entrance fee and 200 who had been admitted for free.

Exactly a month later, the Battalion was in action again, this time against Cardiff City, who they dispatched 1-0. A week later, they were beaten 3-2 by Luton Town.

On Monday, 25 October came news which rocked football to its core. 'Tom Gracie is dead. Wherever football is played in Scotland there will be sincere regret at the untimely end of the Heart of Midlothian centre, of whom may it truly be said, "he always played the game."' So wrote the *Daily Record* in tribute to the Scottish centre-forward.

'Tom passed away in Stobhill hospital, Glasgow, on Saturday morning. He died on service as much as did a brother who fell on the battlefield very recently. Tom's health was never quite the same from the time he joined the Royal Scots last year ... Tom, although aware he was very seriously ill, was quite cheery and assured he was not downhearted. His chief worry was the thought that his comrades who joined the army with him might put him down as a shirker!'

What his teammates had not been aware of was that Gracie, who had signed up to McCrae's Battalion, had been diagnosed with leukaemia in March 1915. Coincidentally, Tom Gracie died on the same day as the famous cricketer W.G. Grace, an early opponent of the continuation of football during wartime.

The weather was described as fine, but as the game kicked off at precisely 3.15 p.m., a light drizzle broke out, which quickly turned into fine rain, making the surface quite greasy. Having lost the toss, Southampton kicked off from the Archer Road End of The Dell.

Even though the battalion was missing several stars, they began strongly, attacking the Southampton goal first. In the first action of the game, Roberts, the Luton Town striker, tested the Saints goalkeeper, Wood, with a long shot.

Despite pressure from the visitors, it was Southampton who got the first goal, the Saints breaking down the wing in their first attacking move of the match.

Shrugging off the goal, the Battalion went back on the attack, Watford's McLoughlin shooting wide after being clear on goal. In the very next attack, Roberts again found the target and this time Wood had no chance, the ball hitting the net and putting the Battalion level with the Saints.

As the first half progressed, it was only the acrobatics of Wood which saved Saints from falling behind. Therefore, it was a bit of a surprise when 10 minutes before the interval, the Southampton striker, Doming, managed to get his head to the ball from a corner and fired it straight into the Battalion net.

There was more bad news when Northampton's Black footballer, Walter Tull, lay on the floor, struggling for breath. In a challenge, he had taken an elbow to the side. It looked as though he was severely winded and unable to continue.

Tull, had an unusual journey to the Battalion, having been placed in an orphanage, where he showed an aptitude for football, passing through Spurs before settling at Northampton Town, the club he was playing for when he joined the 17th Middlesex.

. . . .

After being on the ground for 10 minutes, Tull got to his feet. It was clear to his teammates that he was going to be in no shape to continue with the game. The Football Battalion who went in at half-time 2-1 down would have to play the second half reduced to 10 men.

As the two teams came out for the second half, it seemed as though the Football Battalion was resigned to losing and were simply trying to stop the Saints from running away with the game. And it was only a matter of time before Southampton's Kingston scored the home side's third before Wheeler added a fourth.

Long after the match stopped being competitive, Tim Coleman scored a late consolation goal for the soldiers, meaning the scoreline of 4-2 was a lot more respectable than what it had threatened to be at some points in the second half.

Over 140 miles away, in Birmingham, there would be no shortage of footballing stars for spectators to feast their eyes upon – another eleven made up of men from the 17th Middlesex. The *Birmingham Daily Post*, on Monday, 1 November, reported: 'The primary object of the match was to obtain recruits for the reserve of the Footballers' Battalion.

'Before the game opened, the recruiting sergeants were busy among the crowd. Speeches were delivered by local dignitaries and a few young men answered the call.

'They were heartily cheered by the crowd as they came forward in charge of the recruiting officers. The proceeds of the match will be divided between various charities and battalion funds.'

It would be the second time in three weeks that spectators St Andrews had seen the soldiers come out on top: on 9 October they won 1-0, with the *Birmingham Daily Post* reporting, 'The game, which resulted in victory for soldiers by one goal to nil, provided a pleasant display.

'Judged by the pre-war standard of professional superexcellence it was tame and almost featureless; but regarded as an affair in which football was played for recreative purposes, and without any tangible reward in view, it was satisfactory alike to players and spectators.'

Unlike the game in the south on 30 October, the weather in the Midlands was perfect as 10,000 spectators witnessed well-known footballing stars run out. As in the Cup Final a few months earlier, it was as though a sea of khaki had enveloped the crowd, because of the large number of soldiers.

If the men of the Football Battalion needed reminders of what they potentially faced, they could see that it was the wounded who were being accommodated with seats in the principal stands.

After the publicity surrounding the Liverpool v Manchester United match in April, many eyes would have been on Jackie Sheldon. Sheldon was not the only footballer who had had a brush with the law.

On 18 May, under the headline, 'Famous footballer gives evidence', the *Surrey Mirror* reported, 'Herbert A. Earl, of the 17th Middlesex Regiment, stationed at Holmbury St. Mary, was summoned for driving a motor car without a front identification plate.

'The offence was admitted. P.S. Lightfoot said that at 5.10 p.m. on the 3rd he saw the defendant driving a motor car on the Westcott Road. Witness was unable to stop him at the time, but later saw the car in the town, when he observed that it had no front identification plate.

'Upon searching the car the defendant found the plate in the toolbox. The defendant said he did not know the plate was off until the sergeant told him so.

'Lieut. Vivian J. Woodward, the famous international football player, who belongs to the Footballers' Battalion, said it was no fault of the defendant that the plate was missing. In dismissing the case, the Chairman advised the defendant to be more careful in future.'

Joining Sheldon and Woodward in the side that day was Grimsby's Lonsdale, Martin and Wheelhouse, alongside Bullock of Huddersfield and Booth from Brighton. Completing the line-up was Captain Frank Buckley and Butler of Queens Park Rangers.

From the kick-off, it was clear that the Battalion was the stronger of the two sides. For a start, the Birmingham City players looked leaner than the soldiers who had been in training for the past 10 months.

If Jackie Sheldon had any worries about the verdict of the Football Association's commission into alleged match-fixing, these appeared to be firmly in the back of his mind as he applied pressure in the opening minutes.

Sheldon was not the only one who was performing well, with Frank Buckley making an impression in defence. According to the *Sportsman*, 'Buckley was the most successful in the half-back line, his tackling and placing being admirable.'

For a time, it looked as though the game in Birmingham was about to mirror its counterpart in the south. Despite, Vivian Woodward going close a few times, it was the home side which took the lead after 32 minutes. Three minutes later, the Football Battalion equalised.

A minute after the restart, the Battalion was awarded a penalty, from which Jackie Sheldon confidently slotted home and put the soldiers in front. The dominance displayed by the Battalion in the first half continued and when Sheldon put away his second goal on the 68th minute, the soldiers were cruising at 3-1. The goal from Sheldon capped an outstanding performance for a man who had been accused of fixing matches a few months earlier.

Even when Birmingham managed to hit back two minutes later, any hopes of an exciting finish were extinguished because the Battalion never showed any signs of being troubled by the home side's attack. And there was no doubt who was the man of the match: Jackie Sheldon.

The *Birmingham Advertiser* described what the Liverpool player achieved: 'The work of Sheldon was clever and when he got an opening, he always made the best use of it.'

At the full-time whistle, there followed speeches given by local dignitaries. As the players of both sides walked off, the cheers from the crowd ringing in their ears, the *Sportsman* reported, 'about 100 joined the colours, helping to swell the city's total for the day to 327.' For many of the players, who played in both matches, this would be the last time they would appear on a football pitch.

If the Battalion needed confirmation that the games in Birmingham and Southampton were indeed the 'farewell matches' described in the press, then it came just under a week later. On 5 November, the 17th Middlesex Regiment finally received orders to 'prepare forthwith for France'.

On 16 November, after months of training and practice matches, the Battalion finally arrived in France. Stationed just 16 miles away from the front, the players, so used to hearing the cheers of capacity crowds, heard a different sound for the first time: the sound of gunfire and shelling.

The 17th Middlesex was finally at war.

Chapter 9

Winners!
Morale-boosting games

They knew they were there; they could hear them. At first it sounded like a soft murmuring. The Germans, the enemy, were on the move. The volume, faint at first, slowly rose as they got nearer and nearer the 17th Middlesex Regiment's position.

Soon, voices could be heard. The Football Battalion waited silently, in the mud of the trenches. The sandbags and wooden planks surrounding them offered their only defence. The January rain had been as relentless as the Germans had been with their shelling, and the mud made it almost impossible to stabilise weapons.

As storm after storm rained down, men like Tim Coleman and Jackie Sheldon were unable to go into the trenches. Both stood only 5ft 5in tall and would be up to their chests in dirty water, making them of little use.

Beyond the trench, German voices had turned from mere chatter into song. The Germans were singing in English, their songs directed at the British who waited for them. 'British, how are you? We are coming over!' They were so loud, the Battalion knew they were close.

Privates George Hill and Joseph Adams spoke in hushed tones. They were cold, hungry and tired. They wore only a leather jerkin and a thin waterproof, having left behind their greatcoats, which quickly became waterlogged in rain and rendered their wearers immobile.

The singing and shouting from the Germans was now louder than ever. Even though the men of the Battalion had been here only

10 weeks, they reassured each other this was nothing more than German bravado; no way would they be coming any time soon.

The confidence of Hill and Adams was not shared by their commanding officer, who signalled at the young men to remain quiet. The German singing stopped abruptly: no voices, no shouting, just silence, eery silence. It remained that way for an hour, and with no action from the German side, the commanding officer allowed Private Hill to be relieved of his post along with several others.

Gingerly, Hill and the others inched slowly and silently out of the trench. After easing himself out of the trench, Hill looked back. Suddenly came the loud bang of something resembling a firecracker. Quickly, he dropped to his stomach, the cold air filled with the whistle of bullets over his head.

No one saw the grenade float over the trench and come to rest on the sandbags which made up the walls of the trench. The only indication of its deadly intent was the slight fizzing sound as the fuse burnt out.

Even if anyone had been quick enough to grab hold of the missile, he would have been blown to smithereens before having the chance to throw it back. The fuse burnt out in mere seconds, its explosion splintering the grenade into a thousand tiny pieces, piercing the skin and bone of several of the soldiers in the trench.

Escape was almost impossible, movement hindered by the knee-deep water and thick mud, while the impact of the explosion destroyed the sandbags and wooden planks, almost burying the soldiers alive.

The fuse on the second grenade fired from a German rifle had already burnt out when it landed among the stricken men. This time the trench collapsed, leaving no means of escape. Any hope of rescue would have to be delayed, for fear of more missiles being launched.

Looking on, Private George Hill was sure there would be no survivors. He could see nothing except a sea of smoke and debris. For a moment, and just as before the German advance, there was only silence.

Then came the rat-tat-tat-tat sound of German machine-gun fire, forcing Hill to throw himself on the floor once again, the screams of the men imprisoned in the collapsed trench ringing in his ears.

Two weeks later, on 12 February 1916, Hill was to write of his experiences in a letter published in his local newspaper, the *Leek Times*: 'I am still in the pink after going through tight corners. We did seven days in the trenches without taking things off, but this is only a flea bite to what the boys had to go through at the start, 39 days without leave, it must have been one foul time for them.

'I am sorry to say, I lost a pal, J. Adams, there were two killed and five wounded. We also had Captain Vivian Woodward; the great footballer wounded. I saw them all carried out of the trench.

'I was out of the trench when the Germans exploded two mines and commenced rapid firing on the trench. It was an awful situation when those mines blew up, sandbags and dirt flying about. You must look after yourself or you will get buried. We were 80 yards from the German lines.'

Face down in the mud, sand and water, England's most famous footballer, Vivian Woodward, lay motionless. The shrapnel from the grenade had torn through his skin, burying itself deep into the sinew of his lower legs, and he bled profusely.

Alongside him lay the body of Joseph Adams. Very soon the dreaded news would arrive at his home in Clay Cross. A Post Office telegram from the Army Council, stamped with the words 'regret to inform you', told Mrs Adams that her husband was reported as killed on 22 January 1916. At the age of 23, she was now a widow and her son would grow up without a father.

For an hour, the stretcher bearers waited. Only once the biting wind carried the smoke away, and the heavy rain turned to drizzle and the guns fell silent, did they finally enter the collapsed trench.

Joined by a detachment of Scottish soldiers, the stretcher bearers plunged their hands into the cold slurry, frantically digging out the fallen men. It was a man from Leith who found Vivian Woodward barely recognisable, but alive.

He was taken to a field hospital, where it was initially believed that Woodward had been hit in both thighs. Later, the prognosis seemed much better and doctors assumed that after a period of convalescence, he would be able to return to the front.

Even those who got out of the trench alive were not so lucky. The *Evening Dispatch* reported, 'Dowdeswell, a Wolves junior forward, who joined the Footballers' Battalion, was recently home wounded. He had no fewer than 33 separate injuries, caused by the explosion of a rifle grenade. He was wounded at the same time as Woodward.'

The incident was described in the 17th Middlesex's war diary by Colonel Fenwick: 'During our tour to the frontline, reports of our casualties are "Wounded (Since died) 6, wounded 33."

'The casualties were a result of rifle grenades: The officers and NCOs who have been attached from the 1st King's have returned to their own units, and the officers and NCOs attached to them have returned to us.

'We are now together as a battalion for the first time in six weeks. Wounded, Captain VJ Woodward, Lieutenant EDW Bruton and Major KDL MacLaine of Lochbrie.'

As Fenwick wrote, Woodward lay in a field hospital. On 6 February, he left Dieppe for Dover. On his return he was examined by an army doctor who found that a portion of the grenade had lodged in his right thigh just above his knee – fragments were removed in a painful operation.

When he came before an army board just under a month later, on 13 April, his progress was deemed satisfactory, though he was still not fit for service and given another six weeks before he could return. By then Woodward was showing signs of developing the painful skin condition dermatitis, which meant he was facing the prospect of light duties back in Britain.

. . . .

On 27 February, Colonel Fenwick was settling down for lunch with two other members of the Football Battalion. The bully-beef stew served on tin plates was the only choice on the menu. This was usually washed down with a cup of tepid black tea, served in a tin mug. The venue was a coal cellar in the outskirts of Calonne, which did not benefit from the luxuries of heat, light or ventilation.

As Fenwick swapped stories with his men, he did not notice the old gentleman entering his quarters and when he did look up and acknowledge the man, he did not recognise him. William Joynson-Hicks was usually dressed in top hat and frock coat, but today he was covered in mud, after marching some distance in search of the Battalion.

Fenwick was the son of a prominent and wealthy Northumberland family who had sent him to Eton and he had become a Liberal MP for Houghton-le-Spring. Joynson-Hicks was shocked at seeing the quarters and the state of a man he described as 'practically a millionaire, living this life for his country's sake, when he was long past the age when men were expected to serve in the trenches.'

The purpose of Joynson-Hicks' visit was to reassure the Battalion, 'to make sure that there was nothing that he could not do for them, which was not being done.' In his possession was a letter from the King, giving the Battalion his best wishes, which he hoped to read aloud to the men.

Any amusement the men might have had at the state of the founder of the Football Battalion, now covered in mud, turned to horror when Joynson-Hicks, dissatisfied at the view of the German position from a periscope, ventured into the trench.

When he thrust his head over the parapet to view the enemy lines just over 300 yards away, a German shell came over the top to greet him. Fortunately, it was quickly identified as a dud, resulting in a liberal spraying of mud over the already soiled MP.

A second shell fell just short of the trench, dislodging part of the brick wall which held the structure together. Those in Joynson-Hicks' party decided to bring the impromptu visit to an end, the MP himself later writing, 'The visit was brought to a summary conclusion because the Germans started shelling rather badly.'

• • • •

Back home, any hopes Vivian Woodward would soon be back at the front were quickly dispelled when the former Chelsea man appeared before another army board on 16 March 1915 and was declared unfit for duty.

Just five days later, one of the Battalion's other commissioned footballers, Frank Buckley, took over as commanding officer. Colonel Fenwick, who had been leading the men since their arrival in France, was granted leave to return to British shores.

The appointment of Buckley was certainly not a public relations stunt. As the son of an army instructor, he had signed up for a 12-year engagement on 24 February 1900 with the 2nd Battalion of the King's Liverpool Regiment and seemed set to become a career soldier.

By September 1900, he was promoted to corporal; two years later he was a lance-sergeant, and the following year he gained the rank of gymnastics instructor (first class). Although he expected to serve in the Boer War, he was instead sent to Ireland, where he excelled in various sports.

The whole trajectory of his career changed when Buckley played for the King's Regiment (Liverpool) against the Lancashire Fusiliers in the final of the Irish Cup. He was spotted by a scout from Aston Villa, who suggested he go to England for a trial. In April 1903, his military career was seemingly at an end after he bought himself out of the army for £18 to join Aston Villa.

Over the coming years, he played for a further six teams before joining the Football Battalion on 12 December 1914. His promotion had been rapid, the *Derby Evening Telegraph* reporting on New Year's Day, 1915, 'One of the first players to join the Footballers' Battalion was Frank Buckley, the Bradford City professional, who is in partnership with his brother Chris Buckley, the Arsenal centre-half, as a farmer near Birmingham.

'It will give great satisfaction to the professional footballers when Frank Buckley is gazetted, possibly Monday next, with a commission to the new battalion to which the position has been strongly recommended.

'Buckley will be the second professional footballer to be given a commission in the new army, Evelyn Lintott being the first. Frank Buckley, it will be recalled, was with Derby County two seasons, and was with Birmingham and other clubs.'

Another promotion followed in March, the *Bradford Daily Telegraph* reporting on Monday, 15 March 1915, 'We understand that Lieut Frank Buckley, the Bradford City and England international football player and the first to join the Footballers' Battalion, has been promoted to the rank of captain.

'The heartiest congratulations of football players and followers of the game will be given to Captain Buckley, who has been very popular with the men, and has proved himself a thoroughly efficient and painstaking officer.'

The injury to his former international teammate, Vivian Woodward, on 15 January was not the only incident which affected Buckley deeply that day. Among those retrieved from the collapsed trench was the twisted body of Thomas Brewer, who had played for Queens Park Rangers before the war and had been caught in the crossfire after the grenade went off.

There was no other recruit with whom Buckley had spent more time than Brewer. After receiving his commission, he had been assigned a batman. Brewer became that man and accompanied him everywhere, acting as his personal servant. During their time together in France, the two men had formed a deep bond.

Upon hearing of his death, Buckley fell into a depression. Thomas Brewer was a young man, whose widow was now left with three hungry mouths to feed. Buckley stepped in to help Brewer's family, paying for the children's education.

The appointment of Buckley as commanding officer was greeted by the *Illustrated Police News* on 30 March 1915: 'During the past few days, it has been officially announced that Captain Frank Buckley of the first Football Battalion of the 17th Middlesex Regiment has been promoted to the rank of major. This is very gratifying news.'

Even the man he replaced, Colonel Fenwick, said of his successor, 'If I was walking down the lines with Major Buckley – no matter where we were – the men would salute in the ordinary way, but they took no notice of me. Their eyes were for Buckley. They whispered, "That's Buckley – the footballer."'

On the same day that Buckley's promotion was being reported back home, the 17th Middlesex played the King's Royal Rifle Corps, in the semi-final of the Divisional Tournament, which was played in France. Even though the King's Royal Rifles had won the 99th Brigade competition, they were no match for the professionals of the Football

Battalion, who ran out 6-0 winners. Buckley was to write of the match, 'We are in the final of the Divisional Cup competition and won the semi-final against KRR's 6-0.'

Playing in the Divisional Tournament had initially broken up the boredom, which Walter Tull alluded to when he wrote home to his brother, Edward, in early 1915: 'For the last three weeks my battalion has been resting some miles distant from the firing line, but we are now going up to the trenches for a month or so.

'Afterwards we shall begin to think about coming home on leave. It is a very monotonous life out here when one is supposed to be resting and most of the boys prefer the excitement of the trenches to the comparative inaction whilst in reserve.'

Awarded a bye in the first round of the Divisional Tournament, the 17th Middlesex were drawn against the winners of the game between the 11th Hertfordshire and 13th Essex. A hard-fought, see-saw match saw 13th Essex just edging the match 4-3. Their reward was a fixture against footballing royalty: the 17th Middlesex Regiment, on 7 January 1915.

Five hundred spectators made the 4-mile walk across muddied fields and winding country lanes to arrive at the place which had been commandeered as a football pitch for the hosts, 13th Essex.

Those watching knew they were about to witness a one-sided match – especially not when familiar faces like George Scott of Clapton Orient and Frank Buckley ran out that day. For many, it was also the first time they had ever been this close to a footballing legend, Vivian Woodward.

By any stretch of the imagination, the weather was appalling. Torrential rain soaked the players, turning the makeshift pitch into a mud bath, with huge pools of water appearing. The ball leather, which was showing signs of wear and tear, soon became waterlogged, making it resemble a lump of concrete. The spectators were certainly not going to watch a free-flowing passing game.

If the rain was not bad enough, howling wind made the conditions even worse. Strong gusts threw spray from the rain into the eyes of the players. In the end, the game was more of an exhibition as the 17th Middlesex recorded an emphatic 9-0 victory. Even Buckley, who was not known for his prowess in front of goal, managed to get on the score sheet.

The performance of both Woodward and Buckley was to reach the pages of the *Daily Express*, which praised two outstanding performances. For the players themselves there was no doubt about the eventual outcome of the tournament. One player was quoted as saying, 'We have undoubtedly enough players in the Battalion to produce a dozen teams capable of beating any regimental 11 out here.'

Such confidence was more than justified three days later when the same team that had vanquished the 13th Essex ran out to face the 2nd South Staffordshire in the final. This time they destroyed their opposition 6-0, with Lance Corporal Jack Cock of Huddersfield Town scoring four goals.

In a letter to H.N. Hickson, the secretary at Grimsby Town, Private Sid Wheelhouse lamented the conditions at the match against the 13th Essex and the latest match against the South Staffords. 'The ground we played on was awful. It was over the boot tops in mud and the ball would not bounce. It put me in mind of the Huddersfield ground when we played them two seasons ago, when the ball would not bounce, and we had to hook it out of the mud before we could kick it.'

Before moving to Gorre and the trenches of Givenchy, Frank Buckley lined up alongside Sergeant Richard McFadden of Clapton Orient and Private Tim Coleman to play against a 'Best of Brigade' XI on 15 January.

A 3-1 scoreline flattered the opponents, because, once again, the Football Battalion put on a devastating performance. When the final whistle blew, both players and spectators knew that the next action would be on the battlefield. At least some of them were ready: days filled with rifle drill practice, being taught how to properly fix their gas masks and the correct throwing of grenades may not have been the most stimulating work, but at least they would be well prepared when they finally reached the frontline.

On 20 January, the men reached the trenches at Givenchy, where the lines were as little as 20 yards away from the Germans, and football was the furthest thing from anybody's mind. For nearly two weeks the men who had entertained so many lived in fear of shelling and the constant threat from grenades.

Finally, on 2 February, the 17th Middlesex were relieved of their duties and marched back to billets at Gorre. Again came the tedium and anxiety of preparing for their eventual return to the trenches. Daily gas helmet inspections and lessons in bomb throwing and trench warfare were broken up with the manual work of fortifying trenches with sandbags and barbed wire around Gorre Wood.

If the conditions at Givenchy were extreme, they were nothing compared to those found at the 17th Middlesex's next posting. On 11 February the Battalion reached Festubert, south of the Aubers Ridge, where there were 16 above-ground trenches called breastworks (temporary fortifications which came up to the shoulders or breast).

To construct them, earth, rocks, sandbags, masonry and tree trunks found in the area were used to provide cover for trenches 7–8 feet high. They had been built there because the mud and water at Festubert made it impossible to dig trenches. To add to the danger, soldiers could only be relieved of their duties under the cover of darkness.

While on duty two days later, Tim Coleman could not believe his eyes. Out of the mist and smoke he thought he spied two men walking across no man's land. Sinking slowly down out of view, Coleman wrapped his hands around his rifle as the two figures came into sight.

Soon, he would have a good view of them, young men dressed in German uniform and clearly unarmed. They called out '*Kamerdan*', or 'comrade' and very soon they surrendered to the former Nottingham Forest man.

Writing home, Private Cyril Smith of Croydon Common related what happened next. 'Tim was marching down the trench past the boys (you can imagine how proud he was feeling of himself) when suddenly he sank in about three feet of mud and water. He tried desperately to get out and get a move on to the Battalion headquarters, but each effort he made would send him down a little deeper, much to the amusement of the boys who had collected around.

'While all this was going on Chalmers (Grimsby Town), one of his closest friends, came along and pinched the prisoners off him, marched them to headquarters and naturally got a lot of kind words and praise from the Colonel.

'Eventually, Tim got out with the help of some of the lads, and took an oath that he would never take, or rather attempt to take, any more prisoners. I don't know if he has ever got his own back or not, but if he hasn't – well, he is not the "Tim" Coleman as I know him.

'The "catchphrase" among the lads of the battalion ever since that happened is "What did you do in the Great War, Coleman?"'

The following day, Coleman and the rest of the Battalion were on the move again, this time marching 5 miles to their new billets in Essars, northeast of Bethune. On 26 February, the 17th Middlesex took over the trenches from French troops in Calonne. They quickly made themselves at home by giving this rabbit warren of trenches names like Footballer's Avenue and Middlesex Walk.

After another hard three weeks, which saw some of the coldest weather on the front up to that point, the 17th Middlesex were on the move once more. On 18 March they were told they would finally enjoy a period of rest, including leave. But first the exhausted battalion, which had fought non-stop for 20 days, had to march a demanding 12 miles to their billet in Bruay.

While in Bruay, life fell into a pattern familiar to the Battalion since its arrival in France. There were route marches, rifle inspections and the demonstration of a new 'flame thrower'. The war was never very far away, though excitement was building for the Divisional Cup Final.

In the evening, a detachment of men was ordered to rebuild and repair a large section of the trenches around Souchez, at the north end of Vimy Ridge, where the French and Germans had engaged in heavy fighting.

If working with their bare hands in the freezing night, knee-deep in mud, made conditions bad enough, then the stench and decay of the dead bodies of soldiers scattered across the battlefields, both German and French soldiers, made the work almost insufferable.

After all the build-up, the Divisional Cup Final turned out to be nothing but a damp squib. On 11 April, the 17th Middlesex met the 34th Brigade, Royal Field Artillery, at Hersin.

The team that day – Private Tommy Lonsdale (Southend United) goalkeeper, Private Sid Wheelhouse (Grimsby Town), Lance Corporal Fred Bullock (Huddersfield Town), Private George Scott (Clapton Orient), Private David Kenney (Grimsby Town), Lance Corporal Billy Baker (Plymouth Argyle), Private Hugh Roberts (Luton Town), Private William Jonas (Clapton Orient), Lance Corporal Jack Cock (Huddersfield Town), Lance Corporal Joe Bailey (Reading) and Sergeant Percy Barnfather (Croydon Common) – was simply too powerful and won the Cup, 11-0.

Simply put, the 17th Middlesex had been devastating, scoring a total of 44 goals over the course of the tournament.

The match ball itself would eventually end up in the hands of a renowned comedian of the day, Sammy Shields, which the *Western Morning News* reported on 4 July 1916: 'He sings funnily about a football he produces with an exquisite touch of pathos, recounting how the ball was given to him by Buckley (now Major Buckley), of Bradford, and how it was used in the great contest in Flanders between a team of the Footballers' Battalion (17th Middlesex) and the R.F.A., in which Sergeant McCormick and Corporal Baker played.

'The football bears the signatures of 43 famous footballers serving on the Western Front.'

For the players, a commemorative medal would be struck for each member of the team. The medals were made of silver and were said to be of a 'handsome design'.

Together with the name of the player, each medal bore the following inscription: 'B.E.F. France, Association Football Cup'. Just over a week after the final, the 17th Middlesex would move to begin their eventual journey to the trenches of Calonne.

By the autumn, when the commemorative medal was ready, four of the players would not be alive to receive them.

Chapter 10

Walter Tull
Leaving the field

Something was not right. For weeks now Walter Tull had felt weak and unusually tired, so even if he had been picked for the Divisional Cup Final, he would not have been able to play.

He certainly had a strong claim on the team. In 1909 Tottenham Hotspur had singled out the 21-year-old as the player they wanted to replace the legendary Vivian Woodward at centre-forward. Two years later, though, he headed to Northampton, where he appeared 111 times for the Cobblers.

Such was his fame, it was said that when he went on a visit to Scotland to see his brother, a dentist, the mighty Glasgow Rangers approached him with a view to signing for the team. In the end, and like everyone else in the 17th Middlesex, the war had put paid to any grand plans.

Now, in the middle of April 1915, the trenches were a regular feature of life for the Northampton man, who also had to live with a low-level buzzing in his ears, which was giving him such debilitating headaches he found it difficult to get out in the morning for the regular roll call at 5.30 a.m.

Then there was the nausea, which Tull was sure in some way related to his headaches. Anyway, it could all be explained away: the ringing in his ears came from the noise of the constant German shelling and gunfire, while the nausea came from the stench of the trenches.

Living near one another, almost cheek to jowl, even though they tried maintaining personal hygiene it was extremely difficult. Very often uniforms were caked in mud, and holes dug haphazardly in the trenches served as toilets for the troops on the ground.

Very often men who lost their lives were left where they lay before the stretcher bearers arrived under the cover of darkness to dispose of the bodies. Quicklime was poured on the bodies in the forlorn belief that it would help decomposition (it did the opposite) and prevent the spread of diseases like cholera. The stench, mixed with the heavy fug of gunpowder, could turn even the strongest stomachs.

Then there was the pain which shot through his thighs to reach his shins, making them feel like he had two bags of cement attached to his lower half. Again, Tull put this down to the overexertion. Since they had received their orders to rendezvous at Calonne on 12 April 1915, the Battalion seemed to be constantly marching.

Writing in the Battalion War Diary, Colonel Fenwick, who had returned to the front after his leave, wrote, 'At 8am we left our billets and marched before entraining for Bruay. We marched from there to Calonne, we stopped here for the night and entrained for Aire.

'From Aire to Rudinghan is about 13 miles. This was a very trying march as we had a gale of wind and clouds of dust in our faces all the way.'

On 17 April, the 17th Middlesex then marched all the way back to Calonne. There, they replaced the 13th Hussar Regiment, having marched a round trip of 26 miles over four days.

Even the addition of two officers and 50 other ranks to replace the losses the regiment had already suffered was not enough to make up for the level of exhaustion the Battalion was feeling.

When they arrived, according to the war diary, 'It was a pouring wet afternoon, and everyone got wet through. The trenches are in bad state.' Then there was the dirty water, which soldiers in the trenches had to live with daily.

By the time the Battalion had reached France a painful condition known as trench foot was well known. It causes a tingling, pain and numbness in the feet, and when the condition worsens, the feet become swollen and the skin begins to break down. Left untreated, the foot becomes badly infected as the muscle and tissue decay.

The only way to prevent the condition is to keep feet dry and clean. Soldiers were provided with multiple pairs of socks and told to change their socks and boots as often as possible. The issue for many soldiers, though, was that they found it hard to find time or space to change their socks – especially in water-logged trenches.

By the time Walter Tull was helping to rebuild collapsed trenches, the water was harbouring unseen bacteria. Furthermore, lice were a constant problem, easily finding their way onto clothes and burrowing into the skin of soldiers. Equally, fleas, which usually lived on the mice and voles that had now made their home in the trenches, could be transferring themselves onto the soldiers.

As the 17th Middlesex went about its work in the trenches, Tull found himself getting weaker and weaker. Added to the headaches and nausea came dizziness and backache, which, combined with the pains in his legs, made walking impossible.

For the first six days in Calonne, Tull was too sick to fight; some speculated that the terror of the trenches was adversely affecting him. As he lay on a makeshift bed with tears in his eyes from the severe pain, the man who had written to his brother that he could not wait to get to the trenches because of the tedium of waiting around was long gone.

If Tull was showing the effects of war, then he was not the only one. While on leave in March, Richard McFadden joined his old teammates at Clapton Orient to take on Queens Park Rangers at Homerton. Spectators were less bothered about the 1-1 result than they were about the state of their star striker, who was described as appearing 'altogether not very happy'.

After nearly two weeks, when Tull rallied only to relapse again, he was finally seen by a doctor and then admitted to Lady Hadfield's Anglo-American Hospital on 28 April. There, he was diagnosed as suffering from 'acute mania' or what was commonly known as 'shell shock'.

The condition was well known to the British forces. Private Allen Foster (the former Reading player) wrote to his wife, 'Very trying on the nerves and lots of fellows get what they call shell shock. With the constant bursting of shells etc and the thundering of guns, they seem to go to pieces.'

Walter Tull's condition was so bad that he was transferred by boat back home to Great Britain on 9 May 1915. In 1988, Private Walter Grover, who served with the 2nd Battalion Sussex Regiment on the Western Front and in Germany, 1916-1919, gave an interview to the Imperial War Museum.

In that interview he talked of the fear soldiers felt of being labelled a coward if a soldier was diagnosed with shell shock: 'You can't wonder at it, people cracking up. We had some chaps in our regiment that cracked up with shell shock.

'They called it cowardice, but it wasn't that at all. Nobody knows the effect of a barrage: you are under shells coming over, you could see it out of the corner of your eye these shells coming down and people blowing up and the shells coming down and blowing everybody to pieces.

'You can understand some chaps, they're not all built the same and some couldn't stand it. We had one fellow in our line, and he was as right and as nice as you could wish to meet out of the line and he frankly admitted that, when the shells burst near him, he was like a jelly; he just couldn't stand it.

'I was afraid, oh yes, I'll admit that, but what I didn't want was other people to see that I was afraid, that was the thing. Everybody was afraid, but you didn't want your pal to see it.'

The last thing Walter Tull could be accused of being was a coward.

· · · ·

Just short of seven years earlier, on 20 July 1909, Tull walked among the rows and rows of terrace houses past the Palace Theatre, where the music hall stars of the day plied their trade.

His eventual destination? White Hart Lane, where work was continuing on the West Stand. Just a year after gaining promotion to the top fight, Spurs were a club going places and spectators would no longer get soaked as they cheered on their team, a roof with a

Tudor gable providing shelter in the winter months. The club's new confidence was clear to see, 'Tottenham Hotspur FC' emblazoned in white letters against the blue background of the stand.

Earlier that summer, Vivian Woodward had shocked the football world by announcing his retirement and the race was on to find his successor. The young Walter Tull, making his way along Tottenham High Road on a balmy July day, was the man who had been singled out to replace England's leading goalscorer.

Only 21 years old, standing 5ft 8in and weighing a sturdy 11 stone, Tull had impressed as an amateur for Clapton. On Boxing Day 1908, he made his debut as centre-forward in a 3-1 win against Leytonstone. London's *Daily News* described Walter as 'Clapton's catch of the season'.

At this point, Tull was happy as an amateur and had settled for life as a newspaper printer after completing a four-year apprenticeship. But he jumped at the chance of a trial with Tottenham Hotspur. Successful, he signed a professional contract for a fee of £10 followed by the maximum weekly wage of £4.

After playing for the 'A' and reserve sides, Tull had done enough to be invited on a tour of Argentina, where he played at centre- or inside-forward.

The *Buenos Aires Herald* reported how Tull had 'early in the tour installed himself as a favourite with the crowd'. It was on that trip he was invited to become a professional player. Later, he would apologise in a letter home about this decision, but it was an opportunity to better himself, and in his young life opportunities had been few and far between.

Tull was born on 28 April 1888 at 16 Allendale Street, a small two-up, two-down terraced house in working-class East Folkestone. His father, Daniel, was a carpenter who had sailed from St Lucia to England in 1876, settling in Folkstone, Kent, where he met farm worker, Alice Palmer.

The two married in 1880, and the 1881 census showed the Tull family living at 51 Walton Road, a working-class area of the town. They could be found on Sundays worshipping at Grace Hill Wesleyan Chapel, and in times of need and distress they would turn to the Church.

Tull was the fourth of six children in a mixed-race family that endured the twin evils of abject racism and grinding poverty.

Treated as outsiders, the family lost its anchor when Alice was diagnosed with breast cancer in 1893, quickly succumbing to the disease just as Tull turned seven. Tull's father did the best he could to rear his children with the help of Alice's niece, Clara, who quickly took on a maternal role in the life of young Walter Tull after marrying Daniel in 1896.

A year later in 1897, a daughter, Miriam, came along and it looked as though the family had weathered the storm of Alice's passing. However, it was clear that Daniel was not well. For months he had been complaining of a shortness of breath and a tightness in his chest coupled with extreme tiredness, which he put down to a combination of the grief of losing his first wife and overwork.

Just three months after they had celebrated the arrival of Miriam, however, it was Clara's turn to be dressed in the black of a widow as Daniel succumbed to the undiagnosed heart disease all his symptoms had suggested.

With his death, Clara struggled to make ends meet. The oldest boy, William, was already in work and contributing seven shillings a week to the household income while his sister, Cecelia, the eldest of the girls, was employed as a domestic. Tull's other sister, Elsie, who was then seven, helped by looking after baby Miriam, enabling Clara to take in washing to supplement the Poor Law relief she received.

Still, this was not enough to keep the house going; there was also the problem of what to do with Walter and his brother Edward. Clara turned to the Church and particularly the Reverend George Adcock.

The Wesleyan Chapel had strong links with the Children's Home and Orphanage in Bethnal Green, London, which would become Walter Tull and brother Edward's new home. On 24 February 1897, they were taken away from small-town Folkestone to the unfamiliar sights and sounds of the big city.

After living in a family home, the experience of being thrown into living quarters with 15 other boys, who were then strangers, must have been both disconcerting and frightening. The only adult they would have encountered was the Methodist Sister charged with running the home.

A Form of Agreement held by the orphanage describes Tull in glowing terms as honest and truthful, even if somewhat quick-tempered. He was always repentant, though, and generally dutiful.

Once Clara agreed to send the two boys to the home, she lost all rights over them. She would stay in touch as best she could, sending a basket of fruit or parcels of food when she could afford it. In Victorian England, life was hard for a single mother with two young children, so no one batted an eyelid when she moved on and remarried.

From the time of their arrival at the home, daily life for the boys was regimented. Woken at 5 a.m., each boy had to make his own bed before polishing his shoes for inspection. Breakfast followed at 7 before the rest of the day was taken up with more domestic chores and lessons.

At first it was singing, which provided an outlet for Tull's energies. Both he and Edward were prominent members of the orphanage choir, which travelled the country as a way of raising funds for the home.

In 1900, the choir arrived at a music hall in Glasgow. It had been a gruelling tour and the children were tired, but this did not stop them from giving their best. Among the crowd watching that night was dentist James Warnock and his wife, Jeanne, who both sat mesmerised by a little boy with a huge voice.

Afterwards, they would make enquiries about bringing the boy to Glasgow to live with them on a permanent basis. In November of that year, Edward Tull was officially adopted by them, while his younger brother Walter was left behind in the home.

For seven long years, Walter lived in the home, sustained by Edward's letters. His behaviour deteriorated and it was only cricket and football which provided an outlet for his frustrations.

Finally, in 1907, Walter was old enough to leave the home for a hostel. While completing an apprenticeship at the home's own printworks, he sat down to compose a letter, but this one was not to his brother or anyone else in the family, it was to the secretary of top amateur side, Clapton FC, asking for a trial.

The letter to the secretary had not been unexpected: a friend had told them of Tull's prowess on the football field. Just 10 weeks later, in October 1908, Tull was in the first team and four months later, Tottenham made their move.

On 1 September 1909, the noise from the crowd was deafening as the players ran out for their very first game in the First Division and Walter Tull made history as England's first ever Black professional outfield player.

If Tull was feeling any nerves, he certainly did not show it, throwing himself into the action. There could be no better opponents than Manchester United, who had won their first title the previous year in 1908 and in May had lifted the FA Cup.

At one point, Tull found himself on goal, only to be brought down in the box, winning a penalty for his new side. In the end a 2-2 draw was seen as a fair result.

On 20 September, the *Athletic News and Cyclists' Journal* headline was 'Tottenham's Man of Colour' and it reported, 'The development of young talent is undoubtedly very largely responsible for the present position of Tottenham Hotspur … This season they have introduced yet another youngster in Walter Daniel Tull, who will, if we mistake not, leave an indelible mark in the records of the famous club.

'Tull has the rare distinction of being the only coloured player operating in first-class Association football. He is the son of a West Indian gentleman who married an English lady and was born in Folkestone just twenty-one years ago.

'When nine years of age he came to London, and it is in the great metropolis that he has gained his extensive knowledge of football. He played in a comparatively minor class until last season, when he joined the English Amateur Cup holders, Clapton. He quickly established a claim to the inside-left position and rendered the North London club invaluable assistance in winning the Amateur Cup and the London Senior Cup'.

The *Athletic* went on to describe Tull as a 'brainy forward', who had become 'a professional at the end of last season and was one of the Tottenham team which toured the Argentine last summer. His play in the August practice matches was such that the Tottenham selectors gave him instant promotion to the first team, and though he apparently failed to please the Northern critics in the Sunderland and Everton matches, he demonstrated unmistakably against Manchester United a week ago that he is a player of very high merit.

'There is much of the Corinthian style in his play. His passes are invariably low and accurately placed. He gave evidence of ability as a marksman, which will gain him a place in the goal-scoring records, and in every way he showed himself thoroughly conversant with the finer points of forward play. We commend the Tottenham directors upon their action in persevering with a young player of such promise.'

Nonetheless there were undercurrents of what Tull was to face. The *Greenwich and Deptford Observer*, reporting on Friday, 24 September, noted, 'It was said [when] a lady at a recent Spurs match saw Tull, the coloured forward, she exclaimed, "Now I know why they are called the Hottentots."' Originally used as a term to describe indigenous South African people, it had developed a derogatory meaning by the 18th century, comparable to 'cannibal' or 'barbarian'.

Worse was to come against Bristol City, on 2 October 1909 in his fifth game for Spurs, away at Ashton Gate. The language levelled at Tull appalled a journalist who went by the initials D.D. Writing in the *Daily News* (London), in a report headlined, 'Football and the Colour Prejudice', he said, 'Candidly, Tull has much to contend against on account of his colour. His tactics were absolutely beyond reproach, but he became the butt of the ignorant partisan.

'Once because he "floored" Annan with a perfectly fair shoulder charge, a section of the spectators made a cowardly attack upon him in language lower than Billingsgate.

'Let me tell those Bristol hooligans that Tull is so clean in mind and method as to be a model for all white men who play football. In point of ability, if not actual achievement, Tull was the best forward on the field.'

Even though he had grabbed a goal against Bradford City and his general play had won praise in the press, without explanation Walter Tull now lost his place in Spurs starting eleven and never regained it. It remains a mystery why he never again returned to the Spurs side.

Inevitably, he left the Spurs. In October 1911, he headed for Northampton, after the Cobblers manager, Herbert Chapman, demanded Tull in a swap deal for defender Charlie Brittain. Chapman, a former Spurs man himself, had to fight off stiff competition from Aston Villa, Leicester Fosse and Clapton Orient for Tull's signature. After a shaky start, Tull dropped back to midfield and it was in that position that he was to play over 111 first team games, scoring nine goals by the time he signed up for the Footballers' Battalion.

. . . .

Lying in a hospital bed, back home in Great Britain, the constant ringing in his ears was driving Tull mad, and the stiffness in his legs, which made it almost impossible to walk, led him to believe that both his footballing and army career were at an end.

To the doctors who treated him, the prognosis was clear: Tull was suffering from shell shock. Or some sort of nervous condition. In June 1915, just a month after Tull's return from the front, Major John Graham reported, 'A private from an infantry regiment was admitted to a casualty clearing station … suffering from a febrile illness of three days duration … headache, dizziness, severe lumbago, a feeling of stiffness down the front of the thighs and severe pains referred chiefly to the shins.'

The large number of other cases he was encountering, however, made Major Graham conclude that the cause was an infection caused by lice infecting clothing and irritating the skin, bringing about a condition akin to malaria, which he called trench fever.

Over three months safely away from the unhygienic conditions of the trenches, Walter Tull slowly regained his strength, the *Star Green 'Un* informing readers, 'Walter Tull, the Northampton half-back, who is attached to Footballers' Battalion, is now a convalescent, after being in hospital for three months with pneumonia.'

Walter Tull would never return to the 17th Middlesex Regiment and instead would be sent to officer cadet training school at Gailes, Scotland. Another remarkable chapter of his extraordinary life was about to begin.

Chapter 11

Evelyn Lintott
A teacher on the Somme

It is easy to imagine the scene, the house was quiet, when there came a hard knock at the door. Being in the middle of her morning chores, she hoped she was hearing things. For the past two days she had been determined to keep herself busy. Just a few days earlier, a telegram had arrived with the news that her son had been wounded on the frontline.

There had been tears and prayers, visits to the local parish church, but nothing could take her mind off the dread she felt.

She kept telling herself over and over again that it was all going to be fine, but that did not stop her turning over the contents of the telegram in her head. A few months ago, the telegram had been about another son, but he had been alright. What if the family's luck did not hold up this time?

Over and over again these questions had swirled around her head at night, keeping both her and her husband awake. Neither said what was on their mind, for if they said it out loud it would become real.

The only thing which could stop the constant fretting was to keep busy: the doorstep needed to be cleaned, clothes had to be put through the mangle and the house dusted, but however much she worked, the nagging doubts would not go away. Nothing changed; her son was wounded and missing.

Then there was a second loud bang on the door: she had heard the first knock but had not gone to the door immediately, such was her fear that there might be bad news waiting. However, she knew she could not ignore it any longer.

Straightening up, she put down the rag she had been using to polish the mantlepiece, went to the door and took a deep breath.

Hesitantly, she half opened the door. The sun shone in her eyes, almost blinding her. Standing in front of her was a young boy, dressed in smart, navy-blue trousers, with a sharp crease up the front, and on top a matching tunic with black belt, completed by a peaked hat. This was the uniform of the Post Office.

The boy, who could not have been more than 17, looked down to his shiny black shoes before he handed her an innocuous brown envelope.

Taking the letter in her hands, the woman made her way to the parlour and sat down at the table. She tore open the envelope. Inside was a thin piece of paper, addressed to Mrs Eleanor Lintott of Hazelville, Wolsely Road, Farnscombe, Surrey.

It was dated 7 July and read, 'Regret to inform you that Lieut. EH Lintott of 15th West Yorks Regt reported wounded 1st July is now reported killed 4th July. The Army Council express their sympathy.' It was stamped 'Secretary, War Office'.

Outside in the garden, her husband, Arthur, was tending to the vegetables. Like his wife, he wanted to keep busy. She did not have to tell him that they had lost their son, an England international and schoolmaster, Lieutenant Evelyn Lintott.

· · · ·

Lying in a Fulham Military Hospital in extreme pain and discomfort, Private David Spink was able to explain Lintott's final moments: 'Informant states that he saw Lieut. Lintott killed on July 1st by machine gun at 3pm in advance. He was struck in the chest.'

On 1 July 1916, the first day of the Battle of the Somme, Lintott was one of the 19,240 men who lost their lives. There was no funeral for him; his body would never be recovered and would remain on the battlefield with all his other comrades who fell that day in the worst loss of life in British military history.

By the time that Evelyn Lintott's family had received his effects, which amounted to £500 in cash, some books, a photo case, postcards and photos, a letter dropped through the front door. It was picked up by Lintott's mother and was addressed to her.

She instantly recognised the handwriting: her dead son's. The letter reached her on 29 July and had been written by Evelyn Lintott while he was serving on the front and had received his orders to make an advance: 'If you get this it will mean that I have given all I could. Don't grieve. I would not for one moment have had it otherwise. I'm going into battle happy, confident, and real proud to be in command of the best I have ever met.'

Under the cover of his nom de plume, 'Adjutant', Mr F. Stacey Lintott, a prominent journalist, imagined his brother falling in the field through the pages of the *Yorkshire Sports*: 'I have heard nothing, absolutely nothing of his last hours save the letter from an officer in another battalion who wrote Lieut Lintott's death was particularly gallant, that he was shot three times before he fell.

'We can believe, however, that there was no more ready for that hurricane attack than he, no more quickly over the parapet, no more heroically leading his men – temporarily he was in command of his company. And then the first bullet. But one bullet could not stop the British athlete in the full pride of health and strength. A second bullet but still he pressed forward.

'And then the third. He stumbles and falls, the light of his life dies out of those clear blue eyes, which had been wont to look so fearlessly out on life. The battle rolls forward, but Evelyn Lintott lies there on the ground still yet another victim of the insensate pride and ambition of a mad egotist.'

Had Stacey Lintott not sustained an injury in a childhood accident, he too would have been wearing the colours, like his other brothers. Keith was fighting with the New Zealanders and Morris with the Canadians.

Upon first hearing that Evelyn had been a casualty of the first big push at the Somme, Lintott's parents had held out faint hopes that their son had been wounded, just like his great friend and international teammate, Vivian Woodward.

When the *Yorkshire Post* first reported that Lintott's father had received a telegram informing the family that he had been wounded, the hope was that he would make a full recovery. It was a hope that stemmed from the fact of this not being the first time the family had received a telegram.

A few months earlier, they had been informed that their son, Cuthbert, serving with the First Contingent of the Canadian Expeditionary Force, had been wounded. By the time his older brother fell in battle, Cuthbert had recovered and was engaged in staff work in London, safely behind a desk.

Of the five brothers it was Evelyn who gained fame and his death was mourned as far afield as Toronto. Someone called 'The Critic' wrote to the *West Surrey Times*, 'Au revoir, Evelyn, one of nature's gentleman and looking down upon the disturbed portion of this old world, we feel your spirit will not have fallen in vain.

'We had not thought in times gone by so soon you would have heard the battle cry … Farewell! Evelyn, we ill could spare you, yet transcended in his glory, the grief is ours, the rest is yours, then we cross the great divide we look for you on the other side.'

Long before the war began, the five brothers had stood alongside each other in uniform, in the red and white quartered shirts of Woking Town, the team for which they all played.

A picture still exists featuring Evelyn and Stacey posing for an official team photograph. Sat in the centre, Evelyn holds the ball, his gaze looking at something beyond the camera. At only 20 he is the captain of the side – no doubt down to his goalscoring exploits, which saw him score 66 goals in 108 appearances.

To his right sits his brother, Stacey, sporting a moustache and wearing a muddied bandage on his right knee. Casually resting his arm on the back of the bench, he looks more relaxed and comfortable than the stern, nervous-looking Evelyn. It would not be long before they would be joined by brothers Cuthbert, Morris and Keith.

After excelling as a pupil at the Royal Grammar School in Guildford, Evelyn was employed as a physical training teacher at Maybury School in Walton Road. His days playing for Woking came to an end when he decided to train to become a teacher at St Luke's College, Exeter. There, he began to play for Plymouth Argyle. After being appointed as a teacher at Oldfield Road School in Willesden, he quickly moved on to Queens Park Rangers, and from there he moved to Bradford City and finally, Leeds City.

It was at Queens Park Rangers that he signed professional forms. His brother Stacey took up the story: 'I remember his coming home one Sunday in order we might discuss all the pros and cons. We went for a walk which lasted all afternoon and evening, and when we returned, he had made his mind up to join the paid ranks. I was very much against it for a time and I made every argument to dissuade him.

'His chief contention, however simple, one summarised as follows, "From choice I shall play football for a big professional club every Saturday afternoon and as often as possible other times. Now I am offered over £200 a year to do what I shall do in any event.

'"Not the slightest change will be made to my life. I shall simply drop my initials in the papers and that is about all. I am never likely to make a great deal at my profession and the extra hundreds I have a chance of making at football will come in most useful in the future even more than now. I think I should be a fool to throw away the chance. What is more I believe no one will think the worse of me."'

The *Morning Leader* reported on 8 May 1908, under the headline 'EH Lintott a professional', 'We are officially informed that EH Lintott, the Queens Park Rangers and international half-back, has signed a professional form for Queens Park Rangers. It has been agreed by the directors of the club that Lintott shall be allowed to retain his position as a schoolmaster.'

Lintott made 35 appearances for QPR, scoring one League goal, winning the Southern Football League and playing two Charity Shield matches against the Football League champions, Manchester United. He caught the eye of Bradford City manager Peter O'Rourke, who travelled to London on 21 November 1908 and met Lintott at Paddington station – Rangers were themselves returning from a match at Swindon. Lintott signed for Bradford that night for a fee of over £1000 – which went a long way towards helping QPR out of serious financial problems.

The *Morning Leader* was to write of his transfer on 27 November, 'I haven't had a word to say against the move made by EH Lintott from Queens Park Rangers to Bradford City, which is doubtless all in order, and, if we knew all about it, of simple explanation, but I confess an old-fashioned feeling against these changes.

'However, I wish Lintott every success. He is one of the new type of professionals, the type of superior moral fibre, a type we may justly flatter ourselves is the very outcome of a strong, firm and yet friendly control over the paid elements in the game.

'In the sport wherein, professionalism is not treated as a mean and ignoble thing, but given a helping hand, a touch of camaraderie, the paid player is at his best.'

At City, Lintott was heavily involved with the emerging Players' Union. From 1910 to 1911 he was the organisation's chairman, while his brother Stacey edited the Union's *Football Player Magazine*. Bradford City also found him employment at Sports and Pastimes, the makers of City's shirts.

However, he expressed a wish to return to teaching and found a post at a school in Dudley Hill. According to the 1911 census, Evelyn lived with his brother Stacey and his wife Edith at 22 Granville Road in Bradford, demonstrating just how close the two brothers were.

After 57 appearances and two goals for the Bantams, Lintott moved to Leeds City, which was slowly emerging as a force under Herbert Chapman. On 7 June 1912, the *Leeds Mercury* reported, during pre-season preparations, 'Of the newcomers it was gratifying to see Evelyn Lintott so far recovered as to give a fine exhibition. This erstwhile warrior was ever in the thick of it, and on Saturday's form has evidently recovered from his serious injury when playing with Bradford City.'

Lintott's debut for Leeds came at centre-half, at Fulham on 7 September, the opening day of the season, when City were beaten 4-0. The Sportsman, writing for the *Yorkshire Evening Post*, reported on a promising personal display: 'There was no more energetic man on the field than he, though he met with no success until he had taken a little time to settle down, and then he had to bear the brunt of the attack, which he did right well, especially when it is known that he was up against Pearce, a young man, who seems destined to secure the highest honours of the game.

'In the second half, when the locals were resting a little on their laurels – all four goals were scored before half-time – Lintott was seen at his best in an aggressive mood, and after seeing several chances he gave to his forwards frittered away, he tried hard himself to score, but with no better luck.'

The *Mercury* added: 'Lintott has always played magnificently. Strong in defence, he also found the opportunity to do nearly all the dangerous shooting that was accomplished on behalf of Leeds.

'The new man also has to carry the burden of being the club's new captain, but he has shouldered it confidently, and was soon proving he had lost none of his old ability.'

After his second game, a 2-0 defeat of Barnsley, the *Mercury* reported, 'Lintott gave a fine display of clean tackling, smart headwork, and clever placing. He worked with untiring energy and was largely responsible for the ineffectiveness of the Barnsley forwards.

'Lintott looks like proving an ideal captain, and in him Leeds City have certainly found a treasure. He is the sort of leader who by his play and general conduct on the field encourages and inspires his colleagues.'

By 1908, Lintott had won five amateur caps for England; he broke into the full England team in 1908 when he played in all three Home Internationals.

He rubber-stamped his selection with a promising performance for the South in a trial match against the North on 27 January 1908. *The Times* reported, 'For two-thirds of the game, the South showed themselves distinctly the better side, and with less than half an hour left, they led by four goals to one.

'The North, however, just afterwards secured a second point after a free kick following on a foul and, playing up with great dash and determination, they succeeded in drawing the match at four goals all.

'Although robbed of a victory, the South showed themselves decidedly the cleverer. Ducat and Lintott, the other half-backs, fully justified their selection.'

Lintott's full debut for England came on 15 February 1908 against Ireland in Belfast. The English won 3-1.

In his second full international, on 16 March at Wrexham, England beat Wales 7-1, thanks in part to a hat-trick from Vivian Woodward. Lintott was pitted against the legendary Billy Meredith and by all accounts turned the legendary Welshman inside out.

In his autobiography, *50 Years of Football*, Sir Frederick Wall, secretary of the Football Association, would write of the match, 'A good story relates to the Wales v England match on Wrexham Racecourse in 1908 … Evelyn Lintott, the talented schoolmaster, who was so fine a left half-back, played in all the big matches of 1907/08, and on this occasion, he was ordered never to leave Meredith. He clung to him like an affectionate brother.

'At last, the patience of Meredith gave out and he turned on Lintott with these words, "Go away, you. Go away! Do you hear? You have got seven cursed goals, how many more do you want?" Lintott was silent, but he continued to haunt his jaded adversary.'

On 13 February 1909, Lintott appeared for England on his home pitch at Valley Parade in Bradford (prior to his move to Leeds City) as they defeated Ireland 4-0. *The Times* noted that he 'played quite as well as last year when he took part in the three international games'.

His last international cap on home soil was against Scotland at the Sports Arena, Crystal Palace, Penge, on Saturday, 3 April 1909. England won 2-0, thanks to two goals from Manchester United's George Wall.

For Lintott it had been another strong performance to go along with an earlier game against Ireland in February that year, where he was credited with assisting Woodward in the first of his two goals as England cruised to a 4-0 win.

The two games would be remembered when the *Sporting Chronicle* detailed the death of Lintott on 12 July 1916: 'His last international cap in the old standard matches causes me to ponder of those who played on that occasion when George Wall scored two such splendid goals in the presence of the Prince of Wales, now King George V.'

The *Chronicle* went on to detail what had happened to the players on that day.

Fred Pentland, the outside right, had gone to Germany in May 1914 to coach the German Olympic team. Now, like his contemporary, Steve Bloomer, he was interned at Ruhleben, a civilian detention camp in the Spandau district of Berlin.

The *Chronicle* then went to detail that Harold Fleming was an officer in the army and goalscorer George Wall a sergeant in the Black Watch.

In a tribute to Evelyn Lintott, the *Chronicle* wrote, 'Lintott's heroic end is calculated to cause reflections about the section of athletes which it was alleged had not done their duty in the crisis.'

In January 1915, Evelyn Lintott, Vivian Woodward and Frank Buckley had become the first footballers to be commissioned as officers in the British Army. Lintott had stayed with the Leeds Pals rather than join the Football Battalion, and as the 17th Middlesex prepared to make their own advance on the Somme, he lay dead in the mud of the battlefields.

Woodward was making slow but steady progress back home in Great Britain. Of the three the only one who remained unscathed so far was Frank Buckley. However, for Buckley it was, said a journalist at the *Sporting Chronicle*, 'a merciful dispensation that none can peer into the future.'

The death of Evelyn Lintott would not be the only tragedy which would befall Arthur and Eleanor that year. In October 1915, they would receive another telegram, informing them that another son, Keith, had fallen in battle. They had lost two sons in the same year.

Chapter 12
Brothers
Jonas and McFadden

The small brass box, which the young sergeant major had been carrying around in the pocket of his army tunic for the last 18 months, was now battered and worn. It had been a gift from the Sailors and Soldiers Christmas Fund, in December 1914.

On the front of the box, 5 inches long, was an engraving of Princess Mary, the daughter of King George V. Packed into the Christmas present, which had been sent out to the 2.5 million men serving in the Great War, were cigarettes, sweets and chocolate, a card and a pencil.

By 27 July 1916, the sweets and chocolate were long gone, though the cigarettes were replenished every few days. The pencil had come in handy; whenever there was a lull in the fighting, the sergeant major snatched a few moments to compose a letter back home.

This morning, he reached into his pocket and pulled out his tin to empty its contents on to the makeshift desk in his trench, alongside a locket depicting a man and his wife.

With trembling hands, he lit one of the cigarettes and tried to make sense of the horror which had unfolded before his eyes just hours before. This was going to be the most difficult letter he was ever going to write.

The soldier had been engaged in regular correspondence with his former club, Clapton Orient, writing earlier in the year: 'Your humble servant got two pieces in the head (shrapnel) and one in the chin. I was sent out of the line suffering from shell shock but did not know I was wounded in the head until I got to the dressing station.

'I only knew I was wounded in the chin; but I am right now and back at work. I was sleeping with my "batman" and the shell came through my dug-out and killed him. It must have knocked me out, for when I came to, I had my arm round him, and I was wounded as I have told you. So, I must have been very lucky.'

The serious-looking, athletic young man, with jug ears and dark hair fashioned into a severe centre parting, was more mature than his 26 years. Richard McFadden was a Company Sergeant Major in the 17th Middlesex Regiment, his conduct having marked him out for such responsibility.

A few times over the past few days he had dashed over the top to try to rescue injured men. Delville Wood, which had once boasted birch and oak trees, now looked as though it was carpeted in dirty, thick cotton wool.

In no man's land, among the smoke and gas, he found men dying, tangled up in barbed wire with their bowels hanging out. On several occasions he saw boys who, he was sure, were no older than 16 or 17, with tears running down their faces calling for their mothers. He did what he could, but it was futile; the bodies just stacked up.

The first time he came face to face with a dead body, he vomited. Now, he was injured. After his experiences of the past year, he knew that if a German sniper did not kill him, there was a good chance disease might.

Then there was shell shock. The constant shelling was having a psychological effect on the men. One private, Allen Foster, would write to his wife, 'The whole business was very trying to the nerves, and lots of fellows get what you call shell shock. What with the continual bursting of shells and the thundering of guns they seem to all go to pieces.'

Before he began writing, McFadden picked a piece of paper, yellowing and decaying, which he carried in the tin. Close to disintegrating, it was a photograph of 11 men, arms folded and looking sternly at the camera. He would have remembered that day when they were all dressed in pristine white shirts with a deep red V-shape on their chest, matched with dark blue shorts.

McFadden also remembered when the photograph was taken: Wednesday, 14 January 1914, an FA Cup First Round replay in Nottingham against Forest. He looked at the faces and thought about the journey that had brought them here to Delville Wood, near Longueval in Northern France, where the fighting was particularly fierce. It had quickly been renamed 'Devil's Wood' by those unfortunate enough to be entrenched there.

In the front row was Frederick Parker, nicknamed 'Spider' for his spindly legs and slight frame, and with a prematurely bald head covered by a few strands combed over from the side. Parker looked much older than his 28 years. He was captain of the side and the first man to volunteer for the 17th (Service) Battalion, Middlesex Regiment, the so-called Football Battalion. All the others in the photograph would follow him just minutes later. Also in the photograph was another future recruit, centre-half George Scott, who hailed from Sunderland.

However, the sergeant's gaze focused on the two young men directly in the centre of the photograph. Standing up ramrod straight, looking taller than the others, with a centre parting that shone with brilliantine and the match ball at his feet, was William Jonas.

The young soldier looked at his younger self sitting next to Jonas for the photograph. Richard 'Dick' McFadden was the star striker of Clapton Orient. The two had grown up together in Blyth, Northumberland, and were inseparable.

When the photograph was taken, Clapton Orient had travelled to Nottingham, after they were held to a 2-2 draw at home, with both Jonas and McFadden appearing on the score sheet.

Whenever McFadden looked at the picture, he smiled. After he put Clapton one up after 10 minutes, *Sporting Life* reported that Forest centre-back 'Joe Mercer and Jonas were at loggerheads, resulting in Jonas being dismissed from the field'. It seemed funny to McFadden that the two men who had exchanged blows should now be serving in the same battalion.

For McFadden the game, which had ended 1-0 to the London side, had been a triumph, with the *Daily Record* reporting, 'Clapton Orient go to Nottingham and beat Forest thanks to a goal scored by McFadden about whom there was lately some talk of a transfer to Middlesbrough at a substantial figure. Clapton will be glad he stayed.'

Then his thoughts turned to his last game in a Clapton Orient shirt, when almost 21,000 turned out to witness Orient's last match, a 2-0 victory against Leicester Fosse on 24 April 1915.

Straight after the final whistle, the players had changed into their uniforms and conducted a military parade around the Millfields Road ground.

McFadden now carefully placed the photograph on the desk and reached for the locket. It featured two photographs: William Jonas, dressed in his Clapton Orient shirt, and a beautiful blonde woman, her eyes tinted a blue more piercing than he remembered them.

This was Mary Jane Jonas. Ever since their marriage on 16 December 1911, Jonas had carried the locket with him; here at the frontline it was his most prized possession and he would rather die than let it out of his sight.

Back in their footballing days, McFadden and the other lads had teased Jonas about his good looks and popularity with women. At one stage he was receiving over 50 letters from female admirers. It got so bad that he felt he needed to make a statement in the Clapton Orient matchday programme. *While he appreciates the attention, kind words and good wishes, could these,* he asked, *please cease as he is very happily married to his sweetheart, Mary Jane!*

Any warm memories quickly faded, though, when he remembered how the locket came to be in his possession. Indeed, he had still not quite come to terms with what happened when he finally composed himself and began his letter to the club secretary of Clapton Orient.

McFadden set out what they were doing in Delville Wood. Under the orders of General Haig, the Battalion had attempted to clear the woods of German troops. For the best part of three weeks, British soldiers fought from the trenches before the order to go over the top was given.

Climbing up the last two rungs of the ladder, he jumped out of the trench and ran straight into German fire and certain death. The move was so unexpected, no one could stop him. William Jonas became one of the 485,000 British and French soldiers who fell at the Battle of the Somme.

....

Richard McFadden was a man who had already demonstrated remarkable courage. Just over three years earlier, in February 1913, the *London Evening News* had hailed him a hero after he went to the rescue of a six-year-old girl named Alice Maund, whose clothes had become ignited at her house in Rushmore Road, Lower Clapton.

Flames were raging from the ground floor of the house and McFadden could hear the shrieks of a child. Rushing into the house, he found her enveloped in flames. Tearing the burning clothing from her body, his own hands were severely burned.

Just a fortnight earlier, McFadden had saved two people from drowning in the river Lea.

At the inquest after the fire, the *Evening News* reported that the coroner and the jury commended McFadden for his gallant actions: 'We wish to commend the plucky conduct of Mr McFadden. This is the second attempt within a fortnight, the last being the rescue of two lads from the River Lea.'

As much as this courage brought attention to McFadden, it was his exploits on the football pitch, together with William Jonas, which had brought him fame.

The two had met as young boys, in Blyth. McFadden was born in Cambuslang, Lanarkshire, a town that had fallen on hard times. Blyth, just over the border in Northumberland, provided better opportunities.

The young McFadden had a thick Scottish-Geordie brogue, which made him incomprehensible to most people. To his relief, he was befriended on his first day at school by local lad, William Jonas.

They would remain lifelong friends, comrades on the football pitch and, eventually, the battlefield.

From the moment Richard McFadden arrived at Clapton Orient in a transfer from Wallsend Park Villa in 1911, he was a star player. In his first season he broke the Clapton Orient goalscoring record with 19 goals – a record that would stand for only two years before he broke it with 21 goals.

When the club indicated they wanted more firepower up front, McFadden knew there was only one candidate – William Jonas. However, Jonas was not there simply on a recommendation: his 68 goals over two seasons for North East-based side Havannah Rovers had already made other League sides sit up and take notice.

On one glorious spring day at Highbury, Jonas and McFadden combined to thwart the Gunners' attempt to return to the top flight, forcing a 2-2 draw after McFadden scored a last-gasp equaliser. As they left the field, their names rang out around the famous stadium, underlining their celebrity status.

Now, only a few short years later, Richard McFadden felt he could not let the death of his friend, the man he counted almost as a brother, pass without note.

He wrote to the club secretary: 'I, Richard McFadden, sadly report the death of my friend and O's colleague William Jonas on the morning of Thursday 27th July, aged 26. Both Willie and I were trapped in a trench near the front in Somme, France. Willie turned to me and said, "Goodbye Mac, Best of luck, special love to my sweetheart Mary Jane and best regards to the lads at Orient."

'Before I could reply to him, he was up and over. No sooner had he jumped up out of the trench, my best friend of nearly twenty years was killed before my eyes. Words cannot express my feelings at this time.'

Before jumping over the top, Jonas had pressed his most treasured possession, his locket, into the hand of his lifelong friend.

On the day, the war diary of the Middlesex Regiment simply said, 'On 27th July 1916, the Battle of the Somme, which has commenced on 1st July, was in full flow. The 2nd division was holding the frontline just below Delville Wood, which ran along the road between the village of Longueval and Waterlot Farm.

'The 99th Brigade held the trenches in Princes Street which ran east to west through the middle of the wood, and after being subject to fearsome enemy shellfire which caused many casualties, they were relieved.'

After writing his letter, McFadden put all his possessions, including the locket, into his box and placed it back in his pocket.

After reading and rewriting the letter to make sure he had found the right words, Richard McFadden would date the letter 27 July, then post it in the field post box.

Clapton Orient would mark Jonas' death in their club publication *Oriental Notes* on 26 August 1916: 'It is with regret that we record the death of William Jonas who was one of our most prominent players. "Billy" as he was known to his many friends did not wait for the Derby Groups, but joined up with many of our players in the early stages of the war and now he has paid the great price and died a hero's death on the field of battle. We feel assured that the sympathy of his many admirers will go out to his sorrowing relatives.'

Just a few weeks later, on 21 September 1916, the *Illustrated Police News* reported, 'The first of many Clapton Orient players who joined the colours to receive a decoration for bravery on the field is the popular forward, Company Sergeant Major, R McFadden, Middlesex Regiment who has received the Military Medal.'

An entry in the 17th Middlesex's war diary of 16 October 1916 records that ribbons were presented by Major General Walker OC of the 2nd Division to CSM R. McFadden.

The next time Commanding Officer Fenwick wrote in the diary was on 22 October 1916: 'Battalion relieved the 1st Royal Berks 5th Brigade in the Redan Section at 17.10. We were unfortunate in having a lot of casualties coming in. Company Serjeant-Major McFadden being severely wounded, which was probably due to an extent to the activity of our own artillery to which the Germans retaliated.'

McFadden was seriously injured near Serre-les-Puisieux, by shell blast, while leading a line of troops along a trench on the frontline. One of 19 injured, he died the following day, the third Clapton Orient player to lose his life following William Jonas and former centre-half George Scott.

The letter McFadden wrote to the club informing them of Jonas' death would not be received by the Clapton Orient Secretary until three months later. He opened it on 30 October alongside another letter from Fred 'Spider' Parker, their former captain, who himself had been wounded on the front.

'Dear Mr Deane,' the letter began, 'The first thing I heard on getting back was that poor old "Mac" had died of wounds. It is a terrible blow to all the boys that are left. I could not believe it at first: but it is too true. He was wounded on October 22nd, died on the 23rd, and was buried on the 25th. "Mac" feared nothing. All the boys are going to visit his grave as soon as they get a chance. We have had a splendid cross made for him, with a football at the top of it. No one will miss him like I do out here; we were always together.'

On 4 November, just two months after its obituary to McFadden's lifelong friend, William Jonas, *Oriental Notes* would once again be paying tribute to one of its own: 'It is with feelings of great sorrow and deep regret that we publish the sad news of Company Serjeant Major, Richard McFadden. He died in hospital from wounds received in battle.

'It is hard to realise that the bright and cheerful young man to whom we recently said goodbye should be numbered with the Empire's heroic dead. It would prove a difficult task to do full justice to the memory of our late inside left.

'His knack of making and retaining friends; his loyalty; his innate love of fair play, and his ever-ready hand to succour those in distress was characteristic of the man. Of his brave deeds – both civil and military life – many of us are aware.

'To his lasting honour he volunteered in the early stages of war, and rapid promotion followed. We feel assured that we express the feelings of his numerous friends and admirers when we tender our heart-felt sympathy to Mrs McFadden and the near relatives of our late player.'

Even Arsenal, the club whose promotion ambitions both Jonas and McFadden had done so much to thwart, was to pay tribute in their own programme: 'Orient have our deepest sympathy in the loss of that grand little player. McFadden died the little hero he was, and his name will be largely in the records of all the sacrificing deeds of the men who have proved themselves heroes on the battlefield. Brave men and a very brave football club.'

Even away from the capital, McFadden's loss was felt, the *Manchester Football Chronicle* writing of the fallen football star, 'Two things distinguished Richard McFadden throughout his career as a footballer – his heroism and his goal scoring proclivities. In civil life he was a hero, and he proved himself a hero on the battlefield … one of the noble band of Clapton Orient players … A brave man, he will be mourned by all who knew him.'

Two weeks later, on 18 November 1916, *Oriental Notes* would mourn another loss, when it was confirmed that their former centre-half, Private George Scott, had died: 'It is with feeling of sorrow we inform our readers that another of our players has paid the Great Price. We have received confirmatory evidence that George Scott died on 16 August.

'Big-hearted and daring – as George always was – we can imagine the impetuosity with which he confronted the enemy. To those who knew him personally he was one of the BEST, and the thousands who have witnessed his football career will, undoubtedly, express feelings of sorrow at his untimely end.

'Our warmest sympathy goes forth to his bereaved wife and children and, although condolence may not assuage grief, they have the satisfaction of knowing no man could have sacrificed his life in a nobler cause.'

Company Sergeant Major Richard McFadden, winner of the Military Medal and football hero, is buried at Couin British Cemetery.

The body of William Jonas has never been found.

Chapter 13

Frank Buckley
The Major

Since Colonel Henry Fenwick, the commanding officer of the 17th Middlesex, had received orders to move up to Delville Wood, fighting had been intense. As the Battalion slowly made their way, the mood was sombre.

The attack of Delville Wood was part of the Battle of the Somme, which took place in July 1916. The Somme was the famous plan of General Douglas Haig, who believed it would be the Allied nations' final 'big push' and would end the war on the Western Front. After two years of hard fighting, fatigue had now set in. Everyone engaged in the war hoped that Haig would be proved right.

The Delville Wood attack began on 15 July, when just over 3000 men from the South African 1st Infantry Brigade were tasked with clearing the wood 'at all costs'. As with many other battles, the Allies used artillery bombardment to begin the assault before sending in the infantry. This resulted in the southern part of the woods being quickly cleared of Germans and to those at Headquarters, it looked as though the plan might just be working.

However, the South Africans had placed themselves in a difficult position after coming across 7000 Germans. The trees which had once provided shelter and cover had been reduced to a mass of branches and stumps by the German shelling. The roots left after the artillery bombardment also made it almost impossible to dig trenches, so there was minimal protection against the Germans.

Furthermore, the South Africans were forced for the most part to engage in hand-to-hand combat and this led to a high number of casualties. It was also difficult to retrieve the wounded, but the fighting was so fierce that for every one person wounded, four were killed. The South Africans continued to fight until 19 July when they were relieved, but in that time they suffered some of the worse casualties seen across the Western Front to date.

Captain S.J. Worsley, MC was to write of his experience of Delville Wood, 'Every semblance of a trench seemed full of dead-sodden, squelchy, swollen bodies. Fortunately, the blackening faces were invisible except when Very lights lit up the indescribable scene. Not a tree stood whole in that wood. Food and water were very short, and we had not the faintest idea when any more would be obtainable.

'We stood and lay on putrefying bodies and the wonder was that the disease [dysentery] did not finish off what the shells of the enemy had started. There was hand-to-hand fighting with knives, bombs, and bayonets; cursing and brutality on both sides such as men can be responsible for when it is a question of "your life or mine"; mud and filthy stench; dysentery and unattended wounds; shortage of food and water and ammunition.'

An unnamed German said of the place, 'Delville Wood had disintegrated into a shattered wasteland of shattered trees, charred, and burning stumps, craters thick with mud and blood, and corpses, corpses everywhere. In places they were piled four deep.'

Both Fenwick and his second in command, Major Frank Buckley, were concerned. They were very aware now of how trench fever was affecting their troops. Clean drinking water was a major concern, so as well as ordering the men to be equipped with grenades and bayonets, they also told them to fill empty petrol cans with drinking water.

The last thing the 17th Middlesex needed to deal with was illness or dehydration on top of the constant German shelling. After receiving their orders, they moved through the surrounding villages.

For all regiments, casualties had been too high. Some soldiers had fought for 10 days straight with only an hour here or there for rest. The 17th Middlesex and 2nd South Staffordshire were under orders to hold Delville Wood. All that was left were blackened stumps where trees used to offer shade. It was said not a single tree had not been touched by the carnage. The branches were mixed with discarded equipment and shells. Then there was the stench of the decaying bodies – not to mention those who were injured and drifting somewhere between life and death.

By the time dawn broke on that summer morning, there was still the smoking debris of the battle from the previous day, which had claimed the lives of William Jonas and 13 others. There had been no sleep or rest for the men, who were now the sole defenders of the wood.

From the outset there seemed to be no end to the German bombardment. As the men defended their position, shell after shell seemed to get ever closer to them. The noise and smell of smoke reduced visibility, leaving the soldiers disorientated.

The only hope for shelter came from the shallow trenches surrounding the wood. A few times the heavy artillery blew up the trenches, burying men alive. The lucky ones were dug out but not before they were left with concussion – and mental scarring.

Looking out over the trenches was Major Frank Buckley, now officially the second in command of the 17th Middlesex. Buckley was held in considerable esteem. Commanding Officer Henry Fenwick was to say of him and the footballers who served under him, 'I knew nothing of professional footballers when I took over this battalion. But I have learned to value them. I would go anywhere with such men.

'Their esprit de corps was amazing. The feeling was mainly due to football – the link of fellowship which bound them together. Football has a wonderful grip on these men and the army generally.'

As Buckley surveyed the battlefield, he could see Fenwick motioning to him. In his hand the commanding officer held a piece of paper, which he handed over to Buckley without comment.

Deciphering the quickly scribbled handwriting, he learned that the German troops had assembled to the east of the wood. After quickly asking for artillery and backup, the Battalion then engaged in a waiting game.

For hour upon hour they waited, expecting a German bombardment. Finally, the peace was broken: it was later estimated that nearly 400 shells were landing per minute on the stricken soldiers. A German hand grenade rolled in front of the two commanding officers and exploded at their feet. Fenwick was wounded, but it was Buckley who took the brunt of the blast.

He held his hands up to protect his face, but shrapnel tore through his shoulder, ripping his skin before other parts of the remaining shell splintered through his chest, finally coming to rest in his lung. His body lay in a twisted mess, covered in blood. To eyewitnesses it looked as though Buckley had become the latest footballing casualty.

First on the scene was Newcastle United centre-forward George Pyke. Seeing Buckley, he did not hold out much hope for his survival, later writing, 'A stretcher party was passing the trench at the time. They asked if we had a passenger to go back. They took Major Buckley, but he seemed so badly hit, you would not think he would last out as far as the casualty clearing station.'

Even getting Buckley to the station would have required a major effort. Private Jack Borthwick, a Scotsman who had played centre-half for Hibernian, Everton and Millwall, would write to his manager, Bert Lipsham, 'We were being very heavily shelled, dead and wounded all over the place, Germans as well as our own ... Our captain ... gave orders for four men to take a wounded captain to the dressing station and I was one to be chosen.

'There wasn't a whole stretcher in the place, and all the stretcher bearers were knocked out except one. We got two stout branches of a tree and put two waterproof sheets across them, placed the captain on it, and then started off.

'We had to go three-quarters of a mile to the dressing station, and God knows how we got there with shells flying all around us, scrambling up and down shell holes and over broken tree trunks. I expected that we should all go up in the air any minute.

'However, we arrived all safe and I was thankful as I was well beat. We had an hour's rest before starting back off again.'

Ironically, Borthwick was writing his letter to Lipsham from a hospital bed, having himself sustained wounds later that day. His letter continued, 'Everything was going well until I stopped my packet. I never heard the shell coming but felt it as my neck was very near set in.

'The piece must have been rather large and I was afraid I should be under the turf with a little wooden cross on top. I managed to get back to our trench and the stretcher-bearer dressed the wound. I lay down in the side of the trench for nearly half an hour until the shelling quieted down.

'Our captain wanted to send four men to carry me out, but I didn't fancy it so I told him I would rather walk if he sent a man with me to see I didn't collapse. Jack Nuttall, a teammate at Millwall, came with me and you ought to have seen us dashing across the wood.

'I remember getting to the dressing station, but I must have lost consciousness as I don't remember seeing our doctor. I was operated on next day, but I remember nothing about it. I was placed on the danger list and the missus had word to come, but I took a turn for the better.

'What a ward I was in, not one able to get up. We had six deaths in 24 hours and one fellow off his head. I am glad to say that my wound is going on all right, but I am afraid I am finished with football.

'I feel rather sorry as I am sure the army training had done me a lot of good. I was looking forward to coming home and making good. However, I must be thankful I am alive. My head has been trepanned, as the skull was knocked in. The cut extends from nearly the top of my head down to my eyebrow. It was a near thing of my losing my right eye. This is worse than a whole season of cup ties.'

Among others hit that day was Fred Keenor of Cardiff City, who had enlisted in the 17th Middlesex (Football Battalion) on Friday, 12 February 1915.

His teammate, Ernie Curtis, said of him as a player, 'He was one of the hardest tacklers in the game. Some said he was dirty, but he was just hard. Nobody took liberties with old Fred … could run all night. He couldn't run with the ball, mind you, but he could run all day.'

According to James Leighton's biography, *Fred Keenor: The Man Who*

Never Gave Up, Keenor was quoted as saying of the Delville Wood, 'One must pay tribute to the good work of the Footballers' Battalion. Stationed at Delville Wood, Jerry's artillery threw everything he had at us – and then some. It simply rained shells.

'The wonder was that any of us came out alive. It was attack and counter-attack day and night, but during the battle for possession of this wood there was not a sign of cowardice among our men. Some of them may have been called "windy" on the football fields of England, but out there in France they stood the real test of all.'

Standing near Fenwick and Buckley, Keenor was badly wounded when a piece of artillery shrapnel struck his left leg above the knee, leaving him unable to walk.

An unknown soldier saw him attempting to crawl away from the incoming fire and managed to help him back to the nearby medical facilities, where army doctors were able to tend to his injury. The wound was so severe that they initially considered amputating the leg.

They did not, but even so it looked as though Keenor would be unable to resume his football career when the war finally ended.

Another footballer would join Buckley and Keenor at the casualty clearing station: the former Reading and Manchester City centre-half, Ted Hanney. Like Frank Buckley, Hanney had come from a military family and served in the Royal Berkshire Regiment before buying himself out to play professionally for Reading in 1911.

The following year, he was in the same England team that won the Olympic gold medal in Stockholm, captained by Vivian Woodward. Hanney, now a sergeant, was wounded at the battle of Delville Wood. Suffering injuries to his face, shoulder and the right thigh, he battled on before finally being admitted to the casualty clearing station.

Speaking to the *Berkshire Chronicle*, on 18 August 1916, he said of his experiences, 'I was hit on the night of 28 July about 22.30 but did not leave the trenches until the next morning, about 8.30am. The Germans counterattacked that night three times, and as I felt quite all right, I stopped and gave them a few extra rounds of ammunition ... By gum, I saw some sights there! I shall never forget them.'

By midnight on the day Buckley was injured, 38 men of those who had marched towards Delville Wood just 36 hours earlier were dead, while 150 men, including Fenwick, Buckley, Keenor, Hanney and Borthwick, were wounded.

Among the dead was Sergeant Norman Wood. A promising school career saw Wood play for Bromley before joining Tottenham Hotspur in June 1908. After a year at White Hart Lane without breaking into the first team, he began wandering; he was at Crystal Palace in 1909/10 before moving to Plymouth Argyle in 1910/11, where the handbook referred to him as 'a re-instated amateur, an artistic inside-left'. He then moved to Croydon Common and Chelsea.

He finally achieved the first team football he craved at Stockport County and, after signing in June 1913, he was a regular for the Second Division club.

In February 1915, Wood enlisted in the army, joining the Football Battalion, but then signing for Stalybridge Celtic the following month, and playing for Reading while undergoing military training.

Now he lay dead, a victim of the shelling. The *Athletic News* of 4 September 1916, in tribute, said of him, 'With his brushed dark hair and deft touches of the ball with the side of the foot, his type of play was unselfish … for with a crafty left foot he made openings and opportunities for colleagues. Unquestionably he was a fine initiator but did not make the mark that he should have done.'

With both Fenwick and Buckley down, Captain Edward Inkerman Bell, who had played as outside-forward for Southampton in the 1907/08 season, took over command of the Battalion. For his actions he would himself be awarded the Military Cross. The *London Gazette* reported, on 20 October 1916, that it was given for 'conspicuous gallantry during operations. Finding himself in command of the Battalion he repelled a counterattack with great determination. On another occasion he rescued several men from a blown-in dugout.'

And under his leadership, the 17th Middlesex held its position – but at considerable cost. For 30 July 1916, the war diary of the 17th Middlesex reads simply, 'Men resting and needed it badly.' Over a three-day period, the Battalion had lost one officer and a further eight had been wounded. The diary recorded casualties of 35 killed and 192 wounded.

To underline the horror of those three days, only 13 bodies of those killed were recovered to give the men a burial and a gravestone. The bodies of the others remain in Delville Wood.

．．．．

With no pain relief, he was jolted up and down some distance to reach the casualty station, where the doctors who treated him did not rate his chances. Barely conscious, he was bleeding profusely from the wounds to his shoulder and chest.

For hours, surgeons painstakingly worked to remove the shattered bone, shrapnel and remnants of the German grenade which had ripped through his body. When he came around, he would be forced to wear a sling, but the real damage had been done to his lungs and for weeks afterwards breathing would be difficult.

Months later, Buckley would sit down with a journalist, from the *Sporting Chronicle*, where he explained his injuries, 'Major told me that the clavicle which had been shattered had been repaired and that his arm was comparatively well again, but he carried some shrapnel in one lung, and that he was medically advised to "go slow for a few years."

'Considering his experiences he looked well, but this war has taught us that appearances of men who have been wounded in action are not an index to physical fitness.'

Once deemed well enough to be transferred to a military hospital, Buckley was shipped back to the UK before the first reports of his injuries appeared in the press.

The Globe reported on 7 August 1916, 'Major Frank Buckley, the international footballer, has been severely wounded and is in Birmingham University Military Hospital.'

There was more information in the *Bradford Daily Telegraph* on the same day: 'Great regret will be felt in Bradford at the news that Frank Buckley is back in hospital suffering from severe wounds. He was shot in the shoulder during the great advance, but it is stated that he is now making satisfactory progress towards a return to health. Doubtless the constitution of the old international will stand him in good stead.'

It was felt that Buckley's recovery was going to be slow and painful. However, his attendance at the Birmingham City v Sheffield Wednesday match on 8 September 1916, just over six weeks after he had been wounded in battle, came as something of a surprise.

The *Derby Evening Telegraph* reported, 'Major Frank C Buckley of the Footballers' Battalion who was wounded some weeks ago and was afterwards an inmate of Bounsbrock Hospital is now out of that institution and can get about.

'He still wears his arm in a sling and is decidedly weak, but he can walk in reasonable comfort and is making good progress. Unfortunately, apart from his injury to the arm and shoulder a piece of shrapnel has pierced one of his lungs and it may be accepted as fact that his football career is over. He is living in his old home, Bury Mound, Yardley Wood.'

There was, however, no comfort on the domestic front. The house that Buckley returned to had been decimated by fire and everything inside had been lost. The Buckleys were awaiting permission to rebuild the charred remains when the Major returned from the front.

There was better news on the health front a week later. The *Derby Evening Telegraph* on Monday, 18 September reported, 'Major Frank Buckley, looking considerably better than he appeared to be a few weeks ago, was at the Birmingham match Saturday, and received warm congratulations both upon his improving health, and his military zeal and efficiency.

'Major Buckley speaks in the highest terms of the Footballers' Battalion. He says that they had won the highest commendation from everyone associated with them, although they had been in touch with some of the distinguished regiments in the British Army.

'He paid a high tribute to the worth of the professional footballers connected with the battalion and said that even knowing them as he did before the war, he had never realised that they would devote themselves to their duties as unflinchingly, and they had done or proved themselves such efficient soldiers. He was proud to have been one of the officers in such a battalion.'

When Buckley sat down to watch Birmingham City v Sheffield United on 4 November 1916, he would soon be back on the frontline, although there was a reminder of the threats he would face when he was asked for a comment by the press about the passing of Richard McFadden, which the Major referred to as a 'terrible loss'.

Reporting on his appearance in the crowd, the *Birmingham Daily Mail* wrote, 'Major Frank Buckley, the famous Birmingham and Bradford player, was present at the game between Birmingham and Sheffield United and looks a great deal better than he did six or seven weeks ago.

'He is sounder, but that is only a relative term, for he still has a piece of shrapnel in one of his lungs. But he is due to return to the front in a fortnight's time, having made substantial progress towards recovery. He was much impressed by the sound football manifested by his old colleagues of the Birmingham team.'

Just under two weeks later, on 18 November 1916, the Battle of the Somme had come to an end. It was estimated that the six and a half miles of the British advance equated to a yard for every life lost. Such was the loss of life that conscription was now introduced across the United Kingdom.

Buckley was to arrive back at the front officially on 3 January, where he watched the Football Battalion take on The King's. The 17th Middlesex ran out 6-1 winners.

The appetite for football, on the front and back home, remained undimmed, although, with the men at the front, new football heroes would soon emerge.

Chapter 14

Munitionettes
The war on the home front

On Christmas Day 1917, 10,000 people appeared at Deepdale, the home of Preston North End – a crowd that was unexpected. Tickets cost just 2s 6d, but three days earlier only 200 had been sold.

If the capacity crowd was expecting a festive novelty, it would have quickly understood the error as the two sides ran out. There was no doubt that the Dick, Kerr players were athletic, dressed in black and white shirts with dark blue shorts, topped off with tight-fitting matching caps. Their opponents, also in dark blue shorts, wore red and white striped shirts.

Both teams marched purposely towards the centre circle, where a photographer was waiting to mark this historic match. After the formalities ended, the players dispersed to practise their shooting before the referee, John Lewis, brought both captains together. Taking a coin from the pocket of his blazer, he asked them to call.

Just three days earlier, the *Lancashire Daily Post* had reported that there was some doubt as to whether Mr Lewis would be able to make the trip from his home in Blackburn to referee the match. He had been refused petrol for his car to do the journey and there were no trains running on Christmas Day.

After shaking hands, the two captains took their positions in a typical attacking pyramid formation. From the beginning, the players seemed nervous – a feeling exacerbated by the laughter and jeers from the assembled crowd.

It's fair to say that a large minority in the crowd, many wounded soldiers home from the front or those simply unfit to serve, had come along not just to support the Moor Park Auxiliary War Hospital, but to witness a novelty: football played by women.

As the *Lancashire Evening Post* reported, 'At first the spectators were inclined to treat the game with a little too much levity and they found amusement in almost everything, from the pace, which until they had got used to it, had the same effect as a slow-moving Kinema-picture, to the "how dare you" expression of a player when she was pushed by an opponent.

'But when they saw that the ladies meant business, and were "playing the game", they readily took up the correct attitude and impartially cheered and encouraged each side.'

....

By Christmas 1917, it was clear the country needed something to take their mind away from the Great War, which had now marked its fourth consecutive Christmas. The feelings of many people were summed up by an editorial published in the *Daily Mirror* on Christmas Eve:

'We have the fourth war Christmas with us; but we have not peace with Christmas; and once again, therefore, the festival, for religious people, ought to be purely religious – a season of prayer, and, if not fasting, at any rate not feasting.

'For the rest of us, all the usual efforts of eating and present-buying can most patriotically and usefully be diverted into two other channels – into giving the sick and wounded in the hospitals as good a time as they are able to enjoy; and into buying War Bonds as a saving for future and happier Christmases.

'The great dearness of the ordinary Christmas goods will, as a matter of fact, impose this course on most of the people. War Bonds are not much dearer than turkeys or chickens! – and they are much less wasteful.'

Referring to war fatigue, the editorial went on, 'The people have shown strong common sense, regarding certain aspects of war – its length, for example. They know that, as the King told us some time ago, "the end is not in sight".

'As they have never believed the short-lived prophets, magicians, mediums, and military critics who have told them that it is. Each year "peace before Christmas" – and each year an even more highly explosive Christmas than the last!

'What probably they ask, if they be still wise, is that "we should get it over this time" – whenever we do get it over. The German leaders ask the same. "Peace by victory." But peace final when it comes!

'Otherwise, no thought of the true sense and significance of Christmas will ever again be possible.'

The editorial lamented the use of weapons which had seen a major tank attack by the British Army at the Battle of Cambrai in November 1917: 'You cannot have this feast of brotherhood in the age of high explosives. As each new devastating invention is added to the rest, the danger of humanity increases.

'Slowly, we have been heading for this gulf since the days of gunpowder; the essence of it all being that humanity's power has increased immeasurably beyond its common sense and its morality.

'Power without morality means the death, the suicide, of humanity. The next war, if we have one, will see whole cities and people blown and torn to pieces.

'Let us strive, then, this coming year, to save humanity from that. Let this Christmas be spent, by the faithful, in prayer; by the doubtful ever, in hope, that these bad times may end with humanity's peril out of sight.

'The men who fight and the men who have fought for us are the only ones with a right to regard this year's Christmas as a time of rejoicing and forgetfulness.'

• • • •

After a few minutes it was the Dick, Kerr Ladies who overcame their nerves first, the *Lancashire Evening Post* reporting, 'Woman for woman they were also speedier, and had a larger share of that quality which in football slang is known as "heftiness".

'Quite a few of their shots at goal would not have disgraced the regular professional except in direction, and even professionals have been known on occasion to be a trifle wide of the target.

'Their forward work, indeed, was often surprisingly good, one or two of the ladies displaying quite admirable ball control, whilst combination was by no means a negligible quantity.'

Dick, Kerr's opponents in that first match were the team fielded by Arundel Coulthard Factory, known as Coulthards Ladies. They had been admirable in defence, the goalkeeper managing to defend the goal well, but their attackers were often still like statues whenever the ball came out from the back. Many spectators believed that their initial nerves, caused by playing in front of such a large audience, had given the Coulthards' strikers full-on stage fright.

With so much pressure around the Coulthards' goalmouth and the strikers unable to make any impression on the game, it was not long – just five minutes, in fact – before Dick, Kerr's Miss Whittle made the breakthrough, taking the game by the scruff of the neck.

Dick, Kerr & Co., the leading British manufacturer of light railway equipment, had been converted to a munitions factory and for the first time its workforce was now largely female. Anyone who had seen the kickabouts in the factory yards during tea breaks and lunch hours would know that the women were deadly serious about the game of football. Playing against the young male apprentices no quarter was given, and none was expected.

Even though these were informal friendlies, it was not unknown for shins and legs to be bandaged because hard tackling was the norm. Alice Norris, one of the workers, said of the matches, 'We used to play at shooting at the cloakroom windows. They were little square windows and if the boys beat us at putting a window through, we had to buy them a packet of Woodbines. But if we beat them, they had to buy us a bar of Five Boys chocolate.'

The seriousness of the Dick, Kerr Ladies had even been noted by the *Lancashire Evening Post* on 2 November, when talk of the match at Deepdale was first mooted: 'I am informed that the girls who compose the sides representing Dick, Kerr's, and Coulthards on Christmas Day at Deepdale are practising assiduously, and that indeed the game is being pursued seriously by many more than can be found places on this occasion.

'In all I believe close upon a hundred Dick Kerr's girls have been turning out, but the final selection will be made from about 27.'

Such reports give the impression that women's football was something that had suddenly sprang up. In fact, just over 20 years earlier in 1895, the British Ladies Football Club was formed by socialite Nettie Honeyball at Crouch End Athletic Ground in London, and a match was played between the women of North and South London.

The North London women overcame their southern counterparts 7-1. The British Ladies Football Club had advertised in the *Daily Graphic* for women to play 'a manly game and show that it could be womanly as well'.

The match failed to impress. 'When the novelty has worn off, I do not think that women's football will attract the crowds,' wrote the 'Lady Correspondent' in the *Manchester Guardian*. Thereafter, women's football largely fizzled out.

Then came the Great War. With so many able-bodied men at the front, attitudes towards the role of women had to change – in both the workforce and sport. Middle-class women had generally been discouraged from doing any manual labour, but now they were needed to keep the factories running. The need for weapons, ammunition and equipment was desperate.

As was true of other factories, Dick, Kerr & Co. was brought under government control and now manufactured shells and aircraft for the Armed Services. The first batch of shells were bonded in 1915 and this was the start of an output of missiles which reached 30,000 a week.

The new women workers were known as 'munitionettes' and were encouraged to play sport as a way of keeping them healthy and making sure they were fit for work. The government appointed female welfare supervisors and sent them into the factories to oversee the moral and physical wellbeing of the girls, and they also encouraged the development of sporting activities.

The women started playing football in teams, just like their male counterparts had done, and named them after the factories where they worked. Indeed, football soon became a focal point of factory life.

The women workers were even playing against men, a practice officially banned by the FA in 1902. Nonetheless, believing such enthusiasm should be actively encouraged, the welfare workers employed by the factories organised teams, nurturing an ambition to challenge other factories from further afield.

According to the *Lancashire Evening Post* in November 1917, 'Ladies' football has not seen such a rapid growth in and around Preston as it has been in other munition centres, but is spreading, for one team at least has been formed at Dick, Kerr, and Co.'s works, with others in prospect, representing the different shops, amongst whom a "league" is to be run, while sides or clubs are either in existence or in the course being raised at other munition establishments.'

The paper went on to talk of the growth of the women's game in other major cities, particularly in the north of the country: 'In Manchester, Sheffield, Liverpool and other large centres the feminine workers have played many games and raised considerable sums of money on behalf of war charities, and if I am not mistaken the Munition Girls' League arranged in Manchester has applied to the Football Association for affiliation!

'It is not long since that body removed the embargo that was placed upon ladies' football many years ago, but I think it may be taken for granted that such a step was only dictated by the desirability of first-class grounds being used for raising as much money as possible for war funds, and because the present movement is directed to that end, as distinct from the commercial enterprise which brought the ban into being.'

．．．．

For those who worked in the munitions factories, football acted as a means of escape from the very real threats and dangers in their newfound careers.

Sibbald Stewart worked alongside the women as a civilian munitions worker between 1915 and 1916, and went on serve with 238th Coy

Machine Gun Corps on the Western Front and in Mesopotamia. He described the conditions at Elswick Ordinance Factory in Glasgow: 'We started off at six in the morning and we worked 'til about six at night. Twelve hours on the machine and the night shift came on and took over from us and gone on over midnight.

'So, two twelve-hour days for each machine in the twenty-four hours. Oh for a break for half an hour at midnight in the night shift, but you'd get a full hour's break at lunchtime on the day shift. The only breaks, yes, no cups of tea in the morning or afternoon … heavy going!

'It was tiring work. Of course they were heavy – they were 72 pounds weight per shell, the shell case alone.'

Another man who worked alongside women was Henry Oxley, who worked at Woolwich Arsenal Munitions Factory before becoming a Battalion Gas Instructor for the 23rd Middlesex. He described the sheer monotony of the job: 'My job in the factory was relative to putting holes in fuses of shells. And you worked to a gauge.

'In other words, you did so many, then you put your gauge to the hole you were drilling and if it was oversize, you called your foreman, and he would check it and make it suitable to the gauge.

'In other words, if the job was found to be too big or too small as regards whatever you was doing, it was rejected. We had a special department for inspecting these components we were making for the shells. They were very meticulous and any rejects of course were cast out. And other than that, the work was repetition, so there was no skill required whatsoever.'

Munitions worker Ethel Wilby described how she was treated by management after failing one inspection: 'Every now and again you had to test what you was doing and if it wasn't right, you had to get the tool setter to come and put it right for you.

'On one occasion I found it was wrong and he came and put it right – or thought I'd put it right – and each time I pulled the lever down, so it went wrong again. And he was so annoyed with me on this day that he said, "I'm not putting in any more for you" and swore at me.

'"Go and see the boss." So, I had to go and see the manager in his office, and I explained to him what had gone wrong. I said, "I don't seem to be doing anything right. I don't know if it's the machine or what." So, he said, "Well, perhaps you're not feeling so well today. Go home and come back tomorrow." And I don't know how many drills I broke but I know I was very sorry for myself.'

Then there was the danger of the chemicals involved in their work. Kathleen Gilbert, who worked in the Royal Park Filling Station, explained that even strict safety precautions were not enough to combat the negative effects of the toxins: 'We found work then at the Park Royal Filling Station. And it turned out to be a TNT factory – TNT. And you all had to change when you went in.

'You had to strip and change into other clothes because you weren't allowed a little tiny bit of metal on you at all, not one hook or eye or anything. And of course they had corsets in those days with wires in them, you see. And you had to finish up with an overall and put your head covering on. And they used to give us domes of glass on the table with holes for your hands to go through, and you filled up the gains.

'Gains were something like cartridges but bigger. You filled them up with this black rock stuff. And everyone turned yellow there. And you washed so that the yellow came off, but it was always in your system.'

. . . .

For the women who were married and had husbands serving on the front, there was the constant worry of a dreaded knock at their front door, with a message about a loved one, missing or lost.

In the first week of July 1916, Grace Sibbert received such a telegram, telling her that her husband, John, was missing in action.

A member of the 9th (Service) Battalion of the Loyal North Lancashire Regiment, John had signed up in Preston in September 1914. On 3 July, he went over the top on the third day of the Battle of the Somme.

Then came a second knock at the door. This one informed Grace that intelligence told the War Office that her husband was alive, but had been taken by the Germans and was now a prisoner of war.

Grace threw herself into football.

From the outset she was at the centre of the friendly games in the factory yard, often teasing the apprentices about their play. Legend has it that by this time the Dick, Kerr's men's football team had become a bit of a laughing stock.

Week after week they were being hammered, only to return to the factory after the matches for some good-natured banter from the women there.

By October 1917, the apprentices had had enough. In the canteen over lunch, just after another kickabout where the women had got the better of the lads, a challenge was thrown down. If the girls were so confident, why not face the apprentices in an organised match? Until then the matches had been friendlies.

According to legend, Grace accepted immediately: 'Come on, girls, let's give it a go, it'll be a laugh.' Arrangements were made to play in the Penwortham area, not too far from the factory. The result of the game is lost to history, but this was the beginning of the Dick, Kerr Ladies team.

The original idea for the Christmas Day match came about from the matron of Moor Park. Wanting to raise money for the wounded veterans in her care, she approached Albert Frankland, a clerk and administrator at the factory, with the idea of the women taking part in a charity concert.

Frankland had witnessed the impromptu kickabouts and seen the women take on the apprentices, and knew that the idea of a concert would be rejected out of hand. Perhaps if the matron approached Grace Sibbert with the idea of a football match against the veterans themselves, she would get more joy?

This idea would have been difficult, though: many of the patients were either too injured or infirm to play a full-scale game of football. So Frankland approached Coulthards, who agreed to put together a team of women. Preston North End quickly agreed to loan the ground for £5 and displayed posters advertising the game.

While the revenue from the tickets was donated to the Moor Park Hospital, a further collection at the match was made to raise money for the wounded soldiers. Even before the ball had been kicked, over £600, which equates to £36,000 in today's money, had been raised.

Unfortunately, due to ill health caused by the munitions work, Grace Sibbert herself had to sit out this game. In fact, she never officially played for Dick, Kerr Ladies, but helped manage the team alongside Albert Frankland.

. . . .

Halfway through the first half, a thunderbolt strike from about 15 yards out from Preston-born Elizabeth Berkins saw the once sceptical crowd explode into wild cheers as the Dick, Kerr Ladies doubled their lead. Then Florrie Rance, who towered above her opponents at 5ft 8in, popped up to make it 3-0 before half-time and it looked as though the game was beyond Coulthards.

Partnering Rance up front was Florrie Redford, who was singled out in an otherwise ungenerous match preview by the *Lancashire Evening Post*: 'I do not know what people expect to see at these matches. There are two girls I am told, who are clever, especially one, Florrie Redford, Dick Kerr's inside-right, but whether this kind of thing runs through the lot or not remains to seen.

'One or two old hands of the game have been endeavouring to instil into them the idea of organised, as opposed to what may be described as a mob effort, but as a rule these precepts are apt to be entirely forgotten on the day and it becomes merely a joyous scramble.

'However, the girls pretend to nothing but that which comes within their limited powers in such strenuous and a skilful game as football, and they are to be commended for the effort in the sacred cause of war charity.'

At the start of the second half, Coulthard came out like a team rejuvenated. Any nerves they had been suffering up front disappeared as they launched wave after wave of attacking football. Those watching felt that the type of pressure now being applied to the Dick, Kerr's Ladies backline was surely going to result in a goal.

As the game drew to its close, however, Coulthard had failed to convert any of their chances to score. It was only when they won a penalty that they finally had the chance to get on the scoresheet. Unfortunately, the resulting penalty kick was mishit and rolled harmlessly into the arms of the goalkeeper.

As the Coulthard players trudged back to their half, they were caught on the break. The Dick Kerr, Ladies ran through the opposing centre-halves, and though there was an appeal for handball, it fell on deaf ears as Florrie Rance ran through for her second and the Dick, Kerr Ladies' fourth goal.

Despite the loud cheers and applause at the end of the game, not everyone was impressed. A journalist, writing under the name Perseus in the *Lancashire Evening Post*, would claim about the women's game, 'Of one thing we may be certain – any attempt to establish ladies' football as a regular and recognised pursuit would very quickly fail.

'There is no reason apart from sentimental dislike that many people have to see girls and women taking part in masculine pastimes, why the tendency of the moment should be frowned upon.'

Ultimately Perseus, was proven wrong. Just three years later, football's first woman superstar, Lily Parr, played in a Boxing Day match against St Helen's Ladies which was watched by 53,000 spectators at Goodison Park – where around another 14,000 were left outside the ground, trying to get in.

However, in 1921 women's football was effectively at an end when the Football Association banned women from playing at members' grounds. Officials claimed it was for health reasons, arguing that the game was dangerous to women and adding that charitable donations from matches had been too low.

Men's football, of course, was allowed to resume – but even in the midst of war it was clear that the game would start again without some of its greatest stars.

Chapter 15

John McCartney
Forever Hearts

On 15 August 1914, just over two weeks after Great Britain declared war on Germany, Heart of Midlothian lined up to face the reigning Scottish champions, Celtic – the Edinburgh club led by their paternalistic manager, John McCartney.

Then there were the familiar smells of the west end of the city, the heavy aroma of yeast and hops wafting over Tynecastle, emanating from the Caledonian Brewery. The sun seemed to be smiling on the Hearts team as twin strikers, Tom Gracie and Harry Wattie, scored two fine goals and it finally looked as though there might be a chance that the crucible of power in Scotland would swing from Glasgow to the capital.

While Gracie and Wattie were giving the Celtic defence the runaround, at the other end of the field James Boyd ensured that the waves of attacks launched by the Celtic forwards came to nothing.

These were McCartney's boys. Even after they had left Edinburgh for their eventual destination, the frontline in France, he had not stopped caring. Players including Alfie Briggs, Duncan Currie, Tom Gracie, Jamie Low, Harry Wattie, Willie Wilson, Paddy Crossan and Jimmy Boyd had all joined up.

At the time Hearts were leaders of the Scottish League and news of the players' actions caused a nationwide sensation. They were soon joined by professionals from Raith Rovers, Dunfermline and Falkirk, hundreds of Hearts supporters and many other sportsmen and fans.

Even though they were out of sight, they were never out of mind. McCartney had sent a letter to his players asking if he could send some sort of care package. These could be sent when time and resources permitted. The players responded, asking for a few basics if it wasn't too much trouble… socks, chocolate, soap, a harmonica, tobacco, paper, envelopes, and magazines, please'.

McCartney and his wife went to work. They collected 240 pairs of socks, 141 lb of tobacco, 12 dozen pipes, 5000 cigarettes, 200 boxes of matches, 25 harmonicas, two fiddles, 100 boxes of Edinburgh rock, 400 bars of Fry's milk chocolate, 300 candles, 20 cases of soap, 12 dozen writing pads, 3000 envelopes, 14 pairs of football boots, three balls, two pumps, and an assortment of books and magazines. Finally, in a personal touch, McCartney also included a tin of his wife's special homemade fudge.

The care package was more than welcome: by 1916 the Western Front had settled into a deadly grind of trench warfare. Battalions took turns in the frontline between draining spells labouring in the reserve lines. 'Most of our time is spent digging holes in bits of France to fill other holes in other bits of France,' Company Sergeant Major Annan Ness wrote to McCartney.

The reserve team's half-back, Annan Ness, was well known to McCartney. And as a former soldier he had been charged with leading the drill training sessions between matches once the players signed up.

It must have been with a mixture of fear and trepidation when two letters arrived at his office in Tynecastle, the home of Hearts. One of the letters carried Ness's distinctive copperplate handwriting.

The letter came from Sir James Leishman, a member of the Hearts board, writing to express his sympathy for the family of James Speedie, who had joined the Queen's Own Cameron Highlanders.

On 15 October 1915, the *Dundee Courier* reported the news to the public: 'Intimation has been received of the death in France of Private James Hodge Speedie, Cameron Highlanders, the well-known Heart of Midlothian footballer. Private Speedie was one of the many players of the Hearts who joined the army soon after the outbreak of war.'

Speedie had been killed on 25 September 1915 at the Battle of Loos. He was the first of the Hearts team to lose their life on the battlefield.

Just after the war, in 1918, John McCartney would write a pamphlet, *The 'Hearts' and the Great War*, paying tribute to all the players with a short biography accompanying a photograph. Speedie's entry reads: 'Born at Edinburgh on 17th November 1893. He was by profession an insurance clerk with one of the largest concerns of its kind in the City. He clung to his amateur status and was a great player in his day.

'Like the generality of our men he was modest, unassuming, and kindly. When the call of Country came, he was ready, willing, and anxious to serve the cause of right. Joining the Cameron Highlanders, he was early in France. Jimmy, as he was familiarly known, came through several severe battles, and ultimately fell fighting at Loos, 25th September 1915. His only brother, Lieut. John, has since fallen in action. The parents of these two splendid lads live at Polwarth Gardens.'

A few months later, on a dark evening in early January 1916, McCrae and his men, including McCartney's boys, crossed to France. Three weeks later, they went into the line. 'You sit in the mud and hope the next one won't be near you,' wrote one soldier home.

Back in England, McCartney went every day to Tynecastle, but his thoughts never deviated from his boys. And on 19 March 1916, he heard that a footballer had been lost.

His name was Jimmy Todd, who had played as an outside-forward for Raith Rovers. A former railway clerk, he was barely 20 years of age – and the first footballer of McCrae's Battalion to lose his life.

Todd had been hit in the chest by shell fragments near Armentières, France, on 12 March 1916. He had been taking a break and eating food when he was hit in a dugout – usually earmarked as a safe place to eat and rest.

On a misty morning on 1 July 1916 as the sun struggled to break through the cloudy sky, the soldiers were awoken to the distinctive smell of bacon and eggs sizzling on the makeshift pans in the trenches. As the rest of the Battalion tucked into the treat of an unexpected, cooked breakfast, Hearts wing-half Alfie Briggs hastily wrote a letter.

Just before 7.30 a.m., the whistle blew, the sign for the men to line up for the advance. Gingerly, Briggs climbed out of the trench and stood shoulder to shoulder with his Hearts teammates.

They were a long way from Tynecastle and the air was strong not with the familiar smell of the yeast of the brewery but with the putrid stench of the trenches.

Edwin Ware, a sergeant in the Royal Army Medical Corps (RAMC), wrote later, 'The stench of a battlefield cannot be imagined ... Blood; the dead, both human and animal; the acrid smell of explosives; the smell of lethal gases, whether fresh or stale; chloride of lime, used in the primitive sanitary arrangements; our own seldom washed bodies; and the putrid, churned-up mud. Men, sleeping under these conditions, often looked like the dead, with dull grey, waxen-looking faces which appeared to be moist.'

Looking down the line, Briggs would have seen the familiar faces, older now and sallower as though they had all aged a few decades in a matter of months. One or two of the younger boys were quietly crying, their tears slowly rolling down their cheeks; others vomited.

Looking at his teammates, Briggs may have seen their eyes all focused on Ness, Company Sergeant Major, who looked at his watch and patiently waited as the seconds slowly ticked by. As soon as his watch reached 7.30 a.m., he would blow hard on his whistle and the men would go over the top.

At 7.29 a.m., Ness would have taken the whistle out of his mouth and told his men to get ready. Then he would have looked again at his watch. In preparation for the so-called 'big push', the guns stopped.

If Briggs was tempted to take one last look at the men he had once met on the football field, he would have seen full-back Duncan Currie; his brother Robert, who played for Bury and Hearts; and another brother, Sam, who played for Leicester Fosse.

Then there was Ernest Ellis; the talented forward Henry Wattie, once destined to play for Scotland; and Paddy Crossan, an explosive talent who made for a quick, robust and industrious full-back.

Crossan had signed for Hearts in 1911 and soon became a regular. Handsome and charismatic, he was very popular with his teammates, who took to calling him 'the handsomest man in the world'. Paddy was happy to accept the title. One of his playing colleagues informed a journalist, 'Pat can pass the ball, but he couldn't pass a mirror if he tried.'

Crossan was standing beside his best friend in the Hearts team, Jimmy Hazeldean. The friendship was described by Private Murdie McKay, who said that most of the Hearts men were together at the last. Crossan was quiet, he and Wattie had palled up with Jimmy Hazeldean, and the three of them were now inseparable.

. . . .

At some point in Tynecastle, McCartney opened the letters.

One came from the father of Duncan Currie and confirmed a report in the *Dundee Courier* of 18 July: 'Information has been received in Edinburgh that Sergeant Duncan Currie of the Royal Scots, the Heart of Midlothian football player, has been killed in action. The deceased soldier belonging to Kilwinning, he joined the army in November 1914.'

Currie's father now told him that he had received a letter from a battalion officer notifying him of his son's death.

In *The 'Hearts' and the Great War,* Currie was described as, 'A native of Kilwinning, Ayrshire, where he was born, 13 August 1892. He was assistant to an elder brother as a hairdresser. Of a football family, he came quickly into prominence as a junior, and was early taken hold of by the Heart of Midlothian.

'Like most of the club's players at this period, he gave decided evidence of obtaining highest honours. A strong, resolute player, he took no nonsense, and took the game keenly and seriously.

'His natural proclivities reproduced themselves in his Army career, and the "historic sixteen" gave no one more likely to rise to fame and position in His Majesty's Forces. Duncan soon became a Sergeant. Whilst gallantly leading his platoon at the Somme offensive, 1 July 1916, he fell to rise no more.'

McCartney turned to the second letter, from Annan Ness. It was brisk and businesslike to begin with, telling his manager what Ness saw within seconds of going over the top: 'Teddy McGuire was struck in the arm by flying shrapnel. As he fell, a machine gun round grazed his head.' McGuire, who had played at inside-right, escaped with his life, eventually being invalided out of the army.

The primary aim of the big push was to take the German trenches. Machine-gun fire rang out immediately – and Ernie Ellis fell. 'They came out of the sunken road to find at least three machine-guns trained on them ... Ernie Ellis and Jimmy Hawthorn went down in front of the wire ... It was just cruel. We had no chance.'

In *The 'Hearts' and the Great War*, McCartney wrote of Ellis, 'He made the supreme sacrifice at the Battle of the Somme, 1st July 1916. He left a widow – an Edinburgh lady – and a little girl born after he went to France. His three brothers are on active service.'

Later, Ness would learn that Jimmy Hazeldean took a bullet to the thigh, for which he would be invalided out of the army. Ness himself would be hit, but not before he saw Duncan Currie take a bullet to the shoulder, then fall into the mud and wire. It could not have been more than minutes since the whistle.

Writing in 1918, McCartney was to say of Harry Wattie, 'Alas! poor Harry was not destined to reap a harvest of laurels such as came the way of his confrere. The advent of the world war found him ranking with his clubmates in the 16th Royal Scots. He is presumed to have been killed at the Somme, 1 July 1916.

'Comrades have related that they saw him fall, but a most careful after search failed to trace his body. The ground was ploughed inch by inch with shell fire, so that the reason for non-recovery is obvious. Harry was the youngest of five brothers, one of whom, the Rev. John Wattie, is a Chaplain to the Fleet. Their widowed mother resides in Marchmont Road.'

A month after the action, on 1 August 1916, the *Dundee Courier* reported, 'While no official word has been received by relatives of the men, it is believed that Harry Wattie and Ellis, two of the Hearts players, have been missing since last month.

'Both took part in the assault on the German lines. Wattie belongs to Edinburgh and Ellis to Norwich ... Ellis was knocked about in the 5th German trench and nothing further has been heard of him. Wattie's friends cling to the hope that he is a prisoner at the hands of the Germans.'

It was a hope that would not be met, and there were further casualties among his fellow players.

Crossan was running forward when a shell exploded in front of him, leaving a massive crater, the blast knocking him out. Another blast almost buried him alive. All day and night, Crossan lay there prone, and if he had been found, they would have thought him dead.

Not that there was any hope of his body being recovered. Bombardier J.W. Palmer was to write of his experiences, 'Our lads weren't moved for some days – the dead weren't moved, the wounded were – and for days after when I was laying the wire out, I had to pass over those bodies, whose faces were turning more and more blue and green.'

A Captain Peel, writing in his diary, also described the scene: 'The whole place was littered with debris of all sorts, Boche shrapnel helmets, charge boxes, and thousands of rounds of ammunition, also plenty of dead – worse still, hands and legs.'

However, Crossan was not dead. Covered in mud and chalk, he came around and even though badly concussed, he painstakingly dug himself out of his grave. He knew that standing up, let alone trying to run, was suicide. Instead, he remained on his stomach and slowly crawled away from the Germans.

Inch by inch over three agonising days, Crossan made his way to British lines. Concussion had impaired his vision as he crawled through no man's land, but it had not affected his memory. He later recounted the remarkable journey back to his lines and the horror he had encountered while crawling from shell hole to shell hole, occupied by corpses – and body parts.

He was then taken to a medical station, where it was discovered that despite being buried alive for 24 hours, his wounds were superficial. He was bandaged up and returned to his unit.

A few weeks later, a shell exploded near to him, resulting in some pieces of shrapnel becoming embedded in his left leg. A shard of shell casing also penetrated his left foot, almost taking off his toes. Crossan was removed to a field hospital, where he lost consciousness. When he came round, he noticed that a label had been pinned to his uniform. The label contained the message 'for amputation'. The doctors had decreed that his left leg was coming off.

Writhing in his hospital bed, he screamed at the doctors, 'No, no, I need my leg, I am a footballer!' Crossan did not pay much attention to the orderly in his room, just another unlucky German prisoner of war put to work.

Seeing Crossan in such anguish, the orderly looked at his notes. This was no hospital orderly; the man who tried to calm Crossan, speaking soothing words in a thick German accent, was a surgeon, now caught up in the madness of the war.

The German informed the medical staff that amputation was not necessary as a simple operation would suffice and that he was prepared to carry it out. Remarkably, permission was granted and the kindly enemy surgeon carried out the operation successfully.

After the operation, Crossan was transferred to Stourbridge Hospital in the West Midlands to recover and it was from there that he wrote to his manager, John McCartney. With typical self-belief, he confidently informed the manager that he would soon be kicking a ball again – and he would be as good as his word.

· · · ·

The rest of Ness's letter read, 'Alfie Briggs was not so lucky. He seemed to get caught in the sights of a German sniper. One bullet broke his right leg, another his left foot, another passed directly through his right arm. Another entered his right ankle, travelled all the way up his calf and came out above his knee. The last one glanced across his forehead, knocking him unconscious. Briggs fell just in front of the entrance to Wood Alley, a communication trench which led back to the German third line.'

Even though the recovery was long and hard, Briggs recovered. For the rest of his life, he would live with two bullets lodged near his spine.

He never played football again, although he did some scouting for Partick Thistle. Both family and friends would notice the depression that dogged him, especially around the anniversary of the battle.

It would not be long before the news of casualties sustained by Hearts would reach the newspapers. The *Daily Record and Mail* reported on 13 July 1916, 'Casualties have been heavy in the Royal Scots Battalion, which contained so many of the Heart of Midlothian and other Scottish League footballers.

'Mr McCartney is in receipt of letters which make it clear that a good many well-known players in this noted contingent have been out of action but until official notification is received, names like Briggs, Crossan, Hazeldean and McGuire have all been wounded in the great attack.

'McGuire is in hospital in Glasgow with an injured arm, Hazeldean lies in an English hospital with a bullet wound in the left thigh, while Crossan appears to have left hospital and rejoined his battalion.

'The case of Alf Briggs is more serious. The Clydebank man lies in hospital in Epsom, badly wounded in the head, the arm and foot.'

. . . .

In his letter, Ness was able to offer one moment of relief: the story of Roddy Walker, the old Tynecastle full-back. A German machine-gun team were getting their gun into position when Walker dashed up and knocked out the German who was working on it.

There was a moment of hesitation and the word 'retire' could be heard from a British commanding officer, but Walker was heard to shout, 'To hell with retire! Who ever knew of a Royal Scots retiring?'

Yet the first day of the Somme was as devastating for the Battalion as it was for the entire army. Of the 814 men of McRae's who left the trenches on that day, 636 were killed or wounded. At roll call on 2 July 1916, only 25 men were able to answer.

Of the 11 players who had run out against Celtic two years earlier, Duncan Currie, Ernest Ellis and Wattie, who scored, were all dead. Wattie's body was never found.

Briggs, Crossan, James Hazeldean and Edward McGuire were wounded. Gracie, the other scorer against Celtic, was already dead. Boyd had a month to live. Another Hearts player, John Allan, was killed in action in 1917, the same year that Willie Watson was invalided home.

In December 1918, John McCartney added this dedication to *The 'Hearts' and the Great War*: 'This book is dedicated to our heroes who fought and conquered and died, without knowing that they had conquered, and, equally, to their brave comrades who fought and conquered and lived to return to us.'

McCrae's Battalion would limp on until May 1918, when its capacity had been reduced to 30, but the end had come that bright July day on the Somme. It would not be the last football battalion which that stretch of Northern France would claim.

Chapter 16
Joe Mercer
The hard man did not break

It was a trap, but the Battalion was not to know it. The Germans were not in their trenches but hiding among the trees and branches of Oppy Wood, where their machine guns were firmly sighted on the incoming British Army. What followed was carnage.

Surrounded and with no hope of help, the 17th Middlesex was systematically picked off by the German machine guns.

For those who were not wiped out in the initial barrage, shelter could be found in shell holes. Joe Mercer, a tough-tackling half-back for Nottingham Forest, hid from the machine-gun fire in a shell hole for two long hours. He had been hit a total of eight times.

As he sheltered away from the heavy German shelling, Joe may have thought of the young son, Joe Junior, born only five days after war was declared. He was three now and had spent next to no time with his father.

. . . .

Even before they reached Oppy Wood, things had changed for the Football Battalion. After three years and seeing the Battalion through the Somme, including their actions at Guillemont and Redan Ridge, a weary and tired Colonel Fenwick had finally stepped down. He was 56 years of age but looked much older.

The Battalion was barely recognisable from the one of which Fenwick had first taken command. After sustaining huge losses in the Battle of Delville Wood, the 17th Middlesex needed a draft of 716 men in mid-August 1916 just to bring the Battalion back up to strength. Further action followed, including the Battle of Guillemont.

Fenwick may have relinquished command, but he did not forget the footballers who served under him. In a final act, he contributed £200 to the Footballers Battalion Comforts Fund to ensure there was enough in the fund to buy soft canvas rest shoes, when they were resting way from the front.

The *Sporting Chronicle* of 23 April 1917 said of Fenwick's retirement, 'Colonel Fenwick went to France with the battalion in November 1915, and has been through all their severe fighting and many hardships.

'He was loved by the many fine and famous players under him. He has been the father of the battalion and has looked after the welfare of his men in a manner which they will never forget. As a man of wealth, he has been able to do a great deal for them.'

Fenwick's replacement was Lieutenant-Colonel George Kelly. At 36, he was closer in age to the men he commanded. He was an experienced soldier, seeing action in the Boer War and injured at the Battle of Loos, but proved himself somewhat less popular than his predecessor, described by one soldier as a 'bit of a snotter'.

The man who had first stood as the second in command to Fenwick was no longer in France. In January 1917, the Battalion had attacked German positions at Argenvilliers, and Frank Buckley had been notable for his bravery in hand-to-hand combat, mentioned in dispatches in a special edition of the *London Gazette*.

By June 1917, however, Frederick Wall spoke to delegates at the Annual General Meeting of the Football Association and told them that Buckley was home from the front.

This time, there was no hope that he would be able to return to the Battalion. At this offensive, the Germans had used deadly mustard gas to ward off the allies.

The Germans had first used more than 150 tons of lethal chlorine gas at Ypres, Belgium, on 22 April 1915, decimating two divisions of French and Algerian colonial troops.

By 1917, they had moved on to a more deadly variant: mustard gas. Blistering skins, irritating the nostrils and entering the lungs, it would be responsible for thousands of deaths.

Buckley had donned a sophisticated gas mask when the first wave of the lethal gas was unleashed, but it was already too late. His lungs were damaged by the shrapnel that had forced him out of action the previous year, so he could not withstand even a few breaths of the deadly gas.

He developed a persistent, hacking cough and was unable to stand for even a few minutes without gasping for breath.

Several days later, a doctor declared that Buckley's lungs would be unable to withstand another gas attack, even if he was wearing a mask. Therefore, for the second time in six months, Major Frank Buckley was repatriated, but this time there would be no return.

His place as second in command had already been taken, by Vivian Woodward. Just seven months after being almost buried alive, on 18 August 1916, Woodward had returned to the Battalion.

By 25 November, the *Star Green 'Un* reported, 'We see according to the "London Gazette" Captain Vivian J. Woodward, whilst acting as second in command of his regiment, was given the temporary rank Acting-Major. Congratulations.'

On 13 November 1916, the 17th Middlesex attacked the Redan Ridge, near Serre in the Battle of the Ancre. A heavy fog hung over the battlefield, limiting visibility to 30 yards, and after weeks of heavy rain, some men sank up to their waists in the mud.

The war diary recorded the losses of the day's fighting: three officers killed, two wounded and eight missing; 15 other ranks killed, 145 wounded and 133 missing. By March 1917, a tired Woodward, still struggling with the effects of the wounds to his legs, left the front to become a physical training instructor, eventually being posted to the Physical and Recreation Training School Headquarters at Aldershot.

With Woodward's departure, it meant that of the three original footballers who were commissioned as officers, not one remained. Evelyn Lintott, of the Leeds Pals, had lost his life on the first day of the Somme and Major Frank Buckley would see out the war at home. He would make several attempts to return, but to no avail.

....

On the night of 27 April 1917, the 17th Middlesex lined up for battle opposite some woods, just next to the small village of Oppy.

The wood overlooked British positions and the Germans held it in their possession. It was now well defended with observation posts, machine guns and trench mortars. The aim of the attack was to remove these defensive obstacles and divert German resources away from the main offensive.

Among the soldiers attacking were former Nottingham Forest teammates, Tim Coleman and Joe Mercer.

A tough, no-nonsense man, Mercer started out with Ellesmere Port Town before joining Nottingham Forest in 1910. He had almost signed for Everton but Toffees manager Walter Cuff went to watch him play and then reported back, 'He's a good player alright, but he'd get us thrown out of the League!'

One day after the formation of the Footballers' Battalion, Mercer travelled down to London with teammates Tom Gibson and Harold Iremonger to enlist.

It was still pitch-black when the 17th Middlesex set out. Coleman's wristwatch told him that it was just before 4.30 a.m. when the Battalion launched the charge to take the German trenches.

To the general bewilderment for all involved, the Battalion was occupying the German trenches by 4.40 a.m. What neither the soldiers nor their commanders could have known is that the Germans had left their position and were lying in wait.

The 17th Middlesex faced two problems. Oppy Wood was a strongly defended position, guarded by experienced German soldiers. In front of Oppy Wood lay a well organised trench system, protected by barbed wire with good communications.

The wood itself contained many defences and all along the German lines, machine-gun posts and mortars were well placed to repel any attack. The Germans had strengthened the wood by developing defensive tactics learned from earlier battles.

The British had expected to encounter demoralised troops and thought that the creeping barrage would neutralise all resistance. However, some of the German wire at the south-western corner of the wood was uncut, and it was as though the Germans were about to launch a counterattack.

No preparations had been made for an advance at night, taking compass-bearings or organising intermediate objectives. Sunrise was not until 5.22 a.m. and it would not be possible to see objects in the dark, at 50 yards.

By 8.00, the battalion commander, Lieutenant Kelly, was to write, 'It was now 8 o'clock and a few minutes later a report came in from the OC A Coy, which said that the enemy was working round both his flanks … the enemy also appears to have counter attacked against the front and right flank as well and succeeded in re-entering and getting in between the troops.'

After the initial advance, Tim Coleman lost sight of his mate, Joe Mercer.

Under heavy German gunfire, Mercer was hit in the leg and shoulder. Bleeding profusely and drifting in and out of consciousness, he lay in a shell hole even as the British barrage continued. After two hours, it fell silent and he could hear the faint sound of birdsong.

With an injured leg, he had no way of standing to his full height and his injured shoulder made any movement difficult and painful. Resolving he could no longer stay in the shell hole, Mercer decided to move.

Not knowing that the Battalion had failed to take the wood and that he was surrounded by German troops, Mercer tried to crawl on his stomach back to British lines. Staying just below any potential gunfire, he made a valiant effort, but was too badly injured to get very far. With the whole wood surrounded, it was almost inevitable that he would run into a German machine-gun party who trained their guns directly on him.

Barely able to tell the Germans his name or his rank, Mercer then passed out. When the former Nottingham Forest man awoke, he was strapped to a stretcher in the back of a motor ambulance and unsure of his destination. Neither the driver nor his assistant spoke any English and the pain from his wounds meant that he passed out again, unaware that he was being transported from Oppy Wood to Douai.

If the journey to Douai was uncomfortable, then what followed was even worse. Without pain relief or anyone attending to his wounds, Mercer was laid out on the bare floor of a train. For three days, he was thrown about as the train slowly made its way to the place that would be home for the next few months: Langensalza Camp in Germany.

George Mulford, Sheffield City Battalion (12th Battalion, York & Lancaster Regiment) gave a talk on 12 October 1919, 'My Two Years Amongst the Huns', describing conditions in the camp.

'Think of the conditions of 12,000 men huddled together on a large-sized ploughed field so situated that it caught all the water draining from the surrounding hills. Sanitary arrangements on a par with those of the native quarter in an Egyptian town.

'Food of the vilest and unhealthiest nature for human consumption. Long ramshackle dilapidated barracks to hold 7-800 men with no thought in their construction for comfort and accommodation.'

Lying in a hospital bed, Mercer recovered slowly. Things were not helped by the quality of the food: the menu often consisted of raw fish and black bread with coffee served twice a day. Most of the men baulked at the choice of food and the Russian prisoners were the only ones who could eat it, mainly because they were suffering from the effects of starvation when captured.

Another POW held at the camp in the final year of the conflict, Corporal Golding (235590) of the 8th Battalion Leicestershire Regiment, later observed, 'Captain Alexander was commandant at Langensalza when I arrived … [and] was very strict indeed. We had been told that he was well disposed towards the British prisoners, but he allowed no indulgence or privileges of any sort to the British NCOs.

'In my opinion, he could have done a good deal to improve the conditions of the camp, and particularly the sanitation, which was very bad indeed.'

Looking back, Mercer would later say that he 'was pleased to see Britishers helping in the hospital, and later got in touch with Jim McCormick, Plymouth Argyle's right half-back, who was 'a great help'.

News of Mercer's capture reached the United Kingdom relatively quickly. The *Nottingham Evening Post* reported on Tuesday, 12 June 1917, 'Sergeant Joseph Mercer, who for several seasons played centre-half for Forest, and was very popular with the local football crowd, is slightly wounded and a prisoner in the hands of the Germans.

'Mercer enlisted in 1914, and has been on active service ever since. He was missing a little while ago, and considerable anxiety has been occasioned among his friends, but a postcard giving the information that he is in a prisoners' camp in Germany has just reached his wife, who resides in Cheshire. The news was sent to Nottingham CSM [Company Sergeant Major], T. Gibson and Mr. R. J. Marsters, secretary of Nottingham Forest F.C.'

Eventually, Mercer was well enough to leave the hell of Langensalza for Giessen, the prisoners' camp standing on a hill 1½ miles above the town, flanked on one side by the main highway and on the other by pinewoods. The huts were raised two to three feet from the ground.

One former prisoner described it as a well-ordered camp with good sanitary conditions and clean water. It comprised 50 huts, each of which held 200 men, and these accommodations were described as 'most satisfactory'.

Food was still limited and, as the war progressed and supplies in Germany dwindled, the already meagre rations became even more scarce. However, the other prisoners shared their food parcels.

With a library and band, there were more leisure activities, and five-a-side football contests were even arranged. The prisoners subscribed half a mark each towards the prizes, and the sides were picked in fives as the names came out of a bag. They had to buy wood from the Germans to make goalposts and nets were made from string taken from parcels received from England.

Mercer was to comment later that 'an amusing feature of the contests was that the Germans would not allow the referee to use his whistle because it excited the guard. He had to use a little bell and even at times a mouth organ. To enable the British to have their usual "flutter", a book was made on the matches. The prizes for the contests were all given in cash.'

Unlike the conditions at Langensalza, the commandant at Giessen was usually very fair and held the British up as an example to other nationalities in the camp for their cleanliness – not that this earned them any special treatment.

Unfortunately, on 17 March 1918 Joe Mercer was on the move again – to the camp at Meschede. It had a reputation as one of the worst in Germany and, having spent one night there, he felt as though he had been plunged back into hell.

According to Mercer, 'the commandant at Meschede once met a prisoner coming from the stores carrying two tins of food. The man was too loaded to salute – the commandant led him to a drain and made him pour the contents of the tins down the drain. Later he had to do fourteen days "strafe".'

The regime was brutal. Such were the conditions that 25 per cent of the men who passed through the camp died. Mercer would later recall the sight of five British servicemen being carried from the train, dead.

Guards patrolled the camp carrying switches of barbed wire, which they used to strike prisoners.

In this camp there were no parcels from back home or from the Red Cross, and the men had only the rations given to them. The Germans claimed that food was limited to prevent disease.

In an interview with a journalist from the *Chester Observer*, Mercer was to recall one occasion when one or two NCOs were allowed in to take in the names of newly arrived prisoners. A man brought in a bath of so-called soup and the starving prisoners absolutely mobbed him. There was such a rush that the bath was upset in the crush and all the soup was wasted.

The camp accommodation was ten thousand and when the Armistice was signed, this number had increased to 22,000 by men coming into the camp from working parties.

'The camp authorities asked the prisoners to appoint delegates to visit Army Headquarters, but the British refused to do this, saying it was against their discipline. The German idea was to get the Armistice terms moderated.'

Mercer also noted: 'En route to the frontier, it was pitiful to see the German women and children without food and the prisoners gave a good deal away, even of the little they had. While at Meschede, the Germans pillaged the prisoners' supply of medicine. In fact, the Help Committee wrote home to ask the Depot at Hove not to send further supplies.'

A tunnel was made at Meschede with a view to escape, but it was discovered by the Germans and the prisoners from the whole barracks, about 250, had to do 21 days in dark cells in batches of 30. Mercer insisted that he was not ill-treated himself, adding that the Germans never tackled anyone strong – 'It was always the poor chaps from behind the lines who had no strength.'

After the war's end, Mercer returned to England. The *Chester Observer* carried the news on 4 January 1919 and an interview with him: 'He adds that it was fine the way the Britishers stuck together under all circumstances, and if a man is a prisoner of war it soon brings out the bad or good in him. Except for the stiffness in his arm, Mercer is sound in wind and limb, and soon hopes to be able to take up football in real earnest.'

Mercer did try to resume his playing career, spending some time with Tranmere Rovers, but found it impossible to perform at his former level due to his injuries. He retired from football, going back to bricklaying, his original trade.

He was a changed man, now much quieter and insular.

Mercer passed away in 1927, at the age of just 37, succumbing to health problems brought about by the gassing he had suffered in the trenches. His son Joe was 12 at the time and could only really remember a man who was constantly struggling for breath because of the damage to his lungs.

. . . .

Mercer had not been the only man captured at Oppy Wood. So too were Charles Abbs of Norwich City and Wilf Nixon of Fulham. As for the casualties, there were 11 officers and 451 ranks recorded as killed, wounded or missing. This was not quite the end for the 17th Middlesex, but the Battalion would struggle to regain their previous strength.

Chapter 17

Allastair McReady-Diarmid
Conspicuous bravery

Few would have known the young 12-year-old girl who marched across the Horse Guards Parade to the Cenotaph at Whitehall, London, on 11 November 1929.

The girl, who joined the veterans and various ranks, had come to lay a wreath in memory of her father. By the time the parade took place in November 1929, Alison McReady-Diarmid's father, Allastair, had been dead for 12 years.

Alison's presence did not go unnoticed, with the *Northern Whig* reporting about the ceremony, 'The VC's marched to the Cenotaph from Wellington Barracks with Earl Jellicoe, president of the Royal British Legion, at their head and heralded by the band of the Grenadier Guards. As they took up their places, there stood in the frontline a young girl wearing the VC her father had won at the cost of his life.'

Alison had only met her father once when he was on leave from the Western Front. Too young to remember him, he may have become simply a man in a photograph, wearing a British Army uniform, and the Victoria Cross, which she proudly displayed at the Cenotaph, a reminder of his bravery.

By the time of Alison's birth, on 24 May 1917, Allastair McReady-Diarmid wore the khaki of the British Army. There had been a time when he had been encouraged to take holy orders and wear the black vestments of a priest. Then again, the young captain did not always please his mother and father.

Commonly called Arthur, he had a passion for cricket and at Victoria College in the summer of 1904 he was selected for the cricket XI. His name appears on the cricket shield for 1904 as A M Drew. He tended to be known as 'Drew' – until he was attached to the 14th (Reserve) Battalion. Commissioned as a second lieutenant in March 1915, he changed his name to McReady-Diarmid in September of that year.

The change came about when he was asked by his Colonel to think of a different name, because there were already enough men in the Battalion named Drew. There is no record as to why he chose the name he did, but the change was made legal by deed poll on 10 September 1915, 10 days before he married.

The unit he joined had suffered heavy losses in the early fighting of the war and McReady-Diarmid soon found himself in the trenches on the Western Front. He had been there only a short time when he was blown off a trench fire step by an exploding shell.

He suffered internal injuries, which did not become fully apparent for some weeks, during which time he continued to serve. Eventually he was forced to return home for an operation and a four-month stay in hospital.

To convalesce, he was sent to Dursley in Gloucestershire. To the outrage of his parents – Herbert Drew, a civil servant, and his wife Fanny – McReady-Diarmid married Hilda Dainton, at St James' Parish Church, Dursley, on 20 September 1915. She was a tinsmith's daughter, and a nurse, and his parents considered her beneath their privately schooled son. Things were so bad they would never acknowledge Hilda as their daughter-in-law and it is easy to speculate this may have been the reason for the name change.

Once he had returned to health, Allastair was warned never to throw a bomb or grenade again – advice he chose to ignore. He was posted to a training battalion and in November 1916, he returned to the frontline, first with his former unit and later, under attachment to the 17th Battalion.

Even when McReady-Diarmid was promoted to lieutenant in September 1917 and then to acting captain in October 1917, the rift between his parents remained. Nor did the birth of his daughter, Alison Hilda, reconcile them.

McReady-Diarmid was quickly back in the thick of the battle. Along with the 17th Middlesex, he found himself north of the line near Canal du Nord, just east of Moeuvres, as part of the Battle of Cambrai.

The reason both McReady-Diarmid and the 17th Middlesex found themselves here could be dated back to August 1917 and the advent of tanks. The commander of the newly formed Tank Corps, Brigadier General Hugh Elles, proposed an operation to prove the ability of his tanks. In great secrecy, and under the cover of darkness, around 476 tanks, 1000 guns, eight infantry and five cavalry divisions were massed at Cambrai.

The German frontline was no match for the new British tanks, which drove into the enemies' defences. It was an advance of some 5 miles and even the weather, which had for so long hindered the Allied forces, could not stop the onslaught from the mechanical war machines.

On 30 November, the Germans counter-attacked, firing shells. Colonel Stafford was to note in the war diary that 'a certain number of mustard shells' had fallen on them.

The German infantry gathered in large numbers, ready for attack, and, using intensive artillery fire, gas attacks and infiltrating troops, they advanced deep into British lines, causing panic in some areas and threatening to cut off several divisions.

McReady-Diarmid, the commander of 'D' Company, waited alongside his men for orders.

At 11 a.m. they received the order to attack. Each soldier was carrying only two grenades.

Three hours later, McReady-Diarmid and his men had bombed the oncoming Germans back to their original lines.

At 9 p.m., a tired and exhausted McReady-Diarmid was relieved of his position. The fighting continued non-stop throughout the night, with the Germans beginning yet another advance at 4.30 a.m. The following morning, wave after wave of German attacks forced the

British forces back and it seemed that the allies might be about to succumb to the enemy.

At this point, McReady-Diarmid called for volunteers and then, arming himself with as many bombs as he could carry, disregarded his doctor's orders and began throwing bombs at the Germans.

The actions of McReady-Diarmid were nothing short of spectacular, with the official report stating, 'By throwing all the bombs himself, this officer killed and otherwise disposed of 94 of the enemy – 67 dead and 27 wounded were counted after the recapture of the trench, a feat which can hardly have been equalled in the past.

'Every foot of the 300 yards of the trench was regained, and by his deliberate disregard of danger, his cheerfulness and coolness, Captain McReady-Diarmid inspired all who saw him.'

Though his men were 'tired and shaken' according to the report, the actions of McReady-Diarmid roused them to join him in retaking the land the enemy had overrun. Just as he was about to launch another attack, a stray bomb hit him directly in the head, exploding on impact. He was just 29 years of age.

As a boy, he had attended Victoria College, which included him in the 1920 *Great War Book of Remembrance*. The entry lists the full details of his military career: 'He was admitted at once to the London University OTC and before long received a commission in the 17th Battalion, The Middlesex Regiment. From then till his death, he was almost continuously at the front, apart from four months in hospital in 1915.

'Letters from brother officers show that in a soldier's life he had found his real career. "Apart from his brilliant soldierly ability, he was a most charming companion in the mess. Cheery and full of humour, he was always keeping our spirits up."

'On one occasion one of his brothers, a Captain of RE, was near enough to visit him in the trenches. They only had a few minutes together, as Diarmid was just about to lead a bombing attack: but what impressed his brother was the way the men "rushed out" after him the instant they knew he was to lead.'

The writer Arthur Conan-Doyle, who had criticised the continuation of football after the breakout of war, was to pay fulsome tribute. Describing the action around Cambrai, he wrote: 'There was no more wonderful individual record in the battle than that of Captain McReady-Diarmid, of the 17th Middlesex, who fought like a d'Artagnan of romance, and is said to have killed some eighty of the enemy in two days of fighting before he himself at last met that fate from which he had never shrunk.'

....

Just over a week after McReady-Diarmid's death, his wife, Hilda, received a letter from the 17th Middlesex Commanding Officer, Lieutenant Colonel Stafford: 'Your husband died the finest death that I have ever known a man die. He had personally led a bombing party up a trench and had driven back the enemy more than 300 yards.

'He was killed instantaneously by a bomb, which hit him in the head. Your husband was entirely responsible for the repulse of the enemy at a most critical moment, and nothing can be too much for him. His heroism is the talk of the Brigade. I am sure he died happy.

'He had the true fighting spirit, and his men would have followed him anywhere. His death has left a gap, which we will never be able to fill.

'I cannot say how much I feel for you and your child. It is terrible to have lost such a husband. May God grant you strength to comfort you in your sorrow. I can offer you the sincerest sympathy of every officer and man of the battalion.

'I very much regret to say that we were unable to recover your husband's body, as after he fell, his company were driven back a little way. The place where he was killed is just south of a village called Moeuvres, near Cambrai. The battalion received high praise for its work in repelling the enemy attacks, but your husband stood out by himself among the men.'

There was further praise for the actions of McReady-Diarmid when Brigadier-General Walsh cited him in a report on 12 December about the operations in Cambrai: 'Among so many cases of gallantry and devotion to duty performed by individual officers and other ranks, I wish to draw particular attention to the case of Lieutenant (a/captain)

McReady-Diarmid, 17th Middlesex Regiment, who unfortunately was killed in action on the 1st of December.

'This officer is reported to have killed and otherwise disposed of about 80 of the enemy, to his own hand, a feat which can hardly have been equalled in the past. His display of vigorous offensive action and the splendid example he set to those around him undoubtedly had invaluable effect in keeping back the enemy. His loss to the battalion is a great one.'

Nearly three weeks after his death a special order of the day was issued by Major General Pereira, thanking the officers and men of the Second Division. He paid special tribute to the actions of Captain Allastair McReady-Diarmid.

The first British medal to be created for bravery, the Victoria Cross was instituted in 1856, its first recipients being personnel honoured for their gallantry during the Crimean War. The bronze cross, which bears the inscription 'For Valour', was initially cast from the metal of Russian guns captured at Sevastopol.

The Ministry of Defence explains that it is awarded 'for most conspicuous bravery, or some daring or pre-eminent act of valour or self-sacrifice, or extreme devotion to duty in the presence of the enemy'.

Perhaps through grief and regret about the way he treated his son in life, McReady-Diarmid's father, Herbert Drew, fired off an angry letter to the War Office, complaining about the announcement of his son's death, 'It was a War Office mistake to enter my son's name in the Army List as McReady-Diarmid, as you may see from his papers the change was made when he was in France and was done by the request of his colonel to obviate confusion in orders owing to there being other officers named Drew in the Battalion.'

Then, trying to reclaim his son's name in death, he wrote, 'There was no legal change, and I must ask you to publish his proper name McReady-Drew otherwise it will be no notification to his friends … I trust that there will no further trouble in the matter. I hear unofficially that my son has been recommended for the Victoria Cross and I am therefore anxious that the true name should stand as in Gazette 1915.'

THE FOOTBALL BATTALIONS

The army responded by enclosing the deed poll and the award was officially announced in the *London Gazette*, issue 30578, 15 March 1918: 'His Majesty the KING has been graciously pleased to approve of the award of the Victoria Cross to the undermentioned Officer: -T./ Lt. (A.Capt.) Allastair Malcolm Cluny McReady-Diarmid (formerly Arthur Malcolm McReady-Drew), late Middlesex Regiment.

'For most conspicuous bravery and brilliant leadership. The following day the enemy again attacked and drove back another company which had lost all its officers. This gallant officer at once called for volunteers and attacked. He drove them back again for 300 yards, with heavy casualties. Throughout this attack Captain McReady-Diarmid led the way himself, and it was absolutely and entirely due to his marvellous throwing of bombs that the ground was regained. His absolute disregard for danger, his cheerfulness and coolness at a most trying time inspired all who saw him.

'This most gallant officer was eventually killed by a bomb when the enemy had been driven right back to their starting point.'

On 20 April 1918, Mrs Hilda McReady-Diarmid travelled to London. Her destination, Buckingham Palace. She was shown into the ballroom and given a pin to wear.

The band present struck up the National Anthem and in walked His Majesty King George V flanked by two Gurkha orderly officers, in a tradition begun by his grandmother, Queen Victoria, in 1856. When the Lord Chamberlain called her forward, Mrs Hilda McReady-Diarmid stood in front of the King to receive her husband's Victoria Cross. By the time of the ceremony, the 17th Middlesex Regiment was no more.

At the end of the Battle of Cambrai, 40 soldiers from the Battalion had lost their lives and another 138 had been wounded. Those who inspected the trenches afterwards would find twisted and deformed corpses lying in the cold and wind of Northern France. They made up the 10,000 soldiers lost in battle, many of whom would never be identified.

On 9 December 1917, the Battalion stood at 38 officers and 755 men. And now the 17th Middlesex had to fight the snow, which had fallen heavily in Northern France. The festive season offered no respite: on Boxing Day, the Battalion was back on the frontline, suffering two further casualties when their positions were heavily bombed. There were five more casualties the following day.

Christmas was delayed that year, with the Battalion not sitting down to a traditional dinner until 6 January, when they enjoyed roast beef and pork and Christmas pudding, together with two pints of French beer. Two days later, the Battalion planned a concert, only for a stove to fall over, burning down their hut. The Padre's dog was the only casualty recorded that day.

On 16 January, 40 ordinary soldiers and two non-commissioned officers were received into the Battalion. The war diary noted that these included 'lads who had just turned 19 years old'. It seemed a long time since men had left football teams to join the war effort. Unbeknown to the soldiers or commanders, decisions were being made back home in London that would impact the army in France.

David Lloyd George, now Prime Minister, reacted to the losses sustained by deciding not to send any more reinforcements but wait instead for the Americans, who had joined the war on the side of the Allies in April the previous year. Therefore, General Haig was given a list of 145 battalions, to decide which units to disband. On that list was the 17th Middlesex.

Like for so many people during the Great War, it was a telegram which brought about the end of the Battalion. On 3 February, at a trench near Villers-Plouich, Lieutenant Colonel Stafford read that 'owing to the difficulties in obtaining reinforcements to keep all battalions up to establishment', the 17th Middlesex would be disbanded.

On a moist, bitter winter morning on 11 February 1918, the Football Battalion formed a parade one last time. They were at Metz, on the Western Front, some 15 miles away from the Somme, but a long way from the Fulham Town Hall where it had all begun just over three years earlier.

Colonel Stafford inspected them one last time and would later recall, 'At the final parade of the battalion, I said whatever might happen in later life, I should never be so proud of anything as of having commanded the Footballers Battalion, and now 41 years later, I know that I spoke truly. It was a splendid battalion, and I can imagine that there were few New Army Battalions its equal.'

On that cold February morning as the Battalion fell out for the last time, only 40 footballers remained. Among their number were Tim Coleman, whose death was mistakenly reported just over two years earlier, and Jackie Sheldon, who had begun the war in disgrace as part of the Liverpool-Manchester betting scandal. Both would be changed men by their experiences during the Great War.

For now, the war would not be over for the two old footballers. Very soon, both would board buses which would take them to their new regiment, the 13th Middlesex. The 17th Middlesex was at an end, but for members of the second Football Battalion, the 23rd Middlesex Regiment, the war would rage on. Within their ranks was someone who was about to meet both tragedy and triumph.

Chapter 18

Bookends
The different worlds of Haig-Brown and Tull

Surrounded by advancing German soldiers, with visibility limited by the smoke from days of constant shelling and gunfire, a young goalkeeper from Leicester Fosse ran straight into the enemy fire. Unlike thousands of others in the previous four years, he was not lined up under orders ready to go over the top, his was on a one-man mission.

For three horrific days, Tom Billingham of the 23rd Middlesex Battalion had been part of the heavy fighting that formed the German's Spring Offensive also known as the Second Battle of the Somme, Germany's last-gasp effort to break the British forces and finally bring an end to the war.

On 21 March 1918, the Germans had begun Operation Michael, their big push. Two days later, the allies – including the 23rd Middlesex – were in retreat; casualties were high and all around them was confusion and fear. The gunfire and shelling, including gas, had been non-stop for 72 hours, leaving the fatigued and sleep-deprived soldiers disorientated.

By the time Billingham broke cover, the battalion had taken a position behind a railway embankment at Bihoucourt and Aichet-le-Petit; this came after they had been pushed back from the frontline at Beughy. Now they were digging and digging in a futile effort to improve their defences. But it would come to nothing, the allies were outnumbered and the Germans relentless.

As Billingham tried to take cover from the unending onslaught, the noise of the shells would have rung in his ears. He watched as a fellow footballer – someone he once called a teammate, now his platoon commander – fell, after being hit by enemy gunfire. With no thought for his own safety, he ran to help his comrade.

Once he reached the officer: he would have known there was no chance of survival, the man had taken a direct shot to the head. Perhaps, having seen so many of his comrades left to rot in the mud of the battlefield, their bodies putrefying in the open elements, Billingham felt compelled to load up the body on his shoulders and try desperately to get them both back to safety.

The efforts were futile, the weight of the man's body too much. The smoke would have burned the back of Billingham's throat, his breathing heavy and his eyes stinging. All around him he would have heard the voices of the advancing German soldiers.

Struggling to find his footing and faced with certain death or capture, Billingham had no choice but to abandon his fallen comrade.

The next day, 25 March, the war diary of the 23rd Middlesex Battalion recorded the death of 2nd Lieutenant, W.D. Tull. The first officer of Afro-Caribbean heritage to command a platoon in the British Army, he was just 29 years old and had the previous year agreed to turn out for Glasgow Rangers on his return from war.

Speaking to the *Northampton Mercury*, Tom Billingham would tell of Tull's final moments and his motivation for charging into the German gunfire, risking certain death: 'In a chat with Private T. Billingham, the Leicester goalkeeper, the other day, he told me that Lieut. Walter Tull, of the Footballers' Battalion of the Middlesex Regiment, whose death was such a blow to his many friends, was killed by a machine gun bullet which entered his neck and came out just below his right eye.

'Billingham was about 30 yards from him when he was hit and was the first to go to his assistance. He only lived two minutes, however, and Billingham carried him some distance in the hope of securing for him a decent burial but had to leave him on account of the Germans' rapid advance. Tull, he adds, will be greatly missed. He was a thorough gentleman and was beloved by all.'

Almost 10 days later, on 4 April 1918, Violet Haig-Brown sent a telegram to the Secretary of the War Office: 'Please send news of Lt Colonel Alan Haig-Brown. Haven't heard for fortnight. Anxious.'

Perhaps she was hoping that she would receive a response much like she did a year earlier when her husband was engaged in fighting at the third battle of Ypres, Passchendaele in early August 1917. Then she was told, 'Lieutenant-Colonel A.R. Haig-Brown Middlesex Regt. admitted to 14 General Hospital Boulogne August nineteenth wounded shell shock slight, any further reports sent when received.'

There would no such news this time. What Mrs Haig-Brown would not have been aware of was the same entry in the 23rd Middlesex Battalion's war diary which listed Walter Tull's death also contained the line 'missing believed killed' beside Lt. Col AR Haig-Brown.

The Military Secretary at the War Office would confirm Haig-Brown's death on 6 April 1918, telling his wife he had been instructed by the Secretary of State for War, 'to express his deepest sympathy with Mrs Haig-Brown for the loss of her gallant husband.'

A week later, the Keeper of the Royal Privy Purse, sent a telegram to Edward Tull, Walter's brother, who was then living in Glasgow, informing him that the King and Queen regretted the loss that Edward and the army had been sustained by the death of Walter. Like the telegram sent to Mrs Haig-Brown, this would have provided very little comfort to their families.

The *Northampton Mercury*, which had covered so many of the games Tull played in while at 'the Cobblers' noted his passing on 12 April 1918, writing, 'Tull, Lieut. Walter, Middlesex Regiment, killed in France; well-known as a member of the Cobblers' football team, to which he was transferred from Tottenham Hotspur. Enlisting two years ago, gained his commission by his great ability and merit, which won for him Mention in Despatches.'

The two men could have been mismatched bookends: one privately educated at Charterhouse School and then Pembroke College, Cambridge, the other an orphan brought up in a care home. Although they were both footballers and had passed through Tottenham

Hotspur, there is little chance they would ever have met, had it not been for the Great War.

They had taken differing paths, but days earlier, they now stood together on the Western Front, the inclement winter weather slowly giving way to the milder days of March, both officers in the British Army. If Walter Tull had ever needed a mentor and role model, he would have found it in Alan Haig-Brown.

Whereas Tull's early life was often one of poverty and hardship, Haig-Brown, on the other hand, seemed to have lived a gilded life. His father was the headmaster at Charterhouse School, where he was born and later educated. Later, he read for a degree in Classics at Cambridge, where he earned a Blue sporting award.

In 1901, Haig-Brown signed as an amateur at Spurs, playing alongside Vivian Woodward, but unlike his illustrious teammate, he made only four appearances before moving on, eventually winding his career down at Clapton Orient.

By any stretch of the imagination, Haig-Brown never shone on the football pitch and in all probability would not have made a living from the game in the way Tull did – it was the military in which he excelled.

While working as an assistant schoolmaster at Lancing College, he received a commission as an officer in the 2nd Volunteer Battalion Royal Sussex Regiment. In May 1916, he landed in France, where in September he was appointed commanding officer of the 23rd Middlesex Battalion.

By the time Haig-Brown was desperately trying to stave off the advancing German forces in those three hellish days in March, he already held the Distinguished Service Order. It was he who championed Walter Tull.

After recovering from trench fever and attending officer cadet training at Gailes, Scotland, Tull passed through the 5th Middlesex Battalion, where on 30 May 1916, he became the first Black infantry officer in the British Army.

This appointment came about despite the *Manual of Military Law* (War Office, 1914), stating, 'Once enlisted a man of colour could…

not be capable of holding any higher rank in His Majesty's regular forces than that of warrant officer or non-commissioned officer.'

It would not be long before he was attached to the 23rd Middlesex, commonly known as the second Football Battalion on 29 October 1916. It was here that the children's home product, Tull, would meet the public schoolboy, Haig-Brown.

As officers, both Haig-Brown and Tull would enjoy special privileges – more pay and leave, for one – which tended to cause some resentment among the lower ranks, although it was said that Tull remained a popular member of the Battalion.

After Walter's death, Second Lieutenant Pickard wrote to Edward Tull, 'Allow me to say how popular he was throughout the Battalion. He was brave and conscientious… the commanding officer had every confidence in him, and he was liked by his men.'

It was in Italy where Tull would come to prominence on the battlefield. On 24 October 1917, the Germans and their allies had launched an offensive at Caporetto. The Austro-Hungarian forces, fighting side by side, with the Germans begun making losses. Now they wanted enforcements and to the Germans, this was a real opportunity to draw British attention away from the Western Front.

The attack was so furious and overwhelming for the out-gunned and out-manned Italians that for a time there was a very real threat that Italy could fall into the hands of the Germans, taking them out of the war.

It was decided that five British Divisions were to join six French Divisions in bolstering Italy's resistance. The 41st Division, including the 23rd Middlesex, would see action in Italy.

As Christmas 1917 slowly made its way into New Year's Day 1918, Walter Tull spent the festive season leading his men into the murky, freezing-cold waters of the river Piave on a reconnaissance mission to gather vital intelligence and take prisoners. These river excursions were not for the faint-hearted: Tull and his men would be bare-chested, covered in a thick covering of grease, in water up to their waists. Frequently, the men would carry each other on piggyback.

Even when the mission was successfully completed, there were always the dangers of hypothermia and frostbite. Later, Tull was to receive an official citation for his bravery, with Major-General Sidney Lawford, GOC of the 41st, writing to him, 'I wish to place on record my appreciation of your gallantry and coolness. You were one of the first to cross the river prior to the raid on 1/2 January 1918 and during the raid you took the covering party of the main body across and brought them back without a casualty despite heavy fire.'

Further details of the operation were provided in the *London Gazette*, by General Sir Herbert Plumer, in command of the expeditionary force in Italy: 'On the 1st of January our biggest raid was carried out by the Middlesex Regiment. This was a most difficult and well-planned operation, which had for its objective the capture and surrounding of several buildings held by the enemy to a depth of 2,000 yards inland, provided a surprise could be affected.

'Two hundred and fifty men were passed across by wading and some prisoners were captured, but, unfortunately, the alarm was given by a party of 50 of the enemy that was encountered in an advanced post, and the progress inland had, therefore, in accordance with orders, to be curtailed.

'The re-crossing of the river was successfully affected, and our casualties were very few. An operation of this nature requires much forethought and arrangement, even to wrapping every man in hot blankets immediately on emerging from the icy water.'

Tom Billingham was to make a passing reference to Tull's bravery in an interview with the *Northampton Mercury*. On 18 January 1918, the newspaper reported, 'A visitor to the "Echo" office on Saturday was T. Billingham, who, footballers will remember, played in goal for the Cobblers Reserves, and at the outbreak of war was playing for Leicester Fosse.

'He is a private and physical instructor and is at home on leave from Italy. The weather there is bitterly cold, but warmer weather is due next month. Private Billingham states that Walter Tull, the old Cobbler, is in Italy and is now a lieutenant. On Boxing Day, he took part in a raid, but the enemy had made himself scarce, and only three prisoners were found.'

By the time Walter Tull arrived at Northern France, in March 1918, he had been constantly fighting without leave for eight months. At his side was his mentor and commanding officer, Alan Haig-Brown. The 23rd Middlesex Battalion was now part of the 123 Brigade of 41st Division, they were there in the vain hope of repelling the advancing Germans who could claim an extra 500,000 soldiers from the Eastern Front after the withdrawal of Russia.

It was here that both Tull and Haig-Brown would meet their fate. In letters written to Violet Haig-Brown telling her of how her husband met his demise, Sergeant J. Flaherty wrote, 'The last I saw of my Col. was with his revolver in hand in the trench shouting encouraging words to his men, when I was hit and was sent back.

'He would never go back from the Germans. He was always telling us to die rather than be a prisoner, and I am certain he did that rather than be a prisoner, for we were nearly surrounded when I came away.'

Further information came from Captain B.T. Foss, Adjutant, who wrote to Mrs Haig-Brown, on 11 September 1918, 'Upon receiving order to retire, the Colonel insisted upon remaining where he was until the battalion, and even his personal orderlies and servants, had safely evacuated the position.

'Then, to steady the nerves of his men, he walked slowly back, completely ignoring the very heavy and well-aimed machine gun fire which was hitting the ground around us.

'It was this fire which mortally wounded him and left me the only officer untouched of the party of three. I did my best to get him back to safety, but it was clear to me he has very little chance of recovery.

'Being sent back without an escort I endeavoured to render any assistance I could to the Colonel, but before I could reach him, I was knocked over by a bullet, and before long escorted back by a German soldier, who happened to find me. Since then, the belief that the Colonel was too badly wounded to feel much pain has given me some consolation.'

Lieutenant Alan Haig-Brown now lies at Achiet-le-Grand Communal Cemetery Extension. He was moved there in 1920, having first been buried south of Biefvillers-lès-Bapaume.

For Walter Tull's family, there was still questions in a letter of condolence. While lauding many of Tull's qualities, Major Poole DSO OBE proposed the award of the Military Cross, clearly stating that he had been recommended for such an honour.

Even 100 years after his death in Northern France, despite numerous campaigns throughout the years, by family members and politicians, Walter Tull was never awarded the Military Cross. With no known grave, he is commemorated on the memorial wall of the Faubourg d'Amiens Cemetery in Arras, Nord-pas-de-Calais. Even so, the legacy of Walter Tull continues not only to live on but flourishes to this day.

A befitting tribute can be found in Major Poole's letter, where he said of Tull, 'Now he has paid the supreme sacrifice pro patria; the battalion and company have lost a faithful officer; personally, I have lost a friend. Can I say more! Except that I hope that those who remain may be as true and faithful as he.'

Walter Tull in the colours of Tottenham Hotspur. After serving with the 17th Middlesex, he would go on to be the first person of Afro-Caribbean heritage to be commissioned as an officer with the second Football Battalion, the 23rd Middlesex.

Chapter 19

Reunion
All that is left behind

In the build-up to the 1939 FA Cup Final, there was only one person everyone wanted to talk about. Wolverhampton Wanderers had taken the First Division by storm. But however exciting they were on the pitch, all the headlines were captured by their manager: Major Frank Buckley.

Ever since the end of the Great War in 1918, the old comrades of the 17th Middlesex Regiment had met for a reunion dinner on the evening of the FA Cup Final. The dinner took place at the Bedford Corner Hotel on Tottenham Court Road. Tickets were priced at five shillings, with concessions for those members of the Battalion who were suffering from financial hardship.

When Buckley accepted his invitation to that year's dinner, he must have been hoping that by the time the starter was served, he would have made history. Going into the final weeks of the 1938/39 campaign, it looked as though his Wolves side would become the first side to win the double – the League and FA Cup – in the 20th century.

Even if they failed, all eyes would be on him. For by 1939, Buckley was enjoying a level of fame that more than surpassed his old comrade Vivian Woodward and even Steve Bloomer.

A year after the war ended, Buckley became secretary-manager of Norwich City FC, on the recommendation of the FA secretary, Frederick Wall, but left when the club was suffering severe financial difficulties.

For the next three years, Buckley was lost to football, working as a commercial traveller for a London sweets company, Maskell's.

It was on one of these various sales trips that he found himself in a railway carriage, talking to a gentleman about his former life in football. Unbeknown to Buckley, the man was Albert Hargreaves, a director at Blackpool Football Club.

An offer was made, but Buckley initially had no intention of leaving Maskell's. A subsequent meeting with the club president, Lindsay Parkinson, convinced him that not only would he be well-paid, but also given funds to spend in the transfer market.

At Blackpool, Buckley proved himself to be something of an innovator. He brought in the now-famous tangerine strip and, more importantly, a youth system. He also introduced strict and regimented fitness regimes, including rules about what players could eat and drink.

Even so, Blackpool could never quite achieve the ambitions of a manager who was desperate for First Division football.

The frustration Buckley felt at Blackpool's progress was outlined in a report from the *Lancashire Evening Post* on Thursday, 15 July 1926: 'The manager (Mr Buckley) in review of the club's progress and future remarked it had been said that Blackpool Football Club do not aspire to the First Division. That is all nonsense.

'The one wish of him and the board was to aspire to a higher sphere of football. Last season, he had reached the conclusion, however, the team was not good enough to achieve this distinction. The thing was now to get to work to make it good enough … we hope in the coming season to succeed at last in promotion. Competition is undoubtedly fierce but with a good strong young team we certainly have a chance.'

Only a year later, however, Buckley moved south to the Midlands, becoming the new manager of Wolverhampton Wanderers. The club was not without their own problems, the *London Daily Chronicle* reporting on Wednesday, 10 August 1927, 'It is 21 years since Wolverhampton Wanderers lost their position in the First Division of the League. They have not been nearer than fourth from the top of the Second Division and had considerable anxiety concerning their tenure last season.

'Great faith is entertained in the ability of Major FC Buckley, the new secretary-manager, to produce better results in the coming campaign, although he must make use of practically the same personnel.

'Reinforcements are chiefly of the young and enthusiastic type … The Wanderers have an overdraft of about £17,000 at the bank, this being due in part to the new stand which has been provided, but a movement is on foot to reduce this indebtedness as much as possible.'

As an old soldier, Buckley was something of a disciplinarian. Goalkeeper Don Bilton, who joined Wolves in 1938, recalled, 'If you had a rotten game you'd hardly dare go in at half-time, you were going to get the biggest bawling at … Buckley cursed and swore at you.'

Defender Stan Cullis, who was to become so pivotal to Wolves' future success, wrote of his manager, 'Major Buckley was one out of the top drawer. He did not suffer fools gladly. His style of management was very similar to his attitude in the army.

'He implanted into my mind the direct method which did away with close inter-passing and square-ball play. If you didn't like his style, you'd very soon be on your bicycle to another club.'

Whatever methods Buckley had put in place did not work initially. Despite high hopes in 1928 and 1929, the club which aspired to First Division football only narrowly missed relegation to the Third Division – by three points. It was not until 1932, the fifth year of Buckley's reign, that his tactics with Wolves won the club their longed-for promotion.

According to the *Sheffield Independent* of Monday, 11 April 1932, the success Wolves encountered was down to their manager: 'The Wolves, who put seven goals against Oldham, will now consider themselves justified in celebrating the winning of promotion.

'They are worthy of it, for they have had a good team each year since they fell into the Northern Section. Major Frank Buckley put in some great work at Blackpool, where he laid the foundation of the Seasiders' advance to the top class, and has shown his ability at Wolverhampton, too.

'Major Buckley seldom loses a chance of having a look at some of the Midland League's youngsters, and he is a well-known figure on almost all grounds.'

Wolves steadily moved up the First Division and by 1938 they were able to challenge for the League title, some pundits now tipping them as favourites.

In the penultimate game of the season Wolves won with a game in hand, meaning that even a draw away to Sunderland would be enough to pip rivals Arsenal to the title. Unfortunately, they came unstuck at Roker Park, the 10-man Rokerites winning 1-0.

After learning of Arsenal's title-clinching win at Highbury, several Wolves players burst into floods of tears, to face Buckley's wrath: 'The Major told us only conscientious objectors and men of poor character cried.'

The next season began with a six-match winning streak from 5 November 1938 until they drew at home to Bolton on 17 December 1938. Then they completed a 7-0 battering of Everton, their fellow title challengers, on 22 February 1939. Wolves' fans now dreamed of going one better than the previous year and lifting the title for the very first time in their history.

Going into the last month of the season, the *Bristol Evening Post,* on Wednesday, 5 April 1939, commented on the Black Country side's chances: 'It looks as if the Wolves, still clinging tenaciously to the vision of becoming Cup winners and League champions in one campaign, have a fine chance of getting nearer their ambition.

'They have to travel to Preston, it is true, but the Cup finalists' form is so good now that they can be supported for full points. Everton, at present leading by four points, have stiffer opponents in Chelsea, whom they meet at Stamford Bridge.'

'Chelsea, incidentally, are still fighting hard to make themselves safe from relegation, and victory over Everton would make all the difference in the world. Everton, it must be remembered, partially failed at home last week, but I do not think they will lose at Stamford Bridge.

It was always a tall order; after winning their first six games, Everton led for most of the season and were never outside the top two all season. By 15 April, Everton were six points clear and needed only one point to secure the title.

On the same day as Everton's 0-0 draw with Preston, Wolves kept their hopes alive by beating Charlton Athletic 3-1. Despite having a better goal average, they were now reliant on winning each of their last games and Everton losing their own game with Charlton Athletic, if they were to beat them to the title.

The following week, Everton did lose to Charlton, but a 0-0 draw with Preston meant Wolves had lost all chance of winning their first title. All hopes for silverware would now rest on the FA Cup. It cannot have been lost on Buckley that one of the stars of the Everton side was Joe Mercer Jr – the son of the man he commanded during the war.

After getting past Everton 2-0 in the sixth round and then destroying Grimsby Town 5-0 in the semi-final, Wolves awaited lowly Portsmouth, who had been sucked into a relegation battle all season.

A profile of the Wolves manager, in the *Yorkshire Evening Post* on 12 April 1939, detailed how far the club had come under their manager: 'The Major has brought the Wolves in 12 years from a side bordering on bankruptcy and despondency in the Second Division to be the best club in the country. And this in a town with a population of 133,000.

'Before the war, Major Buckley was a £4 a week professional footballer for Derby County. In the war, he rose to the rank of major. He left Blackpool to manage Wolverhampton Wanderers in 1927.

'In 1931 the club's debts had been wiped off and were back again in the First Division. For two or three years after this they were consistently near the bottom, but they drew by their desperate efforts to avoid relegation.'

. . . .

While it seemed every newspaper in the build-up to the big game was carrying a profile of Frank Buckley, war veteran and forward-thinking manager, the fortunes of the other surviving members of the Football Battalion had been quite different.

In 1939, although still England's top goalscorer, Vivian Woodward was largely forgotten. Following the Armistice, he had coached the British Army football team and captained them to victory in the final of the Inter-Theatre-of-War Championship, in a 3-2 triumph over the French Army at Stamford Bridge.

After finally being demobbed on 23 May 1919, he retired from football, though he served as a director for Chelsea until 1930. According to the 1921 census, Woodward was now a farmer, living with his older sister, Isabella, who managed a dairy farm in The Towers in Weeley, and her four children and a servant.

When Buckley's Wolves were making their way to the FA Cup Final in 1939, Woodward was living at 30 Elm Grove in Camberwell, a retailer of farm produce. He would spend the Second World War as an air raid warden. In 1949, he fell ill from nervous exhaustion and went into a nursing home run by the FA in Ealing, West London.

Woodward died on 31 January 1954 at Castlebar Road Nursing Home, aged 74 years old. The year before he died, he was visited by journalist Bruce Harris and a bus driver J.R. Baxter, who had served with him in France.

Harris reported, 'We found him bedridden, paralysed, infirm beyond his 74 years, well looked after materially. The FA and his two former clubs are good to him; relatives visit him often.

'"But," he told me in halting speech, "no one who used to be with me in football has been to see me for two years. They never come – I wish they would."'

· · · ·

Steve Bloomer spent four years as an internee at Ruhleben, 9 miles from Berlin. Immediately after the war, he coached FC Blauw-Wit Amsterdam before returning to Derby County FC as reserve team coach.

He turned down an approach from Poland to coach their Olympic team in November 1919, but accepted an offer to coach Real Unión Club de Irún, based in Bilbao, Spain. The club won the 1924 Copa del Rey and the Campeonato Regional de Guipúzcoa.

On 16 April 1938, *Derby Evening Telegraph* reported, 'The "Telegraph" announces with regret the death early to-day of Steve

Bloomer, one of football's greatest personalities and the finest inside-right in the history of the game.

'He died at the Great Northern Inn, Junction-street, Derby, the home of his daughter and son-in-law, Mr. and Mrs. Cyril Richards, with whom he had been living since his return on March 25 from a health trip to Australia and New Zealand.

'He was taken ill the day after his return, and his condition gradually became worse. His death, however, was comparatively sudden and will come as a great shock to the countless thousands who knew him affectionately as "Steve." He had been ailing almost since the death of his wife two years ago, and the trip to Australia was arranged in the hope that it would bring the desired recovery.'

Reporting on his funeral a few days later, the *Nottingham Journal* said, 'Wonderful tributes to the memory of "Steve" Bloomer, the former England, Middlesbrough, and Derby County inside-right were paid at his funeral in Derby yesterday.

'Hundreds of people lined the main streets of the town, and the seating accommodation of 1,000 at Derby Cathedral proved inadequate for those who wished to be present.'

．．．．

For Tim Coleman, fortunes had been mixed. There was an unsuccessful spell as the player-manager of Maidstone United.

In March 1925, Dutch club SC Enschede placed an ad in *Athletic News and Cyclists' Journal* inviting applications for the post of trainer. Coleman was the successful candidate. Winning the regional title, the club entered the national section of the season and were crowned national champions of 1926.

In the summer of 1927, he was working as a general labourer. In March 1939, *The People*'s columnist 'Chatterbox' bumped into Coleman and described him as: 'The picture of health. Clear eyed and distinguished, only the greying hair betrays the passing years.'

He died on 20 November 1940 in St Mary Abbot's Hospital, after falling off the roof of a power station in South Kensington while at work. The *Nottingham Evening Post* reported his passing: 'J. G. Coleman, footballer of international renown, who wore the red garibaldi of Nottingham Forest in the first season of the first World War (1914-15) has died following an accident at work when he fell from a roof.

'Tim, a very genial character, joined the City Ground Staff on July 18th 1914, and in his one season with the "Reds" made 39 appearances (two in the Cup) and was top scorer with 16 goals (2 in the Cup).

'He joined the Footballers' Battalion, in numerous games for Forest appearing on the programme as Tim Coleman. Private Coleman, served under Major F. Buckley, and had Tom Gibson, another Forest footballer, as his sergeant major.

'As inside-right Coleman saw service with Northampton, Woolwich Arsenal, Everton, Sunderland, and Fulham, prior to joining Forest. He played for England against Ireland at Goodison Park in 1907, and for the League against Scottish and Irish Leagues the same year. At the outbreak of war in 1939 Coleman was a football coach in Holland.'

....

As the dinner with the Football Battalion approached, Frank Buckley had an opportunity to attempt to make his own piece of history. Predicting the outcome in the *Leicester Evening Mail* on 27 April, it was said no one was expecting anything other than an easy win for Buckley and his team.

For the record, the *Leicester Evening Mail* carried the following quotes from Buckley, 'As at Portsmouth no one at Wolverhampton will hear of defeat for the Wanderers.

'Major Buckley, the manager, however, sounded a note of caution when he gave his views to-day on the likely result.

'"There is no such thing as a 'cert' in the Cup Final," he said. "But I think Wolverhampton can play football good enough to beat Portsmouth." He recalled his team's displays against Everton in League and Cup matches and declared that a reproduction of this form ought to see the Wanderers successful.'

On the same day, the *Staffordshire Sentinel* went so far as to predict the outcome of the Cup Final: 'Beaten in their quest for the League championship, Wolverhampton Wanderers will be the more determined to carry off the F.A. Cup as consolation.

'Portsmouth will put up a stern fight, yet it is hard to see how they can overthrow one of the finest sides of the season.

'The combination picked by Wolverhampton yesterday has not been beaten. Westcott, the centre-forward, and Cullis, the centre-half, are matchwinners out of the ordinary, and the efforts of these two men will play a big part in the decision of an extremely interesting contest.

'Southerners will not hear of Portsmouth's defeat. Elsewhere, the general expectation is a comfortable win for Major Buckley's team.'

Going into the game, most pundits believed Portsmouth's only hope against the powerful Wolves side was that a pair of so-called lucky spats worn by their manager, Jack Tinn, would work the same magic in the final as they had done in the previous rounds.

Any hopes of Buckley turning up to the dinner with the Cup, though, quickly dissolved.

Against all the predictions, Portsmouth ran at the Wolves defence, so it was no surprise when Barlow shot their first goal home from close range after half an hour. Then just before half-time, Anderson added a second. Already the heads of the Wolves players were dropping.

Things did not improve for the team in gold and black when the Wolves goalkeeper Scott dropped a shot on the goal line, allowing Portsmouth's Cliff Parker to slide in to kick the ball from under the keeper's outstretched hands and make it 3–0.

A solitary Dorsett strike from eight yards gave Wolves some hope that a comeback could be mounted, but Portsmouth put the result beyond any doubt when Parker headed in his second and the southern side's fourth from close range.

John Robertson, the sports editor of *Weekly Dispatch* (London), wrote on Sunday, 30 April 1939, of the match, 'The Wolves attack never functioned as we know it can. That was the difference between the two teams. Portsmouth's forward line excelled itself, and even in my wildest dreams I did not believe they could play the thoughtful, devastating football they displayed for 70 minutes.

'After the ineffectual, timid display at Chelsea the week before, this Portsmouth forward line was a revelation in craft, guile, and ideas.

'All five played their part nobly, and the Wolves inside-forwards were novices compared with McAlinden and Barlow. Major Frank Buckley must have watched with mixed feelings the success of Barlow, whose goal in half an hour did so much to sway the destinies of the match.

'Classy winger and seasoned campaigner Fred Worrall, only survivor of the 1934 Portsmouth final team, can look back on this match with pride.

'He was far and away the classiest and most effective winger on the field, and here again it was a case of an old head being best. Worrall always seemed to have time to think a move ahead, and his passes and centres were the soul of discretion.

'Wolverhampton must now, reluctantly, conclude that it takes more than youth and abandon to win the coveted prizes of football. I had to admire the magnificent way Wolves defence kept plugging along to the end. Unfortunately, defences alone cannot win cup finals. In the second half, after Dorsett had reduced the gap to 1-3, the Wolves defenders strained every nerve.

'Cullis began coming through with the ball in the commanding manner we expect, and Galley – hitherto a little disappointing – took a firmer grip on the game. Cup final history is crammed with tragic mistakes, mostly by goalkeepers, and Robert Alexander Scott, the Wolverhampton goalkeeper, walked off Wembley's beautiful turf with dejected countenance, knowing full well that two errors of judgement had contributed largely to the defeat of the hottest Cup favourites for 11 years.'

At the end, speaking to George Casey of the *Daily Mirror*, Buckley was to say of the Cup Final and the season in general, 'The wiseacres will now turn round and say that you just can't win Cup and League in one season. And after Wolverhampton's fate, when they sat pretty to do the trick, what can you say?

'Here's my very best wishes to Jack Tinn and his band of boys. We dished it out to them when things weren't running their way, and they took their medicine like real sportsmen. I wish every side were the same.'

Whatever his disappointment at losing the Cup Final, Buckley was first and foremost a military man. So, after consoling his Wolves players, he joined his former comrades at Bedford Corner Hotel for dinner.

Some 21 years since the end of the Great War, how many of the 500 men who enlisted were still alive? In 1936, only 100. By 1939, just 80 members attended the dinner.

The clouds of a new war were making their way across the European continent, and the reunion would not be held again until 1954 – the same year that Wolves under Buckley protégés Stan Cullis and Billy Wright finally lifted their very first League title to go with their maiden FA Cup won in 1948, the year after Buckley left the club.

He then passed through Notts County and Hull City before ending up at Leeds United, where he signed a young Jackie Charlton and John Charles. He would end his football career as manager at Walsall.

Buckley died on 21 December 1964. Up until the end of his days he would be referred to as Major, a constant reminder of the time football went to war for king and country.

Afterword
Why we remember

At 4.30 p.m. on 11 November 2018, the Premier League Champions walk out to face their fierce cross-city rivals. By the time the teams emerge at the Etihad Stadium, the skies overhead are already dark, and the pitch is floodlit.

A win for Manchester City will mean they return to the top of the Premier League, something which will be all the sweeter if it comes at the expense of Manchester United. However, as the teams walk out, the mood is anything but celebratory. Bernardo Silva, City captain for the day, walks on to the pitch carrying a wreath, as does his Manchester United counterpart, Ashley Young.

Solemnly, they walk to the centre of the ground and lay the wreaths, then the teams line up, side by side across the centre circle.

City wear their home strip of sky-blue shirts, white shorts and navy socks, while Manchester United are in red shirts and black shorts.

Placed prominently and centrally on the shirts of both sides is the poppy, the traditional symbol of remembrance, although the red of United makes the poppy blend into the shirts, making it difficult to be seen by the naked eye.

Even though there are a few shouts and whistles in the crowd, this afternoon they are strangely mute. The announcement over the stadium sound system informs those assembled that when the referee Anthony Taylor blows his whistle the 'Last Post' will begin. This will be followed by a two-minute silence to commemorate the 100th anniversary of the signing of the Armistice, which officially brought the First World War to an end.

As the whistle goes, the 54,316 people in the crowd fall silent.

AFTERWORD

When the final bars of the 'Last Post' sound, both sets of fans erupt into spontaneous applause. Then, as the players run to their allotted positions, both Silva and Young remain at the centre circle and shake hands. Reaching into the pocket of his shorts, Anthony Taylor produces a coin to decide who will kick off the game. On this occasion, the coin he uses is a bespoke commemorative one from the Royal British Legion.

With the formalities over, the game kicks off and the crowd reverts to type, tribal loyalties beginning anew as Manchester City set out on their quest to retain the Premier League title.

Further south in West London, Chelsea take on Everton, the club who won the League Championship in 1915. There, the scenes witnessed in Manchester are repeated – as they are at all the Premier and Football League clubs playing that weekend.

. . . .

A short journey from Chelsea's training ground at Cobham, Surrey, is the Woodland Trust's First World War Centenary Wood at Langley Vale near Epsom.

There, both Manchester City and Chelsea were among the 63 football clubs who pledged to commemorate the role footballers played in the First World War by each planting a grove of trees to commemorate the 100th anniversary of the signing of the Armistice. Every team that donated trees has a plaque to commemorate its contribution to the war effort.

Speaking at the launch of the campaign in 2016, Sir Trevor Brooking, who achieved fame with West Ham and England in the 1970s and '80s, said, 'The Woodland Trust and the National Football Museum's For Club and Country project is the perfect way to commemorate football's important role in the First World War. By planting groves of trees for every club whose players bravely fought for their country we are creating something beautiful and long-lasting for future generations.

'Every football fan needs to get involved and make sure their club is remembered in the football groves at Langley Vale Wood. If you love football as much as I do, please get your team represented and see your own name listed on the supporters' roll of honour.'

Brooking would plant his own tree in the wood in October 2018, to commemorate those footballers who went to war while playing for West Ham United.

Dr Kevin Moore, Director of the National Football Museum, said, 'The partnership between the National Football Museum and the Woodland Trust will give football supporters across the country the opportunity to learn more about their own club's First World War history, plant trees in commemoration and by doing so be part of the supporters' roll of honour.

'We feel passionately that football's involvement in the First World War is remembered by today's generation.'

Clapton, now Leyton Orient, was the first club to enlist in the British Army and so is perhaps the club that is most associated with the Football Battalion. In the week leading up to the anniversary, a young player who had once been loaned to the club was also busy involving himself in the campaign.

Fresh from his exploits leading England into the semi-finals of the World Cup, Tottenham Hotspur superstar Harry Kane planted a tree at Tottenham's training centre at Hotspur Way, Enfield, in memory of one of the 16 Spurs players who played for the club, and served and died during the conflict:

'It's great to have something to remember the players who fought in World War One. It's amazing to think, when you are in this bubble and the world we live in now, that those guys went off from playing football and went off to war.

'They gave the ultimate sacrifice for us. It's an honour to have days like this to remember them by. It's great to be part of it. Days like this are very important, not just for the players but for the community as well.'

At the same ceremony he was pictured on the training ground, his head bowed alongside two teammates and in front of Tommy – the silhouette in wrought iron of a soldier from the First World War. Blazing in the centre of Kane's familiar, lily-white shirt was the blood-red poppy.

AFTERWORD

Kane played the day before the actual anniversary, where he was part of the team which secured a 1-0 win over Crystal Palace at Selhurst Park to take Spurs within two points of top the spot.

That same winter, as part of the campaign 'Football Remembers', the Waterloo East Theatre presented the play, *The Greater Game*. Written by Michael Head and based on the book *They Took the Lead* by Stephen Jenkins, it depicted the lifelong friendship between Clapton Orient players William Jonas and Richard McFadden.

Earlier in the year, in March, the Tull 100 Project had been launched. Continuing through to November, the project used the story of Walter Tull to fund a series of projects at football clubs and community organisations around the country.

But the players of the Football Battalion are remembered even without an anniversary. Every year, thousands of Chelsea fans from all over the world visit Stamford Bridge for the stadium tour and end up in the club museum, where there is a tribute to Vivian Woodward.

On any given Saturday at Pride Park the song 'Steve Bloomer's Watchin'' will be sung by Derby County fans in tribute to their long-dead centre-forward.

And anyone who visits Cardiff City Stadium will be greeted by a statue of a jug-eared Fred Keenor, smiling while cradling the FA Cup, his arm raised triumphantly in the air. The inscription on the plinth underneath details Keenor's success – including the unique achievement of captaining the Bluebirds when they became the first and to date only side outside England to take the FA Cup, in 1927.

．．．．

Even though the Great War ended over a century ago and there are now no survivors, Remembrance Sunday remains firmly fixed in the country's consciousness.

It's easy to forget, given the sombreness of the occasion, how today's perspective is at odds with the way football was viewed when war broke out.

Then football was different and though there are a few exceptions like, Haig-Brown and Woodward, it was played mainly by the working classes. By 1914, in levels of attendance, football was already beginning to outstrip its erstwhile rivals, rugby and cricket.

For example, when Bradford met Burnley in the FA Cup in 1911, 39,146 people turned up at Valley Parade. Total gate attendances peaked at 12.5 million in the 1913/14 season.

The clubs were hugely reliant on gate receipts, meaning that the owners were reluctant to let their best players go to war.

As we have seen, football eventually had to succumb to the inevitable. Clubs faced severe financial and operational difficulties as attendance dropped and many of their key players joined up. Football's very existence was threatened, yet it found ways to endure. The sport adapted by implementing a system of guest players, allowing footballers stationed at military bases to play for nearby clubs.

Football also actively contributed to the war effort. Benefit matches became commonplace, with proceeds often directed to war charities or used to support soldiers and their families.

Clubs embraced their new role, serving as centres for recruitment and morale-building, even as many of their grounds were repurposed for military use or as makeshift hospitals.

Public sentiment towards football shifted as the war dragged on. Initial hostility and scepticism gave way to acceptance as people recognised the value of maintaining some semblance of normalcy and communal spirit. Football proved adaptable and resilient. It bridged the gap between past and present, offering hope that life would one day return to normal.

Many players never returned, leaving an indelible mark on the clubs and their communities, and when the game restarted after the war, it faced the challenge of reinvention.

Clubs resumed operations with reduced squads, financial pressure and a society that had been forever changed.

Like so much else across the country, the experience of loss and resilience shaped the future of football. That is why the story of those footballers from yesteryear demands to be told.

AFTERWORD

No one can play the game or rise to the very top of the profession without a deep love and passion. That is true of any player from any era. The players of the Football Battalions may have lived in a society very different from their more famous descendants today, but the only real difference between them is that they were called upon to fight – and they answered.

In the uncertain world we live in today, let us hope that no young person, whether a footballer or not, is ever called in the same way as those brave men and women so many years ago.

Acknowledgements

Like many football followers, I am guilty of seeing the history of the game in two halves. The first when England won the World Cup in 1966 and the second with the advent of the Premier League in 1992. This does a disservice to all who went before and those who fought for king and country.

Equally, for too long I have felt that we think too easily of the soldiers of the First World War in terms not of the people they were, but the characters in the films and dramas the Great War has inspired over the years. The common misconception has been o the officers, aristocrats who had very little in common with the working-class Tommy. I wanted to move beyond that and remember all the young men who served, regardless of their social class; men who came from all sorts of backgrounds, who scored important goals, slid into tackles, swore at referees and got sent off, just like any footballer who ran onto the field of play.

The war ended over 100 years ago and so, unlike my previous books, there was no one still alive with any memories of that period to share with me. Therefore, I must start where the research began, at the National Archives at Kew, and I would like to thank Dr William Butler, Head of Modern Collections, for all his help and advice when it came to tracking down military records for the members of the Battalion.

I had an enjoyable visit to De Montfort University, Leicester, where I met Professor Matthew Taylor, who is an expert in the history of sport and recreation and gave me some flavour about football and the era of the First World War. Another fantastic archive can be found at the National Football Museum, where I spent a fascinating afternoon with curator Dr Alexander Jackson in Preston. I would like to thank him and his staff for being so generous with their time.

Recently, I have been appointed to the Commonwealth War Graves Commission and I would like to place on record my thanks to the staff at Headquarters in Maidenhead for allowing me to look through the archives of the 17th and 23rd Middlesex regiments.

Over the course of writing this book I have met so many club historians, whose passion for their teams is awe-inspiring. I would like to thank Max Portman, who is the custodian of the West Ham United history. Likewise Rick Glanvill of Chelsea FC. I enjoyed afternoon tea with QPR's Chris Guy and his colleague, Martin Percival, who provided some interesting information about Evelyn Lintott.

For information on Hearts and McCrae's Battalion, I am grateful to David Speed for the knowledge he shared on their last season before they headed off to war. Thanks to my colleague, Ian Murray MP, for putting me in touch with him.

Of all the people I have met in writing this book, a special mention must go to Steve Jenkins of Leyton Orient. He goes beyond being an historian: the players of Clapton Orient are his passion. From his work with his colleagues in the O's Somme Memorial Fund, arranging visits to their memorials in Northern France and the National Memorial Arboretum, to organising charity events and his Orient Line walks, Steve is, simply put, the keeper of the flame.

It is my sincere belief that, thanks to Steve's work, the lives of those from Clapton Orient who served in the Great War will never be forgotten. My thanks to my good friend Jon, now Lord Cryer, for introducing me to Steve.

I would like to thank both my publisher, Matt Lowing at Bloomsbury, and my agent, Nick Walters of David Luxton Associates, for their help and guidance; they are both level-headed and realistic, and are an absolute joy to work with.

Of course, I could never have written this book without so much support from my family. As ever, my mother and my stepfather, Bob, were a constant support. I would like to thank both my children:

Zachariah, who is becoming a football obsessive, and Jasmine, who is not far behind him. I am so privileged to have two kind and caring children.

Being away from home so much means my wife, Julia, does the lion's share of the work, looking after our wonderful children while maintaining a high-pressure job. It blows me away that on top of all that she trained and completed the London Marathon! She really is amazing. Words cannot express my thanks for everything she does for our family. That is why this book is dedicated to her.

As the Member of Parliament for Caerphilly and previously Islwyn, every year I attend cenotaphs all over the constituency on Remembrance Sunday. I am pleased to say the crowds even in the smallest villages are huge. Everyone gathers to remember the names on the war memorials.

Even before I discovered the story of the Football Battalions, I used to look at those names and think beyond the marble in which they are carved that there was a life that was lived with laughter, tears, happiness and anguish. The tragedy is that their lives were cut short.

Through these pages I hope that the voices of the Football Battalions, silent for so long, can be heard again and their story can come back to life. It has been an honour getting to know them: I pay tribute to them and everyone who went to war.

The memorial of the 17th and 23rd Battalions of the Middlesex Regiment at Longueval. Situated on an unassuming corner near Delville Wood, it is the final resting place of so many soldiers, who paid the ultimate sacrifice for king and country.

Bibliography

Books

Alexander, Jack, *McCrae's Battalion: The Story of the 16th Royal Scots* (Mainstream Publishing, 2004)
Andressen, J.H.J., *World War One in Photographs* (Grange Books Ltd, 2003)
Bancroft, James W., *The Early Years of the FA Cup: How the British Army Helped Establish the World's First Football Tournament* (Frontline Books, 2021)
Belton, Brian, *War Hammers I: The Story of West Ham United during the First World War* (The History Press, 2014)
Beujon, Andrew, *A Bigger Field Awaits Us: The Scottish Football Team That Fought the Great War* (Chicago Review Press, 2018)
Brown, Paul, *The Ruhleben Football Association: How Steve Bloomer's Footballers Survived a First World War Prison Camp* (Goal Post, 2020)
Clark, Christopher, *The Sleepwalkers: How Europe Went to War in 1914* (Penguin Books, 2012)
Collins, Damian, *Rivals in the Storm: How Lloyd George Seized Power, Won the War and Lost his Government* (Bloomsbury Continuum, 2024)
Cooper, Stephen, *The Final Whistle: The Great War In Fifteen Players* (The History Press, 2013)
Fairley, John, and Allison, William, *The Monocled Mutineer: The First World War's Best Kept Secret: The Etaples Mutiny* (Souvenir Press, 2015)
Holt, Richard, *Sport and the British: A Modern History* (Oxford University Press, 1990)
Horspool, David, *More Than a Game: A History of How Sport Made Britain* (John Murray Publishers Ltd, 2023)
Hoyer, Katja, *Blood and Iron: The Rise and Fall of the German Empire 1871–1918* (The History Press, 2022)
Inglis, Simon, *Soccer in the Dock* (Collins, 1985)
Jackson, Dr Alexander, *Football's Great War: Association Football on the English Home Front, 1914-1918* (Pen & Sword Military, 2022)
Jacobs, Norman, *Vivian Woodward: Football's Gentleman* (The History Press, 2005)
Jenkins, Stephen, *They Took The Lead: The Story of Clapton Orient's Major Contribution to the Footballers' Battalion in the Great War* (London: DDP One Stop UK, 2005)
Kershaw, Ian, *Hitler (*Penguin Books, 2009)
Lynch, E.P.F., and Davies, Will, *Somme Mud: The Experiences of an Infantryman in France, 1916-1919* (Doubleday, 2008)
McCartney, John, *The Sport in War* (1930)
McCrery, Nigel, *The Final Season: The Footballers Who Fought and Died in the Great War* (Arrow, 2015)
Moran, Lord John, *The Anatomy of Courage: The Classic WWI Study of the Psychological Effects of War* (Robinson, 2007)
Myerson, George, *Fighting for Football: From Woolwich Arsenal to the Western Front – The Story of Football's First Rebel* (Aurum, 2009)
National Football Museum and Jackson, Alexander, *The Greater Game: A History of Football in World War I* (Shire Publications, 2014)
Olusoga, David, *The World's War: Forgotten Soldiers of Europe* (Apollo, 2019)
Quirke, Patrick A., *The Major: The Life and Times of Frank Buckley* (Tempus Publishing, 2006)
Renshaw, Andrew, *Wisden on the Great War: The Lives of Cricket's Fallen 1914-1918* (Wisden, 2014)
Riddoch, Andrew, and Kemp, John, *When the Whistle Blows: The Story of the Footballers' Battalion in the Great War* (J H Haynes & Co Ltd, 2008)
Sandbrook, Dominic, *Adventures in Time: The First World War* (Particular Books, 2021)
Smith, Kevin, *Letters From the Front: Letters and Diaries from the Bef in Flanders and France, 1914-1918* (Fonthill Media Ltd, 2013)

BIBLIOGRAPHY

Stevenson, David, *1914-1918: The History of the First World War* (Penguin Books, 2005)
Strachan, Hew, *The First World War: A New History* (Simon & Schuster UK, 2024)
Taylor, Elliot, and Alston, Barney, *Up the Hammers!: The West Ham Battalion in the Great War 1914-1918* (CreateSpace, 2012)
Tuchman, Barbara, *The Guns of August: The Classic Bestselling Account of the Outbreak of the First World War* (Penguin Books, 2014)
Vasili, Phil, *Walter Tull 1888-1918 Officer Footballer: All the Guns in France Couldn't Wake Me* (Raw Press, 2009)
Vignes, Spencer, *Lost in France: The Remarkable Life and Death of Leigh Roose, Football's First Superstar* (Pitch Publishing Ltd, 2016)
Walvin, James, *The People's Game: The Social History of British Football* (Allen Lane, 1975)
Williamson, Jeff, *Lost Football Heroes of the First World War* (JMD Media Ltd, 2018)
Wynn, Stephen, *Against All Odds: Walter Tull the Black Lieutenant* (Pen & Sword Military, 2018)

Newspapers

The Athletic Chat; The Athletic News and Cyclists Journal; The Berkshire Chronicle; The Birmingham Daily Post; The Birmingham Gazette; The Bolton Independent and Lincoln Advertiser; The Bradford Telegraph; The Chester Observer; The Citizen; The City Press; Cricket and Football Field ; Daily Citizen; Daily Herald; Daily Mail; Daily Mirror; The Daily News and Leader; Daily Sketch; The Daily Telegraph; The Derby Evening Telegraph; The Dorking and Leatherhead Advertiser; The Dundee Courier; East and South Devon Advertiser; Edinburgh Evening News; Empire News; Evening Dispatch; The Football Echo; Football Player Magazine; Greenwich and Deptford Observer; The Hamilton Daily Times; Hampshire Advertiser; The Hull Daily Mail; Illustrated Police News; The Lancashire Evening Post; Leeds Mercury; Leicester Evening Mail; Liverpool Daily Post and Mercury; The Liverpool Echo; London Gazette; Manchester Courier; Manchester Guardian; The Mansfield Reporter; The Morning Leader; Newcastle Chronicle; News Chronicle; Northampton Mercury; The Northern Telegraph; Nottingham Evening Post; The Observer; Pall Mall Gazette; The People; The Scottish Referee; The Scotsman; The Sheffield Daily Telegraph; The Sheffield Independent; Sporting Chronicle; The Sporting Life; The Sports Argus; Sunday Chronicle; Sunday Post; The Sunday Telegraph; The Surrey Advertiser; The Sussex Agricultural Express; The Times; The Week and Sports Special Star Green; Weekly Dispatch (London); West Surrey Times; Western Mail; Yorkshire Evening Post; Yorkshire Sports.

Football programmes

The Arsenal FC official programme; The Chelsea FC Chronicle; The Cottagers Journal (Fulham); *Oriental Notes* (Clapham Orient); *Tottenham Hotspur Football and Athletic Club official programme; The Villa News and Record* (Aston Villa)

Websites and Other

BBC Audio, Voices of World War One; The Imperial War Museum, Sound Archive; Lancing College War Memorial; National Archives, war diaries 17th and 23rd Middlesex; National Football Museum, Football Association minutes

www.footballandthefirstworldwar.org
www.livesofthefirstworldwar.iwm.org.uk
www.mccraesbattaliontrust.org.uk
www.scottishsporthistory.com
www.ww1playingthegame.org.uk

'SUPER' FOOTBALL BOOTS

There are many officers who, full of appreciation of the splendid services of the men under their command, are seeking a means of saying THANKS! in a practical way.

Here is a suggestion—

Tommy will find time hang badly waiting demobilisation and he loves Football, but he cannot get Football Boots. Have a whip round in your mess, and send us an order for sufficient to equip a team of your own.

IN TWO STYLES

19/- & 22/6

Order early as supplies are limited, and state sizes when ordering. Orders executed in rotation.

W. ABBOTT & SONS, LD.,
434, STRAND, W.C.
54 REGENT STREET, W.
(Opposite Swan & Edgars)
121, High Holborn, W.C.